Justification and the New Perspectives on Paul

A REVIEW AND RESPONSE

Guy Prentiss Waters

PUBLISHING

P.O. BOX 817 • PHILLIPSBURG • NEW JERSEY 08865-0817

Unless otherwise indicated, Scripture quotations are from the NEW AMERICAN STANDARD BIBLE®. Copyright © 1960, 1962, 1963, 1968, 1971, 1972, 1973, 1975, 1977, 1995 by The Lockman Foundation. Used by permission.

Scripture quotations marked RSV are from The Holy Bible, Revised Standard Version. Copyright © 1946, 1952, 1971 by the Division of Christian Education of the National Council of the Churches of Christ in the United States of America.

Italics within Scripture quotations indicate emphasis added.

Page design by Lakeside Design Plus
Typesetting by Andrew MacBride.

Printed in the United States of America

Library of Congress Cataloging-in-Publication Data

Waters, Guy Prentiss, 1975–
    Justification and the new perspectives on Paul : a review and response / Guy Prentiss Waters.
       p. cm.
    Includes bibliographical references and index.
    ISBN 0-87552-649-7 (pbk.)
    1. Bible. N.T. Epistles of Paul — Criticism, interpretation, etc. — History. 2. Justification (Christian theology) — Biblical teachings. 3. Bible. N.T. Epistles of Paul — Theology. 4. Reformed Church — Doctrines. I. Title.

BS2655.J8W38 2004
234'.7 — dc22

            2004051004

See Notes & Comments at the end of
Each chapter & summary at the end of
this book.

Contents

Foreword

As part of its program of providing continuing ministerial theological education for the church's ministerial and program staff, and as a resource to the entire presbytery (and larger evangelical community), as well as the local seminary community, the session of First Presbyterian Church, Jackson, Mississippi, established the John Hunter Lecture Series in 2003.

This lecture series is named after the Reverend John Hunter, the sixth pastor of First Presbyterian Church. Hunter was born and reared in North Ireland; received his seminary training at the Presbyterian Seminary in Danville, Kentucky; was a vigorous, faithful, and capable preacher of God's Word; and served as pastor of this congregation for 37 years (1858–1895).

The inaugural Hunter Lectures were devoted to critical issues in New Testament studies. The lecturer was Dr. Guy Waters, assistant professor of biblical studies at Belhaven College. Dr. Waters gave aproximately 20 hours of lectures on the origins and history of what is being called "the New Perspectives on Paul." His purpose was to give an accurate review and description of this approach to reading Paul, and then to assess it from a biblical, confessional, Reformed perspective.

To elaborate, Dr. Waters explained:

> The purpose of these lectures is to give an historical and theological overview of the New Perspective on Paul (NPP). This study will lay

out the theological, historical, and cultural antecedents to the NPP. It will examine representative and leading proponents of so-called "New Perspective" scholarship, and will explore nuances and differences among them. It will then engage in a theological and exegetical critique of the NPP. Finally, it will inquire why the NPP has been received with such enthusiasm within Reformed Christianity, and then underscore what theological and practical consequences adoption of NPP might have within Reformed Christianity.

These lectures were attended, and were met with appreciation, by First Presbyterian staff members, local college and seminary educators, and a number of area clergy, seminarians, and interested laypeople. The lectures were so well received that Dr. Waters was urged to revise them for publication. You now hold the product of those labors in your hand. Dr. Waters's mastery of this material will quickly become apparent. His work throughout manifests his knowledge, judgement, clarity, and care.

J. Ligon Duncan III
Senior Minister
First Presbyterian Church
Jackson, Mississippi

Preface

any in the churches today are hearing for the first time about "the New Perspective(s) on Paul" (NPP). Some have encountered the term through undergraduate or graduate New Testament courses. Some may have heard that their session or presbytery is deliberating on the biblical and theological ramifications of the NPP. Others have been introduced to the NPP through more informal means—conversations with friends, articles posted on the Internet, or Internet discussion groups.

From what quarters has the NPP come? Who are its major academic proponents? What are they saying? What biblical, theological, and confessional issues does the NPP raise? Should individuals in the Reformed community have an interest in this movement that is gaining popularity within the evangelical church? These are the questions that many in the churches are now raising concerning the NPP. These are the questions that I will endeavor to answer in the next nine chapters.

In this work I have at least three objectives. I first want to give an exposition of what leading scholars, recognized as proponents of the NPP, are saying about the theology of Paul and related issues. I have endeavored to quote liberally from these scholars in order to give readers who might not otherwise study this literature a fair sense of the authors' arguments, concerns, and conclusions.

Second, I want to show how the NPP emerges from an academic and theological discussion that predates it by more than two centuries.

This "historical-critical" discussion yielded certain interpretative and theological decisions that, in certain respects, have determined the contours of the NPP. Awareness of the context of this discussion will help us in determining the degree to which persons in confessionally Reformed and evangelical churches may appreciate the NPP.

Third, I want to illustrate the ways in which the NPP deviates from the doctrines set forth in the Westminster Standards. I also want to show how Reformed theology surpasses the NPP in explaining Paul's statements regarding the law, the righteousness of God, justification, and a host of other topics and doctrines. In other words, our critique of the NPP will be not only theological but also exegetical.

I will finally attempt to explain why officers and congregants within Reformed and evangelical churches find the NPP attractive, and why such interest often attends interest in the theology of Norman Shepherd and the theology represented in the September 2002 statement of the session of the Auburn Avenue Presbyterian Church.

At this point, a reader might raise an objection: "Does the author have *nothing* good to say about the NPP? Is there nothing for a Reformed person to appreciate?" To this I answer, "By no means!" I greatly appreciate, to take but one example, N. T. Wright's pressing the lordship of Christ as a focal point of Christian belief and proclamation. He is correct, furthermore, to point to the eschatological inclusion of the Gentiles within the people of God as an important concern of the apostle Paul in his letter to the Romans. To take another example, E. P. Sanders, under whom it was my privilege to study as a doctoral student, has rightly questioned the adequacy of the reigning model of first-century Judaism that has circulated among New Testament scholars for at least a century. Scholarship was long overdue for refinement and correction, and Dr. Sanders has helpfully provoked the kind of academic discussion that is needed to produce a more balanced portrait of first-century Judaism.

Why, then, is this work largely critical in its assessment of the NPP? Let me briefly offer a couple of reasons. The first is that I write from a standpoint of full sympathy with the Westminster Standards. I believe the Confession and catechisms to be the most thorough and faithful confessional statement of biblical teaching in the church's possession. In view of this commitment to the Reformed faith—a commitment that, I emphasize, is rooted in this faith's fidelity to the teaching of the Scripture—I have accordingly examined the NPP and found it defective on several key points of biblical teaching. A second and related reason is that I write this book primarily for individuals who already find themselves within the Reformed community. Some within the Reformed churches have enthusiastically heralded the NPP and its supposed compatibility with Reformed and biblical teaching. Upon examination, however, the NPP both in its particulars and as a system will evidence marked differences with Reformed and biblical teaching. The soteriological sympathies of the NPP, to the degree that these sympathies exist, are not with Protestantism, but with Roman Catholicism. These sympathies are rooted, we will argue, in the historical-critical tradition's previous departure from the Reformational doctrine of justification by faith alone. I have thought it necessary to underscore these concerns in this work in view of the potential dangers to the church that are occasioned by enthusiastic and uncritical receptions of the NPP.

No work is ever undertaken alone. I wish to acknowledge my debt to a number of individuals whose untiring efforts and support have made this work possible. I first want to thank my friend J. Ligon Duncan III, who conceived, spearheaded, and promoted this project alongside his ceaseless labors as the senior minister of First Presbyterian Church, Jackson, Mississippi. It is fair to say that without his direction, assistance, and advocacy, this book would not have come into being. Special thanks must also go to Stephen Tindall and Jennifer Henry, intern and secretary to Dr. Duncan, respectively. Their patient editorial labors have been as invaluable as they are appreciated. I am grateful especially to a father in Zion, the Rev. James T. O'Brien, for his careful, thorough, and critical review of an important portion of this work. I also wish to thank the ministers and elders of the Mississippi Valley Presbytery (PCA), many of whom in the fall of 2003 attended the lectures that formed the foundation of this work and who have encouraged me in the course of this project. I wish to thank the administration and faculty of Belhaven College for their support and encouragement extended to me during this project. I finally wish to thank my wife, Sarah, for her continued encouragement and patience.

This book took its start as the John Hunter Lectures on Critical New Testament Issues, sponsored by the session of First Presbyterian Church, Jackson, Mississippi. These lectures are named in honor of John Hunter, sixth pastor of this congregation (1858–1895). Hunter, in preparation for the gospel ministry, studied under Robert J. Breckinridge and Edward Porter Humphrey at the Theological Seminary at Danville, Kentucky. Both Breckinridge and Humphrey were Old School Presbyterians of the first order. Hunter, having graduated from the seminary, was resident in Danville during the brief tenure of a fellow Irishman, Stuart Robinson, as the chair of church government and pastoral theology in Danville.

I mention this background for two reasons. First, Hunter undoubtedly would have received from his teacher Breckinridge not only sound doctrine, but also the necessity and importance of defending it against the novel views of Scripture, of justification, and of regeneration and conversion that were being propagated by New School Presbyterians in the nineteenth century. Second, Robinson would undoubtedly have endowed in his fellow Irishman a love for the church and the doctrine of its nature and mission, also under attack during the New School controversy.

It is appropriate that this book, which has emerged from lectures named in honor of Hunter and his ministry, should endeavor to defend *the very doctrines* that Hunter and his teachers devoted their ministry to defending. It is also fitting, in recognition of their generosity in supporting these lectures and of their continuation of nearly two centuries of faithful Reformed witness, that I gratefully and affectionately dedicate this work to the ministers, session, staff, and congregation of First Presbyterian Church, Jackson, Mississippi.

"How the Mighty Have Fallen":
From Luther to Schweitzer

In order to understand the New Perspective(s) on Paul (NPP) and the currents that have led into this movement in the academic study of Paul, we must begin with the Reformation and the subsequent rise of historical-critical interpretation. In one sense, the NPP swirls around two figures—Albert Schweitzer and Rudolf Bultmann. In order to understand *them*, we need to trace the historical-critical discussion a century before Schweitzer. In order to understand the rise of *that* discussion, however, we need to explore the impact both of the Reformation and of the subsequent theological declension in Germany on the study of Paul. Why do we begin with the Reformation, a movement that is markedly different from the theological positions of many proponents of the NPP? The NPP is fundamentally centered on Paul, and specifically his understanding of the "law," "works of the law," "righteousness," and other related issues. It is this very cluster of issues with which the Reformation was exercised, and concerning which the NPP will vehemently dissent from the Reformers.

We begin our study by asking two questions of an introductory nature. What impact did the Reformation have on the study of Scripture (generally) and on the study of Paul (particularly)? How did the Lutheran church in Germany decline into patent unbelief in the course of a couple of centuries?

1

The Impact of the Reformation on the Study of Paul

Luther and Calvin

Martin Luther initiated his attempt to reform the church on October 31, 1517, by posting the Ninety-Five Theses on the cathedral door in Wittenberg, Germany. By the time of Luther's death in 1546, it was clear that there could be no reconciliation with Rome. Luther had sought to reform Rome, but had been excommunicated. The Council of Trent, which met from 1546 to 1564 and defined the theological position of the modern Roman Catholic Church, furthermore, placed under *anathema* (curse) those who held to the distinguishing Protestant doctrines—a curse that remains to this day.

John Calvin (1509–1564) represented another wing of the Protestant Reformation and stood shoulder to shoulder with Luther on the key doctrines of grace that were at stake in the sixteenth century. Calvin's study of Paul is representative of the Reformers' close attention to the apostle. Calvin systematically expounded each of Paul's Epistles in commentary form, and also preached through Galatians, Ephesians, the Pastoral Epistles (all of which had been translated into English by the 1570s, thereby influencing English Protestantism), 1 and 2 Thessalonians, and 1 and 2 Corinthians. Much more so than the late medieval church as a whole, emphasis was now laid on the systematic exposition of Scripture in both preaching and teaching. Paul, then, has received careful attention from the heirs of Luther and Calvin. In large measure this is so because Paul provides some of the most detailed scriptural discussion on salvation, not only a matter of intrinsic importance, but also one that has divided and continues to divide Rome and Protestants to this day.

Reformational Interpretation

The Reformers represented a new chapter in the history of interpretation in at least three ways.[1] First, many Reformers had been trained according to the canons of the recent humanist criticism, whose cry was *ad fontes*, or "(back) to the sources." Part of this training involved a resurgence of interest in the "ancient languages" and "rhetorical analysis," an interest that was carried over into Protestant readings

Expository
Sola - Scriptura.

of the Bible.[2] Renewed attention would now be given not only to the historical but also to the grammatical context of the Bible. Second, Protestants self-consciously embraced the theological conviction *sola Scriptura* (Scripture alone). The consistent application of this principle would ensure a vital principle of interpretation: Scripture interpreting Scripture. Third, the historical training and sensibilities of the Reformers ensured that Lutheran and Calvinist biblical interpretation would be sensitive to the history of interpretation. In this way, Protestants could evade Rome's charge that Protestants had not embraced *sola Scriptura* but *nuda Scriptura* (bare Scripture), or Scripture read without the aid of tradition or other such external assistance. The Reformers thereby laid the foundation for exegesis of Paul that was both grammatically and historically grounded, while sensitive to the insights and reflections of past interpreters.

The Stage Set

The magisterial Reformers bequeathed to their heirs a carefully articulated and balanced understanding of the relationship between the doctrines of justification and sanctification. When biblical critics in seventeenth-century Germany began to depart from the *formal* concern of the Reformation (Scripture alone), they soon came to depart from the *material* concern of the Reformation (justification by faith alone). By their doing so, the very soteriology that Luther and Calvin had mightily resisted ironically found its way into these Lutheran churchmen's biblical scholarship.

How Did We Get *Here*?

We jump now from 1564, the year of Calvin's death, to 1826, the year that F. C. Baur began to teach at Tübingen. In the interim, Lutheranism had declined in Germany. We may briefly note one pertinent cause of this decline here. European philosophy had now radically embraced doubt as its epistemological starting point. This skeptical posture extended to biblical authority and the church's understanding of biblical teaching, especially as that understanding came to expression in systematic theology. Exegesis would assume an unprecedented independence from systematic theology and the history of interpretation. H. A. W. Meyer reflects this stance in the 1829 preface to the first installment (1829) of his justly famous New Testament commentary:

> The area of dogmatics and philosophy is to remain off limits for a commentary. For to ascertain the meaning the author intended to convey by his words, impartially and historico-grammatically—that is the duty of the exegete. How the meaning so ascertained stands in relation to the teachings of philosophy, to what extent it agrees with the dogmas of the church or with the view of its theologians, in what way the dogmatician is to make use of it in the interest of his science— to the exegete as an exegete, all that is a matter of no concern.[3]

No longer would exegesis be governed by the teaching of Scripture as a systematic and theological whole. For many German students of the Bible, exegetical and systematic theology had effectively and finally parted ways.

Consequently, many came to view the Bible as simply a document of ancient history. Speculation began concerning the possible origins or sources of the biblical books. The Reformational or "precritical" principle of identifying the "historical sense" of Scripture with its "literal, grammatical meaning" was abandoned.[4] In its place arose the critical principle of seeking "meaning . . . [not] in the received, canonical text," but "behind or under it in hypothetical predecessor-documents or in hypothetically reconstructed life situations of individual pericopes."[5] This principle took the isolation of the text from its systematic-theological context to a new level.

F. C. Baur and the Tübingen School[6]

We are now prepared to consider Baur, who taught at Tübingen from 1826 to 1860. Baur formulated a reconstruction of the history of the apostolic period that dominated New Testament scholarship until the twentieth century and that consciously rejected such key tenets of historical Christian orthodoxy as revelation and miracles.[7] Baur articulated his understanding of the historical and theological development of the early church in an influential article.[8] This article, as Hafemann comments, "laid out the foundation for his understanding of Paul and the history of the early church by applying the dialectical, evolutionary approach of Hegel's philosophy to 1 Corinthians 1:11–12."[9]

Baur advanced a theory of conflict as shaping early Christianity. Traditional Christianity had posited a framework of orthodoxy propagated from Jesus to the apostles to the early church. Traditionally, conflict in the New Testament had been conceived as the struggles between proponents of this orthodoxy and proponents of speculative or practical heterodoxy. Baur, however, understood the conflict to be between two competing forms or species of Christianity: Jewish and Gentile, represented preeminently by Peter and Paul, respectively. He saw evidence of this specific type of conflict in the Corinthian church. These two forms of Christianity had irreconcilably distinctive emphases. *Jewish Christianity* was said to have close ties to Judaism and the Mosaic law. James and Matthew were said to be literary specimens of this form of Christianity.[10] *Gentile Christianity*, on the other hand, was said to focus on the doctrine of justification by faith apart from the works of the law. It was "Law-free" in this sense.[11] Paul's teaching in his letters emphasized, rather, the Spirit (*Geist*).

The conflict between Jewish and Gentile Christianity was a tumultuous one and shaped early Christian history into the second century A.D.[12] But by the second century, Baur argued, an emerging "catholicism" had arisen that stressed ecclesiastical hierarchy, orthodoxy, and organizational unity. The most significant example of the church's march to this "catholicism" is Luke-Acts, which was said to be a "mediating" book that sought to rewrite the history of the first century.[13] The second-century ideals of unity and orthodoxy were projected onto the first century. The author of Luke-Acts had masked conflicts of the past, conflicts that could still be accessed by the modern critical interpreter through such letters as Galatians. Baur, then, came to the conclusion that only four letters of Paul (which he termed *Hauptbriefe*, or the "chief letters") were authentic: Galatians, 1 and 2 Corinthians, and Romans. Baur believed that they were authentic because they demonstrated conflict between Jewish and Gentile Christianity. He rejected the remaining nine letters because, in Baur's judgment, they lacked sufficient evidence of this conflict.

Baur's work was tremendously significant. First, his judgments concerning the authenticity of the Pauline letters stand, although most critical New Testament scholars now admit 1 Thessalonians, Philippians, and Philemon. Second, he gave the first purportedly "historical" framework to early Christianity—one that had been formulated without reference to historic Christianity and "supernatural intervention" in temporal history.[14] Third, while few follow his particular program today, Baur set the terms of subsequent debate for critical Pauline scholarship in the form of three questions:[15]

(1) Who were the opponents of Paul? What did they teach? Baur's thesis placed at the center of the critical study of Paul the apostle's conflicts with his opponents. This meant that the doctrines that occasioned this conflict—justification, faith, works, and the law—would continue to shape generations of discussions within historical-critical scholarship.

(2) What was Paul's view of the law? How did it relate to his views of the gospel? How did he differ on this point from his opponents? Baur raised the question of the role of the Mosaic law in the teaching of both Paul and his opponents. He did so in such a way as to create distance between Paul and his Jewish contemporaries. Back of this question was the nature of Paul's relationship to his Jewish heritage—was it friendly or hostile? Had Paul been influenced by Jewish or Hellenistic beliefs and practices? This concern too would exercise generations of historical-critical scholars.

(3) What is the "generating center" of Paul's thought? Baur had argued that Paul's teaching revolved around two foci: justification by faith alone and the Spirit (*Geist*), which Baur took "in the Hegelian sense as the infinite and absolute in opposition to the finite (the flesh)."[16] The Lutheran tradition had historically maintained Paul's theological center to be justification by faith alone. The question before critical scholarship now was which theological category—the forensic or the transformative—would be regarded as generative of Paul's theology?

Critique of Baur

Before we proceed with our survey of the Pauline interpretation leading up to Albert Schweitzer, we may observe three points of criti-

cism that have been raised against Baur's thesis. One of th
cessful engagements of Baur was mounted by J. B. Light
essay "St. Paul and the Three," Lightfoot demonstrated "th
not stand in opposition to the chief 'apostles of the circ\
James, Peter, and John," as Baur had maintained.[17] Lightfoot also
raised the possibility of different groups opposing Paul. Although modern scholars do not follow Lightfoot in his identifications, they have
picked up his insight and generally argue for diversity or plurality
among Paul's opponents. In other words, those who opposed Paul at
Galatia were not necessarily the same (in person or in doctrine and
practice) as those who opposed him at Corinth.[18]

A second criticism has centered on Baur's view that conflict is at
the heart of Paul's theology. Even if one concedes Baur's point, one
need not make it, as Baur did, a criterion of authenticity. The judgments of authenticity drawn by Baur, after all, countered the virtually
unanimous testimony to the contrary of external evidence.

A third criticism raised against Baur's synthesis is that although
there is an internal consistency to his thesis, it is incapable of independent verification. The testimony of the New Testament documents
themselves is one of harmony and unity of belief, purpose, and mission, even in the *Hauptbriefe*. In Romans 15:30–33, Paul prepares to
take a Gentile-supported offering for the relief of Jewish Christians in
Judea. In 1 Corinthians 8–9, 16, we see evidence of Paul's earlier preparation for this very offering. In Galatians 2:9, the representatives of
the Jerusalem church extend to Paul the "right hand of fellowship."
This is hardly a forced reconciliation of two opponents. We might also
observe 1 Corinthians 1:13 ("Has Christ been divided? Paul was not
crucified for you, was he? Or were you baptized in the name of Paul?").
Paul here explicitly repudiates the whole notion of competing parties
in the church, whatever credence Baur might have given to them.

The Liberal Theology[19]

We turn now to consider the development of historical-critical studies of Paul through the nineteenth century and into the opening decades
of the twentieth century. Our survey takes us through three distinct

movements: liberalism, the history of religions school, and the participationism of Albert Schweitzer. In the nineteenth century, liberal Protestant scholarship in Germany maintained that Paul's thought centered on two central foci: the so-called juridical line of his thought, evidenced in Paul's doctrine of justification by faith alone; and the so-called mystical-ethical line of his thought, evidenced in Paul's language of the Spirit and of union with Christ.[20] This school maintained that these lines were not compatible with one another. Paul often "leaped from the one to the other without sensing the contradiction."[21] But the mystical-ethical line was said to be more fundamental to Paul. Baur had taken Paul's teaching on *Geist* in a philosophical sense. The liberals were now conceiving this teaching in a moral sense.[22] Such a direction suited the ethical or moralistic preaching promoted by liberal theology.[23]

The failure of the liberals to reconcile or harmonize these two lines was also owing to a distinction drawn between Paul's (subjective) experience and Paul's (objective) theology. The latter, it was maintained, not only was the objective expression of the former, but also could not be expected to be consistent. In anticipation of our discussion below, we may note that this distinction was an important root of the consistency/coherency debate in the twentieth century.[24] In employing this distinction, liberal theology recognized that while "theology" reflected Jewish and Hellenistic influences of the day, nevertheless the experience to which it gave expression was timeless. Heinrich J. Holtzmann articulates this very point in his 1897 *New Testament Theology*:

> And so, in the end, we may be permitted to say that the Jewish and the Hellenistic alike are the perishable in Paul, but for Christianity the permanent is what was originally Christian. The former, which are the factors involved in its historical and temporal conditioning, are the concern of our theological and scientific, the latter, which is the resonance of the eternal in the human soul, is concerned with our religious and practical interest.[25]

In summary, liberal theology understood the essence of Pauline soteriology to be that by virtue of one's mystical experience "in Christ," power is given to live a new life. This new piety, we may observe by way of criticism, is very much divorced from the redemptive acts of Jesus' death and resurrection.[26] Ironically, these theologians, many of whom taught within the Lutheran church, had returned full circle to a (de-sacramentalized) Roman Catholic soteriology.

The History of Religions School

Although to this school the question was strictly an academic one, liberal theology had debated the extent to which Pauline thought was indebted to Greek or Jewish thought. The history of religions school weighed heavily on the former: Paul could be explained by pursuing parallels with Hellenistic mystery religions. This interest of the history of religions school paralleled European interest in primitivism and colonial cultures seen, for example, both in music (Igor Stravinsky) and in art (Paul Gauguin). This scholarly movement also arose in the context of a growing European anti-Semitism. The scholarship of this school centered on Wilhelm Bousset's *Kyrios Christos* and Richard Reitzenstein's *Hellenistic Mystery-Religions*.[27] The history of religions school, like Baur, presented a critical reconstruction of Paul independent of historic Christianity and its major tenets.

Unlike Baur, however, these scholars made their recourse almost exclusively to the influence of the Hellenistic environment on early Christianity. That view claimed that Christ came in time to be confessed as "lord" in the sense of the gods of Hellenistic mystery religions; and that he, like other Hellenistic deities, came to be worshiped and venerated as one who had, through death, achieved "victory, resurrection, and immortality."[28]

This group's focus was placed on the participation language of Paul, especially his "in Christ" phraseology and his sacramental theology (e.g., 1 Cor. 11; Rom. 6). The center of Pauline religion, then, was said to be cultic participation in the death and resurrection of this deity. A shift was made from doctrine to cult: the center of Pauline religion was thought to be less doctrinal or propositional than mystical and cultic participation in the risen and ascended Lord. Bousset summarizes this approach in *Kyrios Christos*:

We are now in a position to take a look also at the development and growth of the Pauline Christ-mysticism and the formula "to be in Christ, in the Lord" that sums it up. All that grew out of the cult. The *Kyrios* who was present in the cult became the Lord who rules over the whole personal life of the Christian. Paul's idea of the Spirit, likewise reinterpreted and expanded from the cultic into the ethico-religious, is the vehicle for the introduction of Christ mysticism.[29]

For all the history of religions school's differences from liberal theology (its resistance to the projects of modernizing Jesus and Paul for the modern man, for example), it continued to take the nineteenth-century mystical-ethical line and divorce it even further from the remainder of Pauline thought. This school correspondingly rejected, against Baur, justification as a center for Pauline thought (as Baur had maintained). Hermann Lüdemann had earlier anticipated this rejection, arguing that "there was tension in Paul's thought between the Jewish 'doctrine of salvation' " (focused on justification by faith alone) and the Hellenistic "realistic doctrine of redemption associated with baptism."[30] Hence, Paul was said to have two competing systems of redemption. For Paul, Lüdemann argued, the *real* doctrine that emerged was the Hellenistic, participatory one. Wilhelm Wrede later maintained a similar view. Wrede argued that justification was simply a polemic device to which Paul resorted in his conflict with Judaism.

By way of criticism of the history of religions school, we may observe that few follow this model today. Its central tenet, that the New Testament writers contributed nothing original, and that they simply absorbed and repristinated existing ideas, has been widely discarded. The abiding influence of the history of religions school comes in its stress on participation language in Paul and its corresponding de-emphasis of the so-called juridical language of Paul.

Albert Schweitzer

Albert Schweitzer introduced a new phase in Pauline studies in his two most important works on Paul, *Paul and His Interpreters: A Critical History* and *The Mysticism of Paul the Apostle*.[31] Schweitzer's scholarship signaled an important departure from the history of religions school. Unlike the history of religions school, which posited Pauline thought as taking root on non-Palestinian soil, Schweitzer argued for an organic connection between Judaism and Paul:

> The solution must, therefore, consist in leaving out of the question Greek influence in every form and in every combination, and risk the "one-sidedness" of endeavoring to understand the doctrine of the Apostle of the Gentiles entirely on the basis of Jewish primitive Christianity.[32]

We see, therefore, an explicit step toward a recognition of the "Jewish" roots of Paul. In taking this step, Schweitzer makes a decisive and conscious break from the history of religions school.

The main tenet of Schweitzer's system is what he called "Christ-mysticism." Like the history of religions school, Schweitzer stressed participation language ("being-in-Christ") as central to Paul's thought. While Schweitzer disagreed with the history of religions school concerning the origins of baptism and Lord's Supper,[33] he agreed that Pauline participation was essentially realistic and sacramental. Schweitzer maintains that baptism "effects redemption,"[34] a view that was said to have been transmitted to Paul from John the Baptist. "[Baptism] is, for him, powers that go forth from Christ which cause the redemptive event to take place in it."[35] It further effects the "forgiveness of sins."[36]

With respect to the Lord's Meal (he rejects the term "Lord's Supper"), Schweitzer maintains against Rome that neither Ignatius, Justin, John, nor Paul advanced a doctrine of transubstantiation[37] (although the former three are said to be initiating the process of the change).[38] There is no material change in the elements in the sacramental event. Schweitzer understands the language of "body and blood of Christ" in a horizontal manner, as the communion of the church, the mystical body of Christ. While the Meal is not chiefly vertical, the Meal is also not a bare sign—it "bring[s] about also that union which is to be experienced now in the present with the mystical body of Christ."[39] In sum, in baptism, grace is infused into the participant and redemption is effected. The chief significance of the Lord's Meal consists of both its creation and demonstration of union with Christ.

From this participationist viewpoint, Schweitzer concludes certain things about Paul's forensic language. He addresses this issue by agreeing with the charge that Paul's doctrine of justification rightly leads to antinomianism:

> Ethics are just as natural a resultant phenomenon of the dying and rising again with Christ as is liberation from the flesh, sin and the Law, or the bestowal of the Spirit. It is an operative result of the forgiveness of sin, which God makes a reality by the destruction of the flesh and of sin. Since Paul habitually thinks of redemption on the lines of the mystical doctrine of the being-in-Christ, it does not matter to him that in the subsidiary doctrine of righteousness by faith, he has shut off the road to ethics. What he wants this subsidiary doctrine for is to enable him, on the basis of the traditional conception of the atoning death of Christ, to conduct his controversy with the Law by means of the argument from Scripture. More he does not ask of it.[40]

With Wrede, then, Schweitzer argues that Paul's forensic language is an appendage to Paul—a "subsidiary crater, which has formed within the rim of the main crater; the mystical doctrine of redemption through the being-in-Christ."[41] He employed it for strictly polemical purposes; it does not lie at the heart of his thought. We will see this view surface again later in the twentieth century.

Conclusion

Let's take stock of what we have surveyed. We have seen that a couple of issues have shaped the critical discussion in the nineteenth and early twentieth centuries. First, there is a search for the "core" or heart of Paul's thought. Baur found this in Paul's teaching of the *Geist* in a purely philosophical sense. Liberals also found this in Paul's teaching of the *Geist*, but in a purely ethical sense. The history of religions school rejected (in principle) the distinction between theology and experience drawn by the liberals. It was not concerned with the question, "What is *normative* for the church today?" Its interests were strictly descriptive. They drew a portrait of the New Testament writers as sponges absorbing contemporary Greco-Roman culture, specifically the Hellenistic mystery cults. This school brought to the forefront participation language as being at the heart of Paul. Schweitzer, as we have seen, agreed in principle that participation language was at the heart of Paul. He also agreed that forensic language was a peripheral concern to the apostle.

A second question exercising critical scholarship in the nineteenth and twentieth centuries is whether Paul is Jewish or Gentile in origin. Participants in the critical discussion, many of whom had rejected Scripture's divine origin, sought purely secondary causes to explain the origin and development of the biblical writers' thought. The way in which the discussion had been framed by the turn of the twentieth century meant that one could choose between Jewish and Hellenistic sources. Hermeneutically, this meant that the interpretation of Paul was governed to some degree by (1) one's determination of the location of the sources of his thought and (2) one's prior reconstruction of those determining sources. Baur had resisted substantial Jewish origins for Pauline thought. Paul, after all, was said to be in conflict with Jewish Christianity. The history of religions school argued that Paul's sources were decidedly Hellenistic. Schweitzer was among the first to break with critical orthodoxy and argue for "Jewish primitive Christianity" as the ground from which Paul had sprung.

Into the Twentieth Century:
Bultmann, Davies, and Käsemann

e now turn to three figures, who took two different paths: Rudolf Bultmann, who (in some respects) would take the path of the history of religions school and who would be challenged by his pupil, Ernst Käsemann; and W. D. Davies, who would take the path of Schweitzer.

Rudolf Bultmann

The giant of twentieth-century biblical studies was Rudolf Bultmann. Serving as professor of New Testament at Marburg, Germany, from 1921, Bultmann lived until he was 92, dying in 1976. No single figure in the previous century has had more of an influence in shaping so many departments of New Testament study.

Bultmann set forth his views of Paul most comprehensively in his *Theology of the New Testament*.[1] Following the history of religions school, Bultmann argued that the thought world of the New Testament was to be found in its broader religious environment. Specifically, he pointed to the intermingling of Jewish and Hellenistic thought. John's Christology, for example, derived from a Jewish-Mandaean Wisdom myth of the heavenly primal redeemer-man.[2] Bultmann is clear

15

that the sources that fed into Paul were decidedly Hellenistic. He is, however, agnostic concerning the extent to which Paul, prior to his conversion, had been influenced by Hellenism.

> In his home city he came into contact with Hellenistic culture and became acquainted with popular philosophy and the phenomena of religious syncretism. It remains uncertain, however, to what extent he had already appropriated in his pre-Christian period theological ideas of this syncretism (those of the mystery religions and of Gnosticism) which come out in his Christian theology.[3]

Paul, after his conversion, had adopted the *kērygma* of the Hellenistic church, that is, Hellenistic Christianity.[4] The Hellenistic church did not draw the title *kyrios* (Greek, "lord"), Bultmann argues, from the Septuagint. The Septuagintal references to *kyrios* were only later attributed to Jesus because the church had applied the title *kyrios* to Jesus, having derived this title from the "religious terminology of Hellenism."[5]

Bultmann on Judaism

Bultmann is representative of the ways in which German-speaking New Testament scholarship in the first part of the twentieth century conceived of ancient Judaism. According to E. P. Sanders, Bultmann's portrait of Judaism is secondary and not independently derived from the primary literature of Judaism.[6] Thus, Bultmann's views of Judaism are not uniquely his own, but are representative of German scholarship in that period.

We may ask, then, what were the tenets of Judaism as Bultmann's teachers had taught them to him? Following Sanders, we may identify six such key points of the understanding of ancient Judaism that prevailed among Protestant biblical scholarship in the early and middle parts of the twentieth century:[7] (1) The relationship between the Jew and God was grounded on one's works, namely, one's obedience to the law of God, as set forth in the Torah. (2) Each work was viewed as meritorious: obedience yielded merit; disobedience, demerit to the Jew. (3) One's acceptance with God was a function of whether one's "merits" outweighed one's "demerits." (4) Because one could never know where his balance stood with God, the Jew feared God (in the most negative sense of the word) and did not believe that God loved him. No pure certainty or hope of salvation could be achieved. (5) Supererogation, as reflected in the rabbinic conception of the Treasury of the Fathers, was a consequence of this mentality. (6) Consequently, Judaism was a legalistic religion, that is, it was devoid of grace in any sense of the word.

This construct of Judaism, for Bultmann, was a foil for his construct of Christianity. He regarded Jesus as forward-looking, whereas the Jews were bound to the yoke of the past, epitomized in their slavish adherence to the law. To the Jew, "man's relation to God was inevitably conceived in legalistic terms."[8] Through this system of "merit,"[9] the Jew sought to lay claim on God. Jesus, however, called for an entirely different species of obedience to God. Paul, Bultmann argued, joined Jesus in rejecting Judaism and calling for this new form of obedience.

Bultmann on Pauline Justification

With respect to justification by faith alone, Bultmann departed from his history of religions teachers and colleagues. His views were *formally* Lutheran, that is, he used Lutheran terminology in order to express Pauline thought. Bultmann had *materially* embraced the form of existentialist philosophy that had been taught by Martin Heidegger, and believed that Paul was a suitable exponent of this philosophy. In view of this existentialist commitment, Bultmann departed from scholarship earlier in the century that had largely conceived Paul in corporate or cultic terms. For Bultmann, the "individual" was central, and justification (a "forensic concept") was central to Pauline theology. Justification, then, was not an inward or mystical "change"; rather, it is an "eschatological reality" made present to the believer, a "pure gift of God's grace," not attained or attainable by the works of the law.[10] In this respect, Bultmann argues, Paul was diametrically opposed to Judaism:

> The contrast between Paul and Judaism consists not merely in his assertion of the present reality of righteousness, but also in a much more decisive thesis—the one which concerns the condition to which

> God's acquitting decision is tied. The Jew takes it for granted that
> this condition is keeping the Law, the accomplishing of "works" pre-
> scribed by the Law. In direct contrast to this view, Paul's thesis runs—
> to consider its negative aspect first: *"without works of the Law. . . ."*
> The negative aspect of Paul's thesis does not stand alone; a positive
> statement takes its place beside it: *"by, or from faith."*[11]

For Bultmann, then, not only was justification by faith alone central
to Paul's thought, but it provided the focal point of distinction between
Paul and Judaism.

Bultmann, in formal agreement with traditional Lutheranism,
maintains the following positions: (1) Paul's difference with Judaism
is fundamentally soteriological in nature, that is, Paul is especially concerned to raise and resolve the question, "How am I saved?" (2) This
difference is crystallized in Paul's contrast of "works of the law" and
"faith." (3) "Faith" is exclusive to Christianity; "works of the law"
are the Jew's attempts to merit God's favor by obedience to the law.
All such efforts Paul eschews as unchristian. (4) Judaism, consequently,
is a legalistic religion, and Christianity (alone) is a religion of grace.
Stephen Westerholm nicely summarizes Bultmann's understanding of
the law and of faith:

> For Bultmann's Paul, the pursuit of the "righteousness of the law" is
> the typically Jewish expression of man's universal striving for recog-
> nition on the basis of his accomplishments. Faith is the renunciation
> of such striving as one recognizes one's utter dependence on God. It is
> expressed in genuine, radical obedience to God's demand in the law.[12]

It is in contrast to Bultmann's construction of Paul in particular that
most proponents of the NPP have defined their own understandings
of Paul. One of the first rumblings of discontent with Bultmann occurred in the scholarship of W. D. Davies.

William David Davies

Davies served for much of his scholarly career as a professor at
Duke University. His experience as a Welshman was said to have kin-

dled sympathy with the Jew (as an "underdog"), a sympathy that was encouraged by the support of his mentor and friend, David Daube, and the atrocities perpetrated against Jews when he was drafting *Paul and Rabbinic Judaism* between the years 1942 and 1947.[13]

Paul and Rabbinic Judaism, first published in 1948, was the first significant attempt to examine the relationship between Paul and contemporary Judaism sympathetically. Bultmann and others had conceived the relationship antithetically. Davies claimed, in the preface to the first edition of this book, that his purpose in writing was "[to] help to lead toward a deeper understanding of Judaism among Christians, and of Pauline Christianity among Jews."[14] The burden of Davies's book was to show that Paul was *indebted* to Pharisaical Judaism, as expressed in the works of its heirs, the rabbis. Unlike the approach adopted by Bultmann, then, Davies's approach was fundamentally *comparative* in nature.

One example of this comparative approach concerns the law. For Bultmann, the law in Paul was almost entirely negative. We stand, Paul was thought to argue, under the law's demand, and in our "effort to achieve salvation by keeping the law," we simply sin more. Only when we find ourselves in "dependence on God as Creator" do we experience salvation.[15] For Davies's Paul, however, Christ, as New Wisdom, served to fulfill the role that the Torah had played for Israel. This idea, Davies maintained, had been mediated to Paul through Proverbs, Ecclesiasticus, and Philo. We may note that in this argument continuity with Judaism is stressed, not discontinuity; and that the law has a positive role assigned to it.

Davies carried Schweitzer's mantle in at least two respects. First, the genesis of Pauline thought was to be found in Jewish, not pagan, sources. "Moreover, Schweitzer has convincingly shown, and we shall find so later in our discussion, that Paul's mysticism cannot be Hellenistic."[16] Second, as Sanders has observed, the "center of Pauline thought is not justification by faith." For Davies, it is Christology, *viz.*, the "awareness that with the coming of Christ the Age to Come had become present fact."[17] Of justification Davies remarked that "it is a simplification and even a falsification of the complexity of Paul's thought to pin down Justification by Faith as its quintessence."[18]

Davies maintained positively that

> our work will have made it clear that the centre of that thought is to
> be found not in Paul's attack on the old Torah but in his awareness
> that with the coming of Christ the Age to Come had become present
> fact . . . ; it lies in those conceptions of standing under the judgment
> and mercy of a New Torah, Christ, of dying and rising with that
> same Christ, of undergoing a New Exodus in Him and of so being
> incorporated into a New Israel, the community of the Spirit.[19]

This quotation evidences that in one important respect, Davies differed from virtually all other Pauline interpreters before him. Paul and
the Pharisees had no fundamental soteriological controversy or disagreement. In other words, it was Christology and not soteriology that
distinguished them. "Paul," rather, "found in Christ both Torah and
Spirit. . . . There is found in Paul a 'Christifying' of the Torah; Spirit
and Torah for Paul are coincident as it were in Christ."[20]

Davies's position raises an obvious question. Why then did Paul
make negative comments about the law? Davies argues that Paul held
to the common rabbinic belief that, with the dawn of the Messiah,
there would come a New Law. Paul's critique of the law, then, is an
eschatological one.[21] Paul nevertheless continues to observe the Old
Law because it was his "passport with Judaism."[22] Following Jesus'
example of "universalism in belief and particularism in practice,"[23]
Paul shaped his own belief and practice. Davies will stress, however,
that in so doing Paul was not fundamentally contradictory. Paul "was
being true both to the universalistic tradition of Judaism and at the
same time showing his identification with the Israel according to the
flesh: he was being true to the 'new' and the 'old' Israel."[24] In W. D.
Davies we find, for the first time, the door opened to critical readings
of Paul that would deny fundamental soteriological disagreement between Paul and his Jewish contemporaries.

Ernst Käsemann

Even apart from the scholarship of Davies, there was discontent
with Bultmann's synthesis within Continental scholarship. One such

specimen of this discontent was Bultmann's erstwhile student Ernst Käsemann. Käsemann engaged in what Sanders has called a "war on two fronts"—against Krister Stendahl to his left, and against Bultmann and his loyal disciples (Guenther Bornkamm and Hans Conzelmann) to his right.[25] A postwar student of Bultmann and professor of New Testament at Tübingen, Käsemann maintained that justification was at the center of Paul's thought. On this point, he strenuously opposed Stendahl, directing against the latter his essay "Justification and Salvation History in the Epistle to the Romans."[26] Käsemann concludes that "justification remains the centre, the beginning and the end of salvation history."[27] This concern *not* to subsume justification under salvation history stems, Käsemann informs us, from a concern over recent events:

> This discovery [of justification] immunized us deeply against a conception of salvation history which broke in on us in secularized and political form with the Third Reich and its ideology. It will be understandable that as burnt children we are unwilling to add fuel to the fire which at the present day, for the third time in a century, is awakening such general enthusiasm. Our experience has made a theology of history suspect for us from the very outset, whatever the reasons may be which are urged in its support. It determined the liberalism whose faith in progress was finally shattered by the First World War. However erroneously and improperly, it was capable of serving as a shield for Nazi eschatology. We do not want to be called back to the place where our fathers and grandfathers stood a hundred years ago and where they came to grief fifty years later.[28]

While so distancing Pauline justification from a salvation-historical framework, Käsemann departed from Bultmann by rejecting Bultmann's focus on the individual, that is, the latter's *anthropocentrism*. We may recall that Bultmann had argued that existentialist philosophy lay materially at the core of Paul's message. Sin and redemption, consequently, were perceived in fundamentally individualistic and private categories.

Käsemann, rather, argued that Pauline justification was fundamentally *corporate*. He laid out this case in "The Righteousness of

God in Paul," first published in 1961.[29] The thesis of this essay is that
"the righteousness of God does not, in Paul's understanding, refer primarily to the individual and is not to be understood exclusively in the
context of the doctrine of man."[30] Käsemann positively defined the
righteousness of God in Paul's letters *not* as a gift bestowed by God
to man,[31] but, citing parallels from the Old Testament and the
Gospels,[32] as "a phrase expressing divine activity . . . of the self-
revealing God."[33] Käsemann argued that the tension (or "dialectic")[34]
between Paul's forensic and transformative righteousness language
could be resolved by seeing the righteousness of God as a "gift as
power" with the "lordship of Christ recognized as its peculiar content."[35] He can consequently point to the phrase "righteousness of
God" at Romans 3:25ff. and argue that this means "God's covenant-
faithfulness," *viz.*, God's pledge of saving power that restores his creation. It is "God's victory amid the opposition of the world" or "God's
sovereignty over the world revealing itself eschatologically in Jesus."[36]
There is nevertheless a reserve in Käsemann, and he will not go as far
as Stendahl in the de-individualization of Paul. Käsemann maintains
that "as the acceptance of the divine address, faith in Paul remains primarily a decision of the individual person and its importance must not
therefore be shifted away from anthropology to ecclesiology."[37] In
other words, Käsemann was still willing to see justification in fundamentally *moral* (not *communal*) terms, and focused on (although not
defined by) the individual.

    In summary, we may observe the following conclusions. First,
Käsemann cuts the Gordian knot involved in sorting out the juridi-
cal/transformative language in Paul by resolving the language of righteousness into cosmic, saving power. In so doing, Käsemann has for
all intents and purposes forfeited forensic language. Second, Käsemann, while maintaining a personal dimension to justification, clearly
conceives it to be fundamentally corporate or cosmic in nature.

THREE

Enter the New Perspective:
Krister Stendahl

rister Stendahl, a Swedish Lutheran, served as professor of New Testament at Harvard Divinity School from 1954 to 1984. He is perhaps best known in Pauline studies for two articles, "The Apostle Paul and the Introspective Conscience of the West," and "Paul Among Jews and Gentiles."[1] Stendahl argued that the conversion experiences of Luther and Augustine had tinctured the West's reading of Paul. Western theology, he maintained, had taken a relatively minor component of Paul's thought (justification by faith alone), turning it into *the* center (hence the debate with Käsemann), and had sidelined more significant themes, such as the role of Jews and Gentiles in the plan of God. How did he argue this? We turn now to review these two groundbreaking articles, in the order in which they appeared.

"The Apostle Paul and the Introspective Conscience of the West"

In this paper, Stendahl demurred from the traditional interpretation of Paul, which had understood justification to be a response to a perceived condition of guilt and sin. This condition, traditionalists con-

23

tinued, was occasioned by disobedience to the law, and justification was understood to be a response to that problem. This Reformational model, Stendahl argued, was the product of Luther's unique religious psychology: the blend of Luther's Augustinian background, his conflict with Rome, and his sensitive conscience.[2] Paul had been "read in the framework of late medieval piety."[3] The West "for centuries has wrongly surmised that the biblical writers were grappling with problems which no doubt are ours, but which never entered their consciousness."[4]

Stendahl objected to this model in part because the ancient Eastern churches do not evidence this "plagued conscience."[5] This helped prove to Stendahl that this model was a product of Paul's interpreters, but not of Paul himself. Stendahl also complained that this model had affected "not only . . . those who find themselves more or less dogmatically bound by the confessions of the Reformation," but also "the average student of 'all the great books' in a College course, or the agnostic Westerner in general."[6] On this point, Stendahl faults Bultmann in particular.[7]

Positively, how was Paul to be understood? Stendahl's programmatic statement in this essay explains his approach: "Romans 9–11 is not an appendix to chapters 1–8, but the climax of the letter."[8] It is in these chapters that we reach the central and organizing principle not only of this letter, but of Pauline thought generally: the Jew/Gentile question. Paul was consumed *not* with Luther's question "How do I find a gracious God?,"[9] but rather with two central questions: (1) "What happens to the Law (the Torah, the actual Law of Moses, not the principle of legalism) when the Messiah has come?"[10] (2) "What are the ramifications of the Messiah's arrival for the relation between Jews and Gentiles?" In other words, what is the "place of the Gentiles in the Church and in the plan of God"?[11]

Stendahl argues that traditionally interpreted passages have been misinterpreted. First, Galatians 3:24 does not prove the *usus secundus* (second use, i.e., the law drives us to Christ) in a way that would apply to Jews *and* Gentiles. Paul, rather, is showing that the law uniquely led Jews to the Messiah *in order* to show that "there is no reason to impose the Law on the Gentiles, who now, in God's good Messianic time, have become partakers in the fulfillment of the promises to Abraham (v.29)."[12] The "we"/"our" of this passage, as Stendahl argues in "Paul Among Jews and Gentiles," "means 'me, Paul, with my Jewish compatriots,' and nothing else. It is totally wrong to apply that 'our' to *us Gentiles*."[13] Second, Romans 7, as W. G. Kümmel has argued in his *Römer 7 und die Bekehrung des Paulus* (1929), does not show that Paul is conscientiously anguishing over infractions and transgressions of the law. Rather, Paul is defending the law against the charge that it is sin, and defending its holiness and goodness. This passage is not one of "utter contrition" but "acquittal of the ego," in support of which Stendahl quotes: "But if I am doing the very thing I do not want, I am no longer the one doing it" (v. 20); "I joyfully concur with the law of God in the inner man" (v. 22); and "I myself with my mind am serving the law of God" (v. 25). Stendahl provocatively summarizes his reading of Romans 7 in "Paul Among Jews and Gentiles":

> Thus Paul does not feel responsible for sin; he is on the side of God! He does not get a "Protestant/Puritanical kick" out of the passage at all. Nor does he give it an autobiographical or existential touch. He simply uses an argument known from Stoicism and other ancient philosophies to show that the ego is on God's side, and that it recognizes the law as good. This point is clearly not the epistle's center of gravity.[14]

Such departures from traditional readings of Pauline passages signaled nothing less than a paradigmatical shift in the critical study of Paul.

"Paul Among Jews and Gentiles"

In the previous article, Stendahl had tentatively advanced his argument that Paul had a "robust conscience." Here, he programmatically sets forth the life and teaching of the apostle Paul by means of mutually exclusive polarities (we might say "false dichotomies"). First, Paul's chief concern in Romans is "the relation between Jews and Gentiles—and in the development of *this* concern he used as one of his arguments the idea of justification by faith."[15] This statement virtually reversed the order that most New Testament scholars had previously seen. Stendahl stresses, in explanation of this point, that Paul's concern is not with two systems (Judaism and Christianity) but with "two communities and their coexistence in the mysterious plan of God."[16]

Second, Paul experienced a call, not a conversion.[17] Stendahl argues that there is no evidence from the relevant passages (Acts 9; 22; 26; Gal. 1) that Paul experienced a "change of religion." In Acts 9, Paul is said to be God's "chosen instrument" (9:15), evoking the prophetic-call language of Jeremiah 1:5 and Isaiah 49:1. But there is not a hint that this event is a "conversion from one religion to another."[18] Paul, rather, is called to bear God's name "before the Gentiles and kings and the sons of Israel" (9:15). In Acts 22, we read the same thing: "The God of our fathers appointed you to know his will, to see the Just One and to hear a voice from his mouth; for you will be a witness for him to all men of what you have seen and heard" (22:14–15 RSV). God tells Paul directly, "Depart; for I will send you far away to the Gentiles" (22:21 RSV). Paul argues similarly in Acts 26: "I have appeared to you for this purpose, to appoint you to serve and witness . . . , delivering you from the people and from the Gentiles—to whom I send you to open their eyes, that they may turn from darkness to light and from the power of Satan to God, that they may receive forgiveness of sins and a place among those who are sanctified by faith in me" (vv. 16–18 RSV). Stendahl, overlooking the soteriological import of this passage, sees here once again only the prophetic-call passages (Ezek. 1:28; 2:1, 3; Jer. 1:7), a fact that is highlighted by such other parallel passages in Isaianic prophecy as "the opening of the eyes of the blind" and "salvation" coming to the Gentiles. What of Galatians 1:11–17? Stendahl again sees in Paul's account simply the language of the prophetic-call narratives (Isa. 49:1; Jer. 1:5).

Paul, then, Stendahl argues, did not experience a conversion. He experienced a call on the order of the Hebrew prophets. Paul "felt hand-picked by God after the prophetic model to take the message of God and Christ to the Gentiles."[19] Furthermore, Paul "serve[d] one and the same God" both before and after this encounter. What is emphasized in each of the New Testament narratives is his "assignment" to "bring God's message to the Gentiles."[20]

We explain the transition this way: [Paul's] call brings him to a new understanding of his mission, a new understanding of the law which is otherwise an obstacle to the Gentiles. His ministry is based on the specific conviction that the Gentiles will become part of the people of God without having to pass through the law. This is Paul's secret revelation and knowledge.[21]

It is, therefore, the apostle's sending that is stressed. Considerations of a conversion, classically considered, do not enter into Stendahl's readings of these passages.

In order to stress his point that Paul did not convert in any traditional sense, Stendahl examines passages in which Paul assesses his life both before and after his Damascus Road experience. Even in Philippians 3:5–9, Paul, while mentioning his "former values," speaks of their worth only *relative to* "his knowledge and recognition of Christ."[22] He does not speak of their *intrinsic* demerit. Paul says at 3:6 (RSV)that "as to righteousness under the law [I was] blameless"—consequently, Paul had no "troubles, problems, qualms of conscience, [or] feelings of shortcomings" about his life under Judaism. He was a "very happy and successful Jew."[23] Concerning 1 Corinthians 15:9 ("For I am the least of the apostles, and not fit to be called an apostle, because I persecuted the church of God"), Stendahl observes that "the fact that past glories led him to become a persecutor of the church caused him some remorse *after* his call, but there is no indication of such remorse or doubts prior to his call to the mission."[24] His conscience was robust: "Nowhere in Paul's writings is there any indication that he had any difficulties in fulfilling what he as a Jew understood to be the requirements of the Law."[25]

In defense of Paul's robust Christian conscience, Stendahl addresses three passages. First, concerning 2 Corinthians 5:10–11,[26] Stendahl comments: "That does not sound very modest. That does not sound like a man who is conscious of the fact that he is at the same time justified and sinner, *simul justus et peccator*. So something seems askew in our reading if we think that Paul was troubled by sin."[27] Second, regarding 1 Corinthians 4:1–5,[28] Stendahl argues that this passage self-evidently establishes that Paul has a "robust . . . conscience."[29]

Third, Stendahl sees Paul's comment in 1 Corinthians 15:10 ("I have worked harder than any of them") as evidence that Paul believed that his apostolic labors "made up" for his prior sin of persecution.[30] Paul, of course, recognized that "it was not I, but the grace of God which is with me" (v. 10), but nevertheless "Paul is confident that he has made up for the only sin which he speaks about concretely."[31] We have, then, in Stendahl a category of self-atoning work. If we become aware of any sin (and we probably won't or shouldn't), then, by the assistance of God's grace, we can "make it up" through certain religious activity. Incidentally, when we come to E. P. Sanders's description of rabbinic Judaism (chapter 4), we will see precisely the same doctrine articulated in those Jewish sources that Sanders cites.

A third polarity raised in Stendahl's essay is that Paul taught justification but not a doctrine of forgiveness.[32] When we come to Stendahl's discussion of justification, it is clear that, with Käsemann, he is warring against Bultmann's anthropocentrism (although Käsemann had maintained paradoxically that justification was both corporate and centered on the individual):

> Rudolf Bultmann's whole theological enterprise has *one* great mistake from which all others emanate: he takes for granted that basically the center of gravity—the center from which all interpretation springs—is anthropology, the doctrine of man. This might in fact be so, but if it be so it certainly devastates and destroys the perspective of Pauline thinking.[33]

In Stendahl, then, we continue the revolt against Bultmann's construction of Paul.

Stendahl observes that the word "forgive/ness" is absent from Paul's (authentic) writings. Western emphasis on this concept has arisen from its "anthropocentricity and psychologizing tendencies."[34] The word, of course, *is* present at Ephesians 1:7 and Colossians 1:14 ("redemption [through his blood], the forgiveness of sins"), but these letters are dismissed as non-Pauline. They have been authored by "a writer much in the Pauline tradition."[35] When Paul *does* use some form of the word "forgive," it is because it appears in an Old Testament quotation (Psalm 32 in Romans 4:7: "Blessed are those whose lawless deeds have been forgiven, and whose sins have been covered"). Paul's *real* interest in this passage is righteousness, as he goes on to discuss at Romans 4:9.[36]

Modern readers' corresponding obsession with forgiveness simply evidences that "we happen to be more interested in ourselves than in God or in the fate of his creation."[37] In so doing, we have removed ourselves from the true Paul.

The word "justification," Stendahl observes, occurs predominantly in Romans and Galatians. The phrase "justification by faith and not by works" occurs *exclusively* in Romans and Galatians, both of which letters are occupied with the Jew/Gentile question. Paul, furthermore, explicitly ties justification to the Jew/Gentile question; see Romans 1:16–17 ("For I am not ashamed of the gospel, for it is the power of God for salvation to everyone who believes, to the Jew first and also to the Greek") and Romans 3:28–29 ("For we maintain that a man is justified by faith apart from works of the Law. Or is God the God of Jews only? Is He not the God of Gentiles also? Yes, of Gentiles also"). Regarding Pauline justification, Stendahl observes that it is not the "pervasive, organizing principle or insight of Paul" but "it has a very specific function in his thought."[38] In other words, the doctrine of justification "originates in Paul's theological mind from his grappling with the problem of how to defend the place of the Gentiles in the Kingdom—the task with which he was charged in his call."[39] As Schweitzer had maintained, Stendahl contends that justification's role in Paul's thought is primarily polemical.

Stendahl argues that the rhetorical structure of Romans supports his arguments concerning justification in Paul. In Romans, chapters 9–11 constitute the centerpiece of the book.[40] Romans 1–8 is a "preface" to these chapters. Stendahl expounds the significance of this preface:

> Since justification is by faith it is equally possible for both Jews and Gentiles to come to Christ. In that preface he does not deal with the question of how man is to be saved—be it by works or law or by something else. He is simply pointing out in a very intelligent and powerful theological fashion that the basis for a church of Jews and

Gentiles has already been set forth in Scripture where the prime example is Abraham (Gen. 15:6, cited at Rom. 4:3). In Romans 1–8, both Gentiles and Jews are found equally culpable (Rom. 3:9ff.), yet also equally capable of being saved through justification (Rom. 3:21–30).[41]

Paul, then, argues the way that he does in Romans 1–3 *not* because of his insights of human psychology, but because he taps into a particular strain of Jewish apocalyptic that believed that the Messiah would come in an age of sinfulness.[42] We may outline the reasoning that Stendahl employs here: *because* the Messiah has come, we know that the world is sinful. In maintaining that Paul reasons from solution (the coming of the Messiah) to plight (universal sinfulness), Stendahl anticipates a central plank of Sanders's reading of Paul, and of NPP readings generally.

So what, then, does Paul *mean* by "righteousness" and "justification," according to Stendahl? He argues that we must go to these terms' Hebrew background in order to define them. When we do so, we find that the righteousness of God refers to God's vindication of his people. As a word, "righteousness" means "salvation, rescue, victory, triumph."[43] The people of God celebrate God's righteousness in such a way that they are "absolutely convinced of [their] identity as God's people."[44] Consequently, "any manifestation of God's righteousness must therefore mean that this people is exalted and triumphant and that its enemies are defeated."[45] The language of righteousness in Paul, then, is decidedly nonmoral in nature and communitarian in focus. Stendahl has little positively to say about justification except that it is an ecclesiological term. The term is a device whereby, Paul argues, God includes Jews *and* Gentiles on the same terms within the people of God. He draws a parallel in this respect with the Qumran literature:

> Those who are loyal to the community and to its leader are precisely those who will be saved. At Qumran, loyalty to the sect of the new covenant and to the Righteous Teacher were determinative. In a similar—sectarian—way the early church set loyalty to Jesus Christ and his messianic community as the key to salvation.[46]

Pauline justification, then, when viewed against this Second Temple Jewish background, is explicable as an ecclesiological term.

The fourth polarity addressed by Stendahl in "Paul Among Jews and Gentiles" is that when Paul taught about weakness, he did not teach about sin.[47] On the occasions when Paul *does* speak experientially, it is by the language of weakness that he chooses to speak.[48] Paul's concern with weakness is essentially nonmoral. The apostle never identifies weakness with sin.[49] Nor is this language *anthropologically* moral. It does not come "from within himself—lack of obedience, sanctity, or moral force and achievement" but "from without—it is inflicted by Satan, it is an infliction of the enemy."[50] He *does* admit, however, that Romans 5:6 ("while we were still helpless, Christ died for the ungodly," Stendahl's translation) may be a *possible* exception.[51]

Another polarity explored in this essay is that Paul taught about love, but not integrity.[52] Stendahl states that "church or ethical problems are really group or community problems, because Christianity is not a principle to be followed with utter clarity or precision. Christianity is an experiment in living together—and with a certain flexible ability to take differences into account without being divided."[53] He summarizes:

> As we have wandered through various demonstrations of Paul's principle, *love rather than integrity*, we may now be ready to rephrase it and sharpen it by saying: love allows for not insisting on one's own integrity at the expense of the unity of the community. . . . Love allows for the full respect of the integrity of the other, and overcomes the divisiveness of my zeal for having it my way in the name of my own integrity.[54]

We might note, for example, that he takes Paul's phrase "discerning the body" (1 Cor. 11:29 RSV) to mean, with Schweitzer, "recogniz[ing] the community of the church."[55] The Pauline ethic, as with justification, is therefore one that does not stress objective standards (sin, uprightness), but focuses on issues of community harmony. Such formulations flow from Stendahl's overarching conception of the center of Paul's thought as consisting of the inclusion of the Gentiles into the people of God. When we later turn to N. T. Wright and his ethics, we will hear reverberations of Stendahl's conception of Pauline ethics.

Summary

We may now, in preparation for our review of more recent NPP proponents, draw some concluding observations:

1. According to Stendahl, Paul was never concerned (personally or corporately) with a change of religions—rather, Paul's ministry was to follow a call that God had given him to proclaim the Messiah to Jew and Gentile. Paul, therefore, had no *soteriological* objection to Judaism. Stendahl, then, unlike Bultmann and Käsemann, posits fundamental continuity among the Old Testament, first-century Judaism, and Paul.
2. Paul never suffered, whether as a Jew or as a Christian, a tormented conscience, as Augustine and Luther had argued. On the contrary, he possessed a robust conscience, even to the point of believing that his apostolic labors made up for his persecutions in Judaism (1 Cor. 15:10).
3. Pauline thought is not anthropocentric (whether in a Reformational Lutheran or a Bultmannian Lutheran sense), but fundamentally concerned with the Jew/Gentile question. Romans 9–11, consequently, and not Romans 1–8, constitutes the center of Romans. We may recall Stendahl's comments concerning the goal of Romans 1–8 in the structure of Romans. These chapters are "a preface . . . in which Paul argues that since justification is by faith it is equally possible for both Jews and Gentiles to come to Christ. In that preface he does not deal with the question of how man is to be saved—be it by works or law or by something else."[56]
4. Paul's doctrine of justification by faith alone is a polemical doctrine and does not rest at the center of his thought.
5. Paul's doctrine of justification is not *soteriological* but *ecclesiological* in nature. Paul is not concerned with sin or any other moral issue, but with the disclosure of the victory of God in

including Jews and Gentiles into one people. The office of faith was to be an instrument whereby "the church knows itself as belonging to God, knows its enemies to be God's enemies."[57] The doctrine of justification was explicitly formulated in service of the Jew/Gentile question: how can we warrant Gentile membership in the people of God? Justification stems, then, from the unique circumstances surrounding Paul's call. The doctrine also is tied to a unique system of ethics focused on the cohesion of the community (not transcendent and objective moral standards).

6. Why, then, does Paul employ moral language in Romans 1–3? It is because Paul reasons from solution to plight. Paul's statements regarding man's universal sinfulness are a consequence of his Jewish heritage. They stem from a prior belief that *if* the Messiah has come, *then* the world must be sinful. Stendahl does not argue that such statements are grounded on Adamic solidarity in sin (as traditionally argued from Romans 5:12–21), or on an empirical assessment of the human condition.

Ad Fontes?:
E. P. Sanders on Judaism

ver the next two chapters, we will turn our attention to E. P. Sanders, admittedly a pivotal figure not only in the NPP but also in Pauline studies. Sanders has published three works that are especially pertinent to our studies. Sanders's magnum opus is *Paul and Palestinian Judaism*, written during the mid-1970s and published in 1977.[1] Its discussion on Pauline theology is incomplete, so Sanders elaborates his conception of that topic in *Paul, the Law, and the Jewish People* (1983).[2] A nonpolemic and in-depth survey of ancient Judaism was published in 1992, *Judaism: Practice and Belief.*[3]

We will argue that Sanders does not argue any single point that was substantially new. His genius consists in synthesizing many diverse strands of Pauline interpretation that have preceded him, and in presenting a case grounded on a fresh reading of the primary sources pertinent to ancient Judaism. In the present chapter, we will explore his research into Judaism—why it is significant, and what he has concluded. In the next chapter, we will turn to Sanders's research into Paul, and the way in which he rereads Paul in light of his readings of rabbinic Judaism.

The Background: Questions of Method

We observed above that for most twentieth-century New Testament scholars, Judaism contemporary to Paul had been mediated through a handful of secondary sources.[4] In a blistering overview of prior scholarship in *Paul and Palestinian Judaism*, Sanders dismantles the pantheon of works on ancient Judaism as distorted and inaccurate.

Sanders not only dissents from the literature on questions of interpretation of data, but also proposes a new methodology. Sanders specifically charges that past scholarship has limited its attention to what Sanders has termed "reduced essences" (i.e., faith versus works; liberty versus law; spiritual versus material/commercial religion) or an "individual motif."[5] This stemmed, in part, from a desire to construct a "systematic theology" from the rabbinic sources, as though "there was one systematic theology operative in the entire period."[6]

What is needed, Sanders argues, is a holistic comparison of one "pattern" or "whole religion" with another system. This approach, Sanders contends, is least vulnerable to abuse. The approach that Sanders proposes focuses on two questions that inquire into how a religion functions: how does one *get* in and how does one *stay* in the community of the saved? Sanders's pattern is not quite soteriology because it does not address, for instance, questions about the afterlife, original sin, and other matters with which Sanders argues Judaism is relatively unconcerned. Rather, the pattern stresses, Sanders tells us, "how religion and the religious life *worked*, how the religion *functioned*." In other words, from attention to functional considerations, a "common pattern" of religion will emerge from the sources.[7]

Sanders further argues that we should not expect systematic precision on important questions that we might bring to the system, or that the system raises but *do not touch the functional dimensions of religion* (the importance of this argument will become evident below). This state of affairs is owing, according to Sanders, to the diverse character of the literature. Rabbinic literature is the compilation of the opinions of hundreds of teachers, is not creedal in character, and does not strive to achieve the same levels of definition that a church council would. To anticipate a criticism to which we'll return below, however, we should note that the consensus of rabbinic opinion on some issues (*that* God elected Israel), but the diversity of rabbinic opinion on other issues (*why* God elected Israel) is significant in a way that Sanders does not grasp.

A final methodological contribution of Sanders's scholarship of ancient Judaism is that he constructs his pattern of Judaism from sources dating between 200 B.C. and A.D. 200. The pattern concentrates on three broad categories of material: the Tannaitic literature, the Dead Sea Scrolls, and the Apocrypha and Pseudepigrapha. New Testament scholars had previously read the Talmudic literature (dating not earlier than late antiquity) and had assumed that this literature provided an accurate representation of Jewish belief and practice contemporary to Jesus and Paul. Jacob Neusner's work *The Rabbinic Traditions about the Pharisees Before 70* convinced many scholars that drawing statements from the Palestinian and Babylonian Talmud uncritically in order to construct a picture of pre–A.D. 70 Judaism was wrongheaded.[8] Sanders concurs.[9] He does not deny the continuity between Pharisaic and rabbinic Judaism (as some skeptical scholars of Judaism have done), but neither does he equate them. When he attempts to construct a portrait of the Pharisees from the rabbinic sources, Sanders restricts himself to the works of the *Tannaim* (the repeaters), whose works represent the earliest stratum of the rabbinic literature. The works of the Tannaim, portions of which date to the first century A.D., include the Mishnah, the Tosefta, and the Tannaitic or *halakhic midrashim*. We consequently have a revolution of sorts in the study of ancient Judaism. Much rabbinic material that *had* been used to construct a portrait of Judaism was now being ruled out of court by Neusner, Sanders, and other scholars of Judaism.

Questions of Substance

Sanders has chiefly objected to conventional (i.e., liberal Protestant) reconstructions of ancient Judaism on grounds of substance. He argued that what characterized Judaism globally, as a pattern of religion, at this time was what he has termed "covenantal nomism," consisting of eight constituent elements:[10]

(1) God has chosen Israel and (2) given the law. The law implies both (3) God's promise to maintain the election and (4) the requirement to obey. (5) God rewards obedience and punishes transgression. (6) The law provides for means of atonement, and atonement results in (7) maintenance or re-establishment of the covenantal relationship. (8) All those who are maintained in the covenant by obedience, atonement, and God's mercy belong to the group which will be saved. An important interpretation of the first and last points is that election and ultimately salvation are considered to be by God's mercy rather than human achievement.

In view of this universal pattern, Sanders argues that ancient Judaism, according to its own sources, was not a religion of works righteousness. We now examine this argument from the standpoint of the Tannaitic literature, which represents that strand of Judaism with which Paul was most intimate and familiar. We will consider the evidence that Sanders has produced from this literature concerning election, obedience, salvation by membership in the covenant, and atonement.

Election

Election, Sanders argues, was generally conceived to be "totally gratuitous without prior cause in those being elected."[11] And yet, the rabbis offered three reasons "why God chose Israel."[12] First, God was thought to have "offered the covenant to all."[13] This belief was occasioned by rabbinic speculation that since Sinai was not located within the geographical bounds of Israel, the covenant must have been offered to nations other than Israel:

> *They encamped in the wilderness* (Exodus 19:2b). The Torah was given in public openly in a free place. For had the Torah been given in the land of Israel, the Israelites could have said to the nations of the world: You have no share in it. But now that it was given in the wilderness publicly and openly in a place that is free for all, everyone wishing to accept it could come and accept it.[14]

Although God offered the covenant to all nations, the rabbis argued, "only Israel accepted it."[15]

Another interpretation: "And he said, 'The Lord came from Sinai' "
(Deut 33.2). When the Holy One, blessed be he, revealed himself to
give [the] Torah to Israel, he revealed himself not to Israel alone, but
to all the nations. He came first to the sons of Esau and said to them,
"You accept the Torah." They said to him, "What is written in it?"
He answered, "Thou shalt not murder." They answered that the very
nature of their father was that he killed (referring to Gen 27).[16]

A second reason that God chose Israel, the rabbis argued, was
"because of some merit found either in the patriarchs or in the exodus generation or on the condition of future obedience."[17] The following two rabbinic discussions illustrate these two grounds of election,
respectively.

And Ye Shall Keep It until the Fourteenth Day of the Same Month.
Why did the Scripture require the purchase of the paschal lamb to
take place four days before its slaughter? R. Matia the son of Cheresh
used to say: Behold it says: "Now when I passed by thee, and looked
upon thee, and behold, thy time was the time of love" (Exodus 16.8).
This means, the time has arrived for the fulfillment of the oath which
the Holy One, blessed be He, had sworn unto Abraham, to deliver
his children. But as yet they had no religious duties [*mitzvoth*] by
which to merit redemption, as it further says: "thy breasts were fash-
ioned and thy hair was grown; yet thou wast naked and bare," which
means bare of any religious deeds. Therefore the Holy One, blessed
be He, assigned them two duties, the duty of the paschal sacrifice and
the duty of circumcision, which they should perform so as to be worthy of redemption. For this reason Scripture required that the purchase of the paschal lamb take place four days before its slaughter.
For one cannot obtain rewards except for deeds. R. Eleazar ha Kap-
par says: Did not Israel possess four virtues than which nothing in
the whole world is more worthy: that they were above suspicion in
regard to chastity and in regard to tale bearing, that they did not
change their names and that they did not change their language . . . ?[18]

"When the Most High gave to the nations their inheritance." When
the Holy One, blessed be He, gave [the] Torah to Israel, he stopped,
looked (into the future, *tsafah*) and perceived . . . , and there being

no nation among the nations which was worthy to receive the Torah except Israel, "he fixed the bounds of the peoples."[19]

A third reason offered is that "God chose Israel for his name's sake."[20] The passage that Sanders offers as evidence of this reason nevertheless does not maintain God's name's sake as an *exclusive* ground of Israel's election:

> R. Jose the Galilean said: "And God said." The Holy One, blessed be He, said to Moses, "Israel deserves extinction in Egypt . . . because they are unclean [through worshipping] the idols of Egypt. . . . But for the sake of my great name and because of the merits of the Fathers [I will bring them out], as it is written" [citing Exodus 2:24, Ezekiel 20:9]. . . . R. Joshua b. Karha said: "And God said." The Holy One, blessed be He, said, "Israel was not worthy that I should give them manna in the wilderness, but rather they deserved hunger and thirst and nakedness. But I completed [paying] to them the reward of Abraham their father who 'stood' and 'made' before the ministering angels, as it is said, 'And he took the curds and milk . . . [which he made . . . and he stood by them . . .].' " (Genesis 18.8).[21]

Let us note some observations on these data that Sanders has offered concerning rabbinic opinions of the reason back of God's election of Israel. First, as we commented above, even rabbinic opinions that Sanders cites in the third category above ("God chose Israel for His name's sake") do not evidence God choosing *solely* for his name's sake. The act of divine election, rather, consistently contemplates the good deeds of certain Israelites. Second, for Sanders, the conflicting diversity of opinions concerning *why* Israel was elected arose from a rabbinic desire to "make God's choice seem non-arbitrary."[22]

Third, Sanders explains the significance of the diversity of these explanations by observing that "from debates about *why* God chose Israel we infer the centrality of the conviction *that* he chose Israel."[23] The passages in the rabbinic literature that speak of God's delivering Israel at the exodus because of the merit of their deeds were attempts "to find a reason for the election," and so were not themselves "a systematic explanation of God's election of Israel" and therefore do not entail merit.[24] Sanders also observes that "for whatever reason God chose Israel in the past, the *a priori* expectation would be that in subsequent generations the covenant would remain effective, that God would keep his promises to redeem and preserve his people."[25] In summary: "All three [kinds of statements] are explanations of the same conviction, the conviction that God chose Israel, and all three are based on the same logic, that God's choice was not capricious or arbitrary. For our purpose, the underlying agreement is more significant than the dispute."[26]

Obedience

Sanders argues that obedience to the commandments is in this literature a consequence of Israel's election.[27] Sanders reminds readers that contrary to prevailing academic conceptions of obedience in rabbinic Judaism, the rabbis themselves took into account intention, not simply the outward deed; believed in an "essential . . . core" to the commandments, namely, the love of God and neighbor; did not regard the law to be a burden; and believed that one ought to obey God primarily from the motive of love.[28]

Regarding man's nature, Sanders offers a brief summary of the rabbinic discussions:

> It is important to note that the Rabbis did not have a doctrine of original sin or of the essential sinfulness of each man in the Christian sense. It is a matter of observation that all men sin. Men have, apparently, the inborn drive towards rebellion and disobedience. But this is not the same as being born in a state of sinfulness from which liberation is necessary. Sin comes only when man actually disobeys; if he were not to disobey he would not be a sinner. The possibility exists that one might not sin. Despite the tendency to disobey, man is free to obey or disobey.[29]

In other words, nothing within the nature of man determines him to sin. He is, to use traditional theological language, *posse peccare et posse non peccare* (able to sin and able not to sin).

Regarding the acceptability of one's obedience, Sanders cites two rabbinic discussions as evidence that God's "quality of rewarding" exceeds his "quality of punishing":

> If he that commits one transgression thereby forfeits his soul, how much more, if he performs one religious duty (*mitzvah*), shall his soul be restored to him![30]

> In a *qal vachomer* argument R. Jose reasoned that, if Adam's transgression caused death to fall to countless future generations because of God's "quality of punishing," much more will God's "quality of rewarding," which is greater, cause one's descendants to reap benefits from one's fulfillment of commandments.[31]

There is, however, an inherent vagueness to such statements. This imprecision is further problematized by the fact that affirmations can be found in the rabbinic literature to the effect that "God is just and pays to each his due" *and* "God's mercy predominates over his justice." It is at this juncture that Sanders reminds us that the rabbis do not give us a "doctrinal system in which every statement has a logical place."[32] He assures us that the predominance of mercy "reflects the Rabbinic attitude towards God at its most basic level."[33] These rabbinic statements nevertheless beg the question on what ground one may have hopeful expectations at the final judgment. Sanders observes that there are "three groups of sayings" concerning the final judgment: "damnation for one transgression," "salvation for one fulfillment," and "judgment according to the majority of deeds." We will now consider each of these groups.

1. *Judgment According to the Majority of Deeds.* The discussion concerning the judgment according to the majority of deeds especially swirls around one Mishnah and the rabbinic interpretative tradition subsequent to it.

> Everyone who fulfills one *mitzvah*—God benefits (they benefit) him and lengthens his days and he inherits the land. And everyone who does not fulfill one *mitzvah*—God does not benefit him nor lengthen his days; and he does not inherit the land.[34]

On the above Mishnah, a number of comments arose in the Tosefta.

> Whoever fulfills one *mitzvah*—God benefits (they benefit) him and lengthens his days and his years, and he inherits the earth. And everyone who commits one transgression, God harms him and shortens his days, and he does not inherit the land. And concerning this one it is said: "One sinner destroys much good" (Ecclesiastes 9.18): with a single sin this one loses for himself much good. He should always consider himself as if he were half innocent and half guilty. If he fulfils one *mitzvah*, happy is he for weighting himself down in the scale of innocence (*kaf zekut*). If he commits one transgression, [it is as] if he weighted himself down in the scale of guilt (*kaf chobah*). . . .[35]

> R. Simeon b. Leazar said in the name of R. Meir: Since the individual is judged according to the majority [and] the world is judged according to the majority, if he fulfills one *mitzvah*, happy is he for weighting himself and the world down in the scale of innocence. If he commits one transgression, [it is as] if he weighted himself and the world down in the scale of guilt. . . .[36]

How does Sanders interpret these passages? First, he comments that the passages state that "a man should consider himself *as if* he were half innocent and half guilty and *as if* his every next act would determine his fate. . . . It means that one should repent every day."[37] In other words, the rabbis have offered a hypothetical construct (with no necessary bearing in reality) in order to assist the faithful person's obedience. Second, what of R. Simeon b. Leazar's statement that one is "judged according to the majority"? Sanders observes that R. Meir, in whose name R. Simeon speaks, elsewhere said that "charity saves from Gehinnom" (Baba Bathra 10a), and so "he can hardly have held the systematic belief that one is judged strictly according to the majority of deeds."[38] Third, Sanders concedes that a later interpreter, cited in the Babylonian Talmud, understood *Kiddushin* 1.10 to refer "to one whose deeds are otherwise in balance."[39] In the Palestinian Talmud, furthermore, Akiba is reported to have said: "[It refers to] whoever does not have one *mitzvah* which can prove in his favour [and so make the scales incline] to the side of innocence [*kaf zekut*]."[40]

In support of the above statement, Sanders notes, one might quote Akiba elsewhere (*Aboth* 3.15, "all is foreseen but freedom of choice is given, and the world is judged by grace, yet all is according to the majority of works"). Sanders, however, maintains that Akiba was "not . . . a systematic theologian" and so "did not explain how the two parts of the saying fit together."[41] Sanders stresses, furthermore, that Akiba simply says in the Palestinian Talmud that "the fulfillment of one *mitzvah* produces much good."[42]

Against Sanders's explanations of these statements we may register a couple of objections. First, in view of the fact that *later* rabbinic interpreters understood Akiba to take a "majority of deeds" view, we ought to consider quite seriously the likelihood that they did not misinterpret, but were correctly interpreting, their forebears. Second, why would the hypothetical language ("as if") employed in the Tosefta be put to practical use unless it had "more-than-hypothetical" significance? Could this not indicate the way that at least *some* practitioners viewed the judgment, especially in view of Akiba's paradoxical statement at *Aboth* 3.15? The totality of the evidence makes Sanders's explanations appear to be special pleading in the face of the evidence. Sanders will concede below that "it is true that there are some sayings which do indicate that God judges strictly according to the majority of a man's deeds."[43] In one sense, then, the question is moot. We may note for the time being that for the rabbis, this "majority of deeds" view was tempered by the sense that God would, in the end, be gracious to Israel. The rabbis seem, however, unable to give expression *in what way* these two conceptions could be reconciled.

2. *Damnation for One Transgression.* A second class of statements regarding the assessment of one's obedience at the last judgment speak of "damnation for one transgression." Sanders summarizes the rabbinic opinions proffered within this category:

> The most important passages in this connection, however, are those which state that those who sin with the intention of denying the God who forbade the sin break or cast off the yoke. That is to say, they exclude themselves from the covenant and consequently from the

> world to come. . . . The particular sin mentioned is *either tantamount to denying God explicitly or is a deliberate sin against one's fellow which violates not only the letter of the law but its basic moral principles and which could only have been committed with calculation and intent.*[44]

Examples of such transgressions include idolatry (*Mek. Pischah* 5) and the "rejection of one commandment with the intent to deny the God who gave it" (*Sifra Behar* 5.3). Sanders also comments that while Galatians 3:10 (where Paul quotes Deuteronomy 27:26) sets forth the view that the law required "legal perfection" (as also did IV Ezra, Sanders concedes), the rabbis never understood Deuteronomy 27:26 in this way.[45] Rather, they rendered as "confirm" the verb that most translators of Galatians 3:10 render "abide by." The issue for the rabbis, Sanders notes, was one's pattern of covenantal faithfulness, antecedent to which was the intent to bear all the obligations of the covenant. "What is required is submission to God's commandments and the intent to obey them."[46] Provided that one intentionally undertook *this* yoke, Sanders argues, then the question of legal perfection simply did not enter the picture. Such an intention was all that was needed to render the kind of obedience that was acceptable.

3. *Salvation by a Single Righteous Act.* A third class of statements regarding the acceptability of one's obedience at the last judgment addresses the question of how one is saved in the rabbinic literature. On this question Sanders pairs two important quotes by Akiba. We have an interpretation of Isaiah 5:14 by R. Akiba, followed by an interchange between two rabbis from *Sanhedrin* 81a:

> Only those who possess no good deeds at all will descend into the netherworld.[47]

> When R. Gamaliel [II] read this verse (i.e. Ezek 18.5–9) he wept, saying, "Only he who does all these things shall live, but not merely one of them!" Thereupon R. Akiba said to him, "If so, *Defile not yourselves in all these things* (Leviticus 18.24). Is the prohibition against *all* [combined] only, but not against one?" [Surely not!] But it means,

in one of these things; so here too, for doing one of these things [shall he live].[48]

What can we say of these statements? At the very least, Akiba indicates that the ground of one's acceptance (i.e., life) is to be found in one's obedience (defined here as "one" of the precepts), and *that complete obedience cannot be and will not be required of the sinner*. What we do not have is harmonized consistency in Akiba's statements. At *Aboth* 3.15 (cited above), he takes a *quantitative* ("majority of deeds") view of one's acceptance; here, he takes a *qualitative* ("one good deed") view of one's acceptance. Sanders says at this point that these views render it "clearly impossible to attribute to him [i.e., Akiba] the view that God judges by saving those who have one more fulfillment than the number of their transgressions," as *Aboth* 3.15 is often taken. Rather, "all three statements could be made without intellectual embarrassment by anyone but a systematic theologian. Each type of saying is an effective way of urging people to obey the commandments as best they can and of insisting upon the importance of doing so."[49] Sanders further notes that rabbinic statements that "God judges strictly according to the majority of a man's deeds" cannot be taken as rabbinic doctrine because of the attestation and number of statements that speak of "fulfilling one commandment merit[ing] salvation."[50] In two distinct arguments ("the rabbis are not systematic theologians" and "there are numerous 'fulfillment of one command' statements as well as 'majority of deeds' statements"), Sanders dismisses the significance of the "majority of deeds" comments.

Sanders's proposed solution to this difficulty is at the expense of the data before us. Even if we are unable to reconcile the two classes of statements as they stand, yet we may draw the following observations: (1) Akiba, in both instances, held to the view that the *ground* of one's acceptance lay in one's deed(s). (2) Akiba, in both instances, held to the view that God would not require complete obedience of the sinner. (3) At *Aboth* 3.15, Akiba was content to let the two propositions stand together without an effort to resolve them—presumably, he held to the frequently expressed rabbinic opinion that God's mercy would triumph over his judgment. (4) This imprecision or failure to resolve the issue, to be sure, is a necessary consequence of accepting the following propositions: God does not require perfect obedience; works are the ground of acceptance before a holy God. The question remains, of course, as to what quality or quantity of obedience is required to successfully sustain the divine scrutiny at the Day of Judgment. (5) Notice as well that any divine grace evidenced in the judgment is conceived only *after* the performance of works of obedience. In other words, grace does not have a logical priority in the system, but appears to fill in the cracks left by the imperfections of human obedience.

Some rabbis admitted that there was a third class of men who stood between the righteous and the wicked:

> The School of Shammai say: There are three classes; one for "everlasting life," another for "shame and everlasting contempt" (Daniel 12.2) (these are the wholly wicked) [and a third class which is] evenly balanced. These go down to Gehenna, where they scream and again come up and receive healing, as it is written: "And I will bring the third part through the fire, and will refine them as silver is refined and will try them as gold is tried; and they will call on my name and I will be their God" (Zechariah 13.9). And of these last Hannah said: "The Lord killeth and the Lord maketh alive, he bringeth down to Sheol and bringeth up" (1 Samuel 2.6). The School of Hillel say: He is "great in mercy" (Exodus 34.6), that is, he leans in the direction of mercy; and of them David said: "I am well pleased that the Lord hath heard the voice of my prayer," etc. (Psalm 116.1); and of them, the whole psalm is written.[51]

This debate is telling in many respects. First, for all three classes of men, the ground of their acceptance is seen again to lie within themselves. Members of the middle group are not admitted to life until they have been purged by the purgatorial pains of Gehenna. Second, the rabbis do not evidence consensus concerning *how* the mercy of God was to be exercised in the judgment, only *that* it could be expected to be exercised. The Hillelites, who offer the most lenient terms in the above debate, claim that God "leans in the direction of mercy." Even this statement, however, could have provided no adherent to this system with any specific guidance!

Salvation by Membership in the Covenant and *Atonement*

1. *Salvation by Membership in the Covenant.* If one is in the covenant, according to Sanders's summary of the rabbinic literature, then only renunciation of God and his covenant can put one out of the covenant. This principle holds even if any other sin is committed within the covenant, provided that one "indicates his basic intention to keep the covenant by atoning, especially by repenting of transgression."[52] One evidence of the grace of God in the covenant was that he provided "a means of atonement for every transgression."[53]

2. *Atonement.* Sanders comments that the rabbis opined that "the wholly wicked are paid here for their few good deeds, while the completely righteous are punished here for their few bad deeds."[54] The sufferings of the righteous were consequently regarded as atoning in character. This leads to the question of how God dealt with the transgressions of his people, or the question of atonement: What did the rabbis mean by "atone"? Sanders argues that rabbinic usage of this word embraces "both man's act of atonement and God's act of forgiveness."[55] Noteworthy is the apparently universal rabbinic view that certain acts of the Jew effected atonement. We turn to examine them *seriatim*. There were four means of atonement, according to the rabbis: repentance, the sacrifices of the Old Testament (culminating in the annual Day of Atonement), one's sufferings, and one's own death.

a. *Repentance.* On several occasions the rabbis affirmed that the act of repentance was in some instances atoning:

> One scriptural passage says: "Return, O backsliding children" (Jer. 3.14), from which we learn that repentance effects atonement. . . . If one has transgressed a positive commandment and repents of it, he is forgiven on the spot. Concerning this it is said: "Return, O backsliding children."[56]

> R. Judah said: [For the transgression of] every [commandment] following "Thou shalt not take [the name of the Lord thy God in vain]," repentance atones. . . .[57]

Sanders notes that repentance is not technically an independent means of atonement but "the attitude which is always necessary for God's forgiveness."[58] Even so, the rabbis do list repentance above as an independent means of atonement. Further, Sanders explains, "repentance, like obedience, is best undertaken simply from love of God; but even repentance made from fear is better than none at all. The rabbis do not praise it, but they do not deny its efficacy."[59] This observation tells us that the rabbis placed emphasis (although not *exclusive* emphasis) upon the act itself rather than on the *quality* of the act. Sanders concludes that repentance "is not a 'status-achieving' activity by which one initially courts and wins the mercy of God. It is a 'status-maintaining' or 'status-restoring' attitude which indicates that one intends to remain in the covenant. . . . one is already 'saved;' what is needed is the maintenance of a right attitude toward God."[60]

b. *The Old Testament sacrifices (Day of Atonement)*. The question of the atoning efficacy of the sacrifices required by the Old Testament was moot at the time of the compilation of the Mishnah, by which time these sacrifices had long since ceased. The reflections of the Tannaim are important nonetheless in establishing rabbinic understandings of these sacrifices' significance. The Day of Atonement in particular was regarded as having its own province with respect to the atonement of Israel's transgressions:

> And another scriptural passage says: "for on this day shall atonement be made for you" (Leviticus 16.30), from which we learn that the Day of Atonement effects atonement.[61]

> If one has violated a negative commandment and repents, repentance alone has not the power of atonement. It merely leaves the matter pending and the Day of Atonement effects atonement. [This is proved by reference to the second passage (i.e., Lev 16.30).][62]

We may observe from the quotations above that the Day of Atonement was regarded as having atoning efficacy independent of repentance. As Sanders reminds us, however, the Day *did* command repentance, so in one sense the question is "entirely academic."[63] It is unlikely that the rabbis officially or formally assigned an *ex opere operato* efficacy to the sacrifice.

c. *Sufferings.* Sufferings or chastisements were also regarded as atoning:

> And still another scriptural passage says: "Then will I visit their transgressions with the rod, and their iniquity with strokes" (Psalm 89.33), from which we learn that chastisements effect atonement.[64] If one willfully commits transgressions punishable by extinction or by death at the hands of the court and repents, repentance cannot leave the matter pending nor can the Day of Atonement effect atonement. But both repentance and the Day of Atonement together atone for one half. And chastisements atone for half.[65]

> R. Ishmael reasoned that if a slave could obtain his release by virtue of losing "tooth," "eye," or any "other of his chief external organs;" *how much more* could "a person at the price of suffering . . . obtain his pardon from heaven," citing Psalm 118:18, "The Lord hast chastened me sore: but He hath not given me over unto death" (Psalm 118.18).[66]

The rationale for attributing atoning value to suffering was twofold: (1) Sufferings lead to repentance, which is atoning; and (2) it was necessary that the righteous be "punished on earth for their sins in order to enjoy uninterrupted bliss hereafter: payment *must* be exacted if we are not to deny that God is just."[67]

d. *Death.* As Sanders rightly observes, if one concedes that human suffering atones, then "it is only a small step to saying that death atones."[68] In this respect, the atoning efficacy of death did not contemplate the act of death apart from repentance:

> And another Scripture passage says: "Surely this iniquity shall not be expiated by you till ye die" (Isaiah 22.14), from which we learn that death effects atonement.[69]

> However, if one has profaned the name of God and repents, his repentance cannot make the case pending, neither can the Day of Atone-

ment effect atonement, nor can sufferings cleanse him of his guilt. But repentance and the Day of Atonement both can make the matter pend. And the day of death with the suffering preceding it cleanses him. To this applies: "Surely this iniquity shall not be expiated by you till ye die." And so also when it says: "That the iniquity of Eli's house shall not be expiated with sacrifices nor offering" (I Samuel 3:14) it means: With sacrifice and offering it cannot be expiated, but it will be expiated by the day of death.[70]

Sanders notes that "there was an opinion, however, that death would atone for all but the most serious sin even without repentance."[71]

Summary

From the preceding, we can construct our own summary of the "pattern" of rabbinic religion, based on the evidence that Sanders has presented to us. While Sanders might differ with some of these conclusions, we nevertheless present them as grounded on the very data that Sanders himself has provided in *Paul and Palestinian Judaism* and that we have cited in the course of this chapter.

1. Election was, at least in part, by God's grace. Yet it was also at least partially grounded on the merits of the patriarchs or Israel's foreseen obedience.
2. Many rabbis gave no evidence of concern with the law's demand for perfect obedience.
3. Humans were not regarded as being determined by nature to sin, although the impulse to sin was thought to be within each person.
4. The rabbis did not believe that divine grace had to overcome and overpower the will in order that a good work might be certainly rendered. God's grace, rather, helped to make up the deficiencies of the obedience rendered (however those deficiencies were conceived, whether qualitatively or quantitatively).
5. The rabbis' concern with obedience did not exclude considerations of intent or the necessity of the motive of love underlying all obedience.

6. True obedience, according to the rabbis, consisted of one's intentional pattern of covenantal faithfulness, *viz.*, one's desire to accept the bounds and obligations of the covenant and to live within it faithfully.

7. The rabbis recognized four means of atonement that one could make in order to address his sins (repentance, Old Testament sacrifices [Day of Atonement], sufferings, death).

    (a) The emphasis, we saw, was placed on the act of atonement rather than on the quality of the act of atonement.

    (b) Certain means of atonement (sufferings, death) were explicitly said, on certain occasions, to be God's own means of satisfying his justice.

    (c) The rabbis developed an elaborate extrabiblical system that not only created means of atonement not found within the Old Testament (repentance, suffering, death) but also assigned to these means of atonement varying levels of atoning efficacy for applicable sins.

8. One could be assured of salvation by virtue of membership within the covenant if that membership was accompanied by the kind of obedience mentioned above.

9. The rabbis believed that the ground of one's acceptance in the judgment was the rendering of covenantal obedience to God (however such obedience was conceived—on this there was disagreement), an obedience that God accepted graciously.

10. The rabbis were not agreed on what constituted sufficient covenantal obedience to render one secure in the judgment (recall the Hillel/Shammai debate), or along what lines the mercy of God would (or could) be exercised to remedy the sinner's deficiencies.

11. Back of the debates concerning the judgment is the assumption that grace enters *after the work is performed*, and that without the work performed there can be no grace. Works, then, may rightly be said to have priority over grace in this system, and that not by number count, but by their place in the system. Works are therefore fundamental and essential to this religion. To anticipate our discussion below, Paul will be right to say that the Jews think that their works will save them.

12. Such an anthropology as evidenced in the rabbinic literature leads to a view of the law that will inevitably render the law suitable to one's capacity. In other words, provided that human ability is retained (at least in some fashion), and that divine grace is seen merely as moral or suasory, and not physical, such an anthropology is incapable of producing a law that can't be reasonably kept. This understanding of the law is expressed in three lines of evidence that we have observed above: (a) an understanding of the law that does not require its perfect obedience, (b) a minimization of heart sins with a corresponding exaltation of the external, and (c) a freedom and impunity to add to the requirements of the law. Consequently, while there may be a *formal* exalting of the law (in the guise of a legal theology), we have *materially* a rejection of the law and its authority.

Religious Experience

In view of the preceding discussion and summary, it is worthwhile to examine briefly the nature and quality of religious experience among practitioners within the rabbinic system. Sanders argues that, by and large, the rabbis felt close to God and were "confident of God's presence and accessibility."[72] What about the celebrated case of R. Jochanan b. Zakkai?

When Rabban Jochanan ben Zakkai fell ill, his disciples went in to visit him. When he saw them he began to weep. His disciples said to him: Lamp of Israel, pillar of the right hand, mighty hammer! Wherefore weepest thou? He replied: If I were being taken today before a human king who is here today and tomorrow in the grave, whose anger if he is angry with me does not last for ever, who if he imprisons me does not imprison me for ever and who if he puts me to death does not put me to everlasting death, and whom I can persuade with words and bribe with money, even so I would weep. Now that I am being taken before the supreme King of Kings, the Holy One, blessed be He, who lives and endures for ever and ever, whose anger, if He is angry with me, is an everlasting anger, who if He imprisons me imprisons me for ever, who if He puts me to death puts me to death for ever, and whom I cannot persuade with words or bribe with money—nay more, when there are two ways before me, one leading to Paradise and the other to Gehinnom, and I do not know by which I shall be taken, shall I not weep? They said to him: Master, bless us. He said to them: May it be [God's] will that the fear of heaven shall be upon you like the fear and flesh of blood. His disciples said to him: Is that all? He said to them: If only [you can attain to this]! You can see [how important this is], for when a man wants to commit a transgression, he says, I hope no man will see me. At the moment of his departure he said to them: Remove the vessels so that they shall not become unclean, and prepare a throne for Hezekiah the king of Judah who is coming.[73]

Sanders says that this story, "rather than proving that God was perceived as remote, that a man had to obey more commandments than he committed transgressions in order to be saved, and that anxiety was the resultant religious attitude, shows rather that the Rabbi felt close to God, had a real perception of living in his sight, and was conscious of his own unworthiness."[74] Such "consciousness" is "to be expected in prayer and at the time of death" and is "not at all incompatible with a modest certainty of salvation which we have seen repeatedly in the literature. . . ."[75] Sanders will also point to other prayers: "Master of the Universe, I have examined the two hundred and forty-eight limbs which you have put in me, and I have not found that I have offended you with one of them. [If you gave me the limbs], how much more should you give me my life!" "May neither our host nor we be confronted with any evil thought or sin or transgression or iniquity from now or for all time." Sanders concludes that the above specimens, when read not in isolation from one another but together, demonstrate a religion not of "uncertainty and anxiety" nor of "self righteousness" but of "modest certainty."[76]

Critique

We now proceed to analyze and critique Sanders's synthesis of rabbinic Judaism. In so doing, we will restrict ourselves to the evidence that Sanders has produced in *Paul and Palestinian Judaism*. First, let us recognize that Sanders has provided a more balanced picture than prevailed in earlier German scholarship, *viz.*, of a purely Pelagian system. Sanders correctly reminds us that the rabbis were conversant with the language of grace and forgiveness, and were certainly aware of their own sinfulness and, at times, of God's holiness. Sanders's service to scholarship consists in his construction of a fuller portrait of the evidence than we possessed in the earlier model. It is, rather, his interpretation of that evidence to which we will chiefly object. We might say in passing, however, that Sanders did not uncover anything substantially new with respect to the evidence itself, or with respect to a more sympathetic reading of the evidence.[77]

Second, we protest against Sanders's restriction of his consideration to the so-called functional dimensions of religion (e.g., getting in and staying in). We have seen that certain discussions of such doctrines as original sin and native (in)ability are ruled out of court, and that certain discussions concerning the *reasons* for God's election of Israel are ruled out of court as irrelevant when in fact they *are* relevant. Because of these unwarranted restrictions, Sanders's conclusions are often not sustained by the evidence he adduces.

Third, Sanders too hastily dismisses evidence that does not support his conclusions. At points he even recognizes that there are several rabbinic statements that seem to contradict or at least to weaken his thesis. He will consequently stress that the rabbis aren't systematic theologians or that the majority of one class of statements nullifies a numerical majority of another class by virtue of that majority. Against Sanders we stress that any satisfactory portrait of rabbinic Judaism must take into account all the evidence. When we do, we find that Sanders's conclusions inadequately account for the data.

Fourth, Sanders has not established that Judaism contemporary to Paul was a religion of grace. This may be seen from the rabbinic evidence addressing election, human ability, the obedience required by the law, the obedience assessed at the divine judgment, means of atonement, and assurance of salvation. The fact that the rabbis could inquire *why* God elected Israel is more significant than Sanders admits. We cannot afford to pass over such statements because they are allegedly peripheral to the central conviction *that* God elected Israel. Any system of theology that conceives God as electing a person on the grounds of his or her foreseen or actual deeds is not gracious in the biblical sense. The Old Testament itself precludes such reasoning (see Deut. 7:7–8; 9:4–5), for the biblical position is that God has chosen his people solely because it pleased him to do so.

Sanders registers no objections to the view of human nature that emerges from the rabbinic writings, namely, that men are by nature sick but not dead, and still capable of rendering some obedience that, with the subsequent assistance of God's grace, will be proved acceptable to God. When we approach such a critic of Judaism as Paul, whose conceptions of human ability and divine grace are equally radical, then we will see the differences between the two systems emerge more clearly. If, to anticipate our discussion below, we approach Paul with an *a priori* judgment that he will not or cannot differ from the rabbis soteriologically, we are bound to misunderstand the depth of Paul's criticism of human nature *or* the heights of divine grace to which he points us.

Sanders argues that the rabbis were not exercised about (if they even conceded) the law's requirement of perfect obedience. Further, while obedience was seen as the means of staying in the covenant into which God had graciously placed a person, and while obedience was not conceived to the exclusion of considerations of motive, we have seen comparatively little concern displayed by the rabbinic evidence that Sanders has summarized for the *quality* of the act and motive of obedience (i.e., questions of sincerity and hypocrisy). The emphasis tends to fall upon the act itself. The absence of this concern for the quality of the act was prompted, undoubtedly, by the prior denials of the radical character of sin and of the radical demand of the law. Here lie the roots of the externalism against which Paul would rebel.

Sanders is too willing to pass over the tensions inherent in the different classes of rabbinic statements concerning the final judgment ["damnation for one transgression," "salvation for one fulfillment," and "judgment according to the majority of deeds"]. Sanders points to a common *functional* purpose underlying all three classes (i.e., to promote obedience), but overlooks their *theoretical significance, viz.,* that at least some rabbis believed that the judgment would be not simply *according to* but *of* [the majority of] deeds. It is hard to defend a religion as gracious when at least some of its teachers on some occasions proclaim that an adherent is ultimately accepted at the bar of judgment because the sum total of his good deeds outweighs the sum total of his bad deeds. What is chiefly objectionable here, of course, is the view that the ground of the believer's acceptance rested in his own deeds (whether conceived as acts of obedience or acts of atonement); and that the believer was not bound to keep the whole law. When Paul comes to critique this religion, he has not only a true sense of the value of even the best works that man is able to render, but also a firm belief that the atonement required far exceeds what any ordinary son of Adam can render to God.

Sanders points to the fact that the rabbis saw sacrifices, death, suffering, and repentance as atoning, and understands this fact as evidence that this religion was gracious. But one must ask how God can accept the imperfect deeds (even if well-intentioned) of a sinful human being as satisfaction for sin. Further, to see one's suffering, one's death, or repentance as atoning puts God under human obligation. There is no biblical warrant for these actions as atoning. To reason in this way is frankly presumptive.

Sanders again sees the deathbed scene of Jochanan b. Zakkai as evidence of the "modest certainty" of this religion. We must inquire, however, of the value of such certainty to an adherent of this religion. Jochanan b. Zakkai had declared that "when there are two ways before me, one leading to Paradise and the other to Gehinnom, and I do not know by which I shall be taken, shall I not weep?"[78] Our objection is not the problem of certainty *as such*,[79] but that this particular species of uncertainty belies the weakness of this religion, *viz.*, that the adherent's acceptance before God lay ultimately in himself and not in God.

In summary, Sanders has corrected the portrait of Judaism as a religion of pure Pelagianism, and has demonstrated that this religion is semi-Pelagian in nature. In election, human ability, obedience, atonement, and acceptance at the judgment, rabbinic opinion is universally and incontrovertibly synergistic. Human actions and endeavors have preeminence over divine grace. In a very real sense, salvation (notwithstanding the *language* of grace) was by works of the law. We can see, then, the elements of Paul's critique in the very evidence that Sanders musters to prove that Paul had no disagreement with contemporary Judaism.

We are assured, finally, that the Reformers' recovery of the doctrine of justification and their appeal to Paul was no mere reading of late-medieval soteriology into the mouths of Paul's opponents. While we must appreciate the differences between late-medieval soteriology and ancient Judaism, we must also recognize their fundamental soteriological identity: both are semi-Pelagian systems. The Reformers were *right*, then, to go to Paul in the way that they did—both were concerned to strip down religions that mingled the grace of God with human merit and therefore placed the believer's ultimate confidence not in the grace of God but in his own labor and activity. We can see and appreciate why the cross brought Paul, Luther, and Calvin such rest and comfort of soul.

FIVE

Schweitzer *Revivus:*
E. P. Sanders on Paul

aving examined E. P. Sanders's paradigmatic revolution in the study of rabbinic Judaism, let us see how he interprets Paul. First, we'll consider how various streams of scholarship already surveyed have merged to form the river of Sanders's understanding of Paul. Second, we'll explore the most salient points of Sanders's thought with respect to Paul, highlighting how his scholarship in Judaism has informed his understanding of Paul.

Sanders's Debt to Prior Scholarship

Sanders's contribution to the critical study of Paul consists not in the novelty of his particular insights, but in the synthesis into which they have been forged. With Albert Schweitzer, Sanders isolates "being-in-Christ" as the center of Paul's thought, a point to which we will return.[1] There are, to be sure, differences between the proposals of Schweitzer and Sanders. They differ both terminologically (Sanders rejects the term "mystical" in favor of "participationist") and substantively (Schweitzer saw justification as an appendage to Pauline thought, while Sanders sees it as generically tied to Paul's view of "being-in-

Christ"). Nevertheless, the similarities underlying the writings of both scholars far outweigh such disagreements.

With W. D. Davies, Sanders takes a conciliatory and appreciative view of Paul's relationship with contemporary Judaism. The "Paul" of both constructions is far more Jewish than the "Paul" of Wilhelm Bousset and Rudolf Bultmann. More thoroughly than Davies ever endeavored, Sanders undertakes a *comparative* study of Paul and rabbinic Judaism.[2]

With Bultmann, Sanders examines Pauline soteriology largely as the dealings of God and the individual, without explicitly commending Bultmann's anthropocentrism and without adopting Bultmann's existentialism. Sanders will explicitly disagree with Ernst Käsemann's view that justification is a corporate category. There are, nevertheless, formal similarities in the way that both scholars conceive righteousness in Paul. Notwithstanding their disagreements in defining the term "righteousness," neither allows for a forensic dimension of the terminology.

With Krister Stendahl, Sanders argues several things: (1) Paul did not experience a conversion so much as a call. (2) Paul did not labor in Christian ministry out of any sense of dissatisfaction with the Judaism he (admittedly) left behind. (3) Paul had a robust conscience and was not plagued by guilt from which he sought relief. (4) Forgiveness is not a dominant category in Pauline thought. (5) Paul's moral objections to Jewish and Gentile behavior in Romans 1–3 are *logically subsequent to* his conviction that Jesus is the Messiah. In other words, Paul reasons from solution to plight.

Paul and Judaism

Sanders, we observed, concluded that the prevailing view that "Judaism necessarily tends towards petty legalism, self-serving and self-deceiving casuistry, and a mixture of arrogance and lack of confidence in God"[3] was in error. Ancient Judaism, rather, had a healthy appreciation of the covenant, and of the grace of God in election, obedience, and the final judgment. Sanders consequently concludes that Paul's disagreement with Judaism could not have been that Judaism is a religion of works and Christianity is a religion of grace.

Covenantal Nomism

Sanders argues that, far from rejecting his Jewish heritage, Paul transforms it in light of "two primary convictions" from which the whole of his theology is developed: (1) Jesus is Lord, in whom "God has provided salvation for all who believe and who will soon return." (2) Paul was called to be the "apostle to the Gentiles."[4] What we have in Paul, then, is a transformed covenantal nomism. Sanders breaks, then, from Davies's conception of Paul as reconstituting "Exodus, Covenant, Torah" into "New Exodus, New Covenant, and New Torah."

The covenantal nomism takes the following basic form: (1) "One enters" the covenant "by baptism." Sanders, however, rejects Schweitzer's *ex opere operato* doctrine of baptismal regeneration. Baptism, furthermore, does not play a significant role in the thought of Sanders's Paul. (2) Once one enters the covenant, then membership "provides salvation." (3) Obedience to (or "repentance for the transgression of") a "specific set of commandments" "keeps one in the covenantal relationship, while repeated or heinous transgression removes one from membership."[5] The overarching assumption, then, is that, excepting the notable specific instances (as above), we are to assume *continuity* between Paul and Judaism.

Notwithstanding this continuity, Sanders recognizes the limitations of calling Paul a covenantal nomist. First, Sanders argues, Paul primarily grounds ethics not in commandments or in the covenant, but in the "mutually exclusive union" of the participant "with Christ":

> We must note the inadequacy of the covenantal categories for understanding Paul. Although at one point he does view heinous immorality coupled with defiance of him as transgression which must be repented of if the offending member is to remain in the body of Christ, it seems more germane and natural to his thought when he grounds his admonitions not on the threat of the expulsion for unrepentant transgression, but on the fact that certain acts constitute a union which is mutually exclusive with the union with Christ (1 Corinthians 10:1–5). The fault of eating and drinking with idols and of fornication is not their character as transgression against the

will of God (although Paul could have quoted the Bible to show that they are transgressions), nor their character as transgressions of the apostle's ordinances, but their result in forming a union which is antithetical to the union with Christ.[6]

Notice in the preceding quotation that Sanders effects a dichotomy: Paul's real thought grounds ethics either in union with Christ *or* in the commandments. Paul, of course, evidences both tendencies without apparent tension between them. In similar fashion, Sanders will establish a dichotomy between Spirit and law as the ground of Pauline ethics:

> There is an important respect in which behavior is not conceived in the manner common in Judaism. Paul understands it to be the "fruit of the Spirit." Despite his well-known lists of vices and virtues, his general tendency was not to give concrete rules for living; and we discover most clearly that he had some when someone strays too far from the sort of behavior which should flow from the indwelling Spirit. But the principal point is that, in Pauline theory, deeds do flow from the Spirit, not from commandments.[7]

These arguments of Sanders will be especially important to our consideration of Paul and the law below.

Second, this term ("covenantal nomism") does not "take account of his participationist transfer terms," *viz.*, "dying with Christ and thus to the old aeon and the power of sin," that trump the covenantal categories that Paul might have inherited from Judaism:

> The heart of Paul's thought is not that one ratifies and agrees to a covenant relation with God and remaining in it on the condition of proper behaviour; but that one dies with Christ, obtaining new life and the initial transformation which leads to the resurrection and ultimate transformation, that one is a member of the body of Christ and one Spirit with him, and that one remains so unless one breaks the participatory union by forming another.[8]

How do we explain Paul's appropriation of the language of the new covenant (e.g., 1 Cor. 11:25; 2 Cor. 3:6)? Paul has here "doubtless follow[ed] traditional Christian terminology."[9] Further, "What Christ has done is not, as we said just above, contrasted with what Moses did, but with what Adam did. Adam did not establish a covenant, but his transgression did determine the entire fate of mankind; and so has Christ's act determined the fate of the world. Here again we see the covenantal categories transcended."[10] There are genuine limitations, then, to understanding the covenant as the organizing principle of Paul's thought.

Given these limitations, how are we to conceive the apostle Paul and his relationship with Judaism? In a summary discussion of Paul and his relationship with Judaism, Sanders stresses that in many respects Paul is fundamentally still a Jew.

> Paul's thought was largely Jewish, and his work as an apostle to the Gentiles is to be understood within the framework of Jewish escha tological speculation, as Romans 15:16 makes clear. Paul interpreted his task of bringing the Gentiles into the people of God in such a way, however, that the church, in both his understanding and practice, became in effect a third entity. Paul nevertheless seems not to have perceived that his gospel and his missionary activity imply a break with Judaism.[11]

Sanders continues by observing that there are two places in Paul's writings where this break is "clearly perceptible."[12] First, Paul rejected the "traditional Jewish doctrine of election" by maintaining "that the covenant 'skips' from Abraham to Christ, and now includes those in Christ, but not Jews by descent."[13] Second, Paul maintained that "it is through faith in Christ, not by accepting the law, that one enters the people of God."[14] Paul, then, differs from Judaism not only by defining the people of God to be "in theory universal," but also by defining the boundaries around the people of God around Christ.[15] Hence, "heinous sin, unrepented of" will result in "expulsion (though not . . . damnation)," as well as "behavior which denies Christ, such as worshipping idols as if they were real gods or accepting some requirement other than faith as essential for membership."[16] In conclusion, while one might speak of Paul as a covenantal nomist, it is important to recognize that what distinguishes the church as the people of God is its reorganization around Christ—with respect to election, constitution of membership, ethics, and entrance rite (i.e., baptism). New boundaries and new boundary markers have been erected. This constitutes the primary difference between Judaism and Christianity.

Solution Preceding Plight

If Paul's religion is a transformed covenantal nomism (notwithstanding the differences observed above), then why does Paul fault Judaism as he does? Traditionally, Judaism has been conceived in New Testament scholarship as a legalistic, or works-based, religion. Paul's dissatisfaction with Judaism was said to attend his grasping of Christianity as a religion of grace. But Sanders argues that Paul's discontent with Judaism does not stem from some prior dissatisfaction but is a logical consequence of his two fundamental convictions:

> As far as I can determine, inability and self-righteousness do not figure at all in his statements about the law (except for the extreme statement of fleshly inability in Romans 7:14–25). When he criticizes Judaism, he does so in a sweeping manner, and the criticism has two focuses: the lack of faith in Christ and the lack of equality for the Gentiles. Both of these points figure in Romans 9:30–10:13, both are related to his call to be apostle to the Gentiles, and both strike at Judaism as such.[17]

In a now-famous formulation, to which we have been making reference, Sanders argues that Paul proceeds logically from solution to plight. In other words, "in short, this is what Paul finds wrong in Judaism: it is not Christianity."[18] Sanders elsewhere presses the necessity of distinguishing one's reasons from his arguments. In assessing Paul's discontent with Judaism, one must trace out his reasons (his fundamental convictions, as above) from his arguments (the argumentation offered in support of his fundamental convictions). In view of his two underlying and fundamental reasons, Paul proceeds with argumentation.

In proof of this solution/plight scheme, Sanders points to what he argues are irreconcilable inconsistencies in the plight passages in

Paul. The first example is Romans 7:7–25. Sanders first outlines Bult-mann's understanding of these verses:

> And is there a necessity that natural human "life in the flesh" must without exception become "life in the flesh" in the negatively qual-ified sense—i.e. must it become "life according to the flesh"? That is evidently Paul's opinion. In man—because his substance is flesh—sin slumbers from the beginning. Must it necessarily awaken? Yes, be-cause man encounters the Torah with its commandment: "you shall not desire" (Romans 7.7ff.).[19]

Sanders, however, argues that Bultmann mistakenly attributed Paul's *reason* behind this *argument* to a psychologically derived analy-sis of man's fleshly weakness:

> It is certainly true that Bultmann is pointing to an *explanation* in Paul of how it is that every man sins and is under the power of sin, but it should be equally clear that it was not *from* the analysis of the weak-ness of the flesh and the challenge of the commandment that Paul ac-tually came to the conclusion that all men are enslaved to sin. This is a view which springs from the conviction that God has provided for universal salvation in Christ; thus it follows that all men must need salvation, and Romans 7 is a somewhat tortured explanation of the law and its purpose in the light of this.[20]

In other words, Paul is on the horns of a dilemma: "As a good Jew [he thought] that God gave the law, while he was also convinced, on the basis of the revelation of Christ to him, that the law could not produce righteousness."[21]

How does Paul respond to this dilemma? He assigns to "the law a negative role in God's plan of salvation." Paul, however, was not consistent in this assignment, an inconsistency that surfaces especially in Romans 7. Why does Sanders call Romans 7 "a somewhat tortured explanation of the law and its purpose"? Sanders does so because he believes there to be explanations of "God's will, sin, and the law" in Romans 7 that are incompatible with similar expressions elsewhere in Paul's writings.[22]

First, Sanders sees Galatians 3:22–24 and Romans 5:20ff. (cf. Rom. 3:20; 4:15) as giving us Paul's "majority statement," *viz.*, God's will gave man the law, which has resulted in human sin defined as transgression and bondage. Sanders sees such claims ("for through the Law comes the knowledge of sin" [Rom. 3:20]; "The Law came in so that the transgression would increase" [Romans 5:20]) as mere assertion on Paul's part. He finds Romans 3:20 and 5:20 as finding *formal* parallel in 7:13 ("so that through the commandment sin would become utterly sinful"). Paul's main expression of the law's "negative role in God's plan of salvation," therefore, is to say that "it produces sin *so that* salvation would be on the basis of faith."[23]

Second, in Romans 6:1–7:6, Paul now depicts sin as a power that "can be escaped only by death, and which is thus not entirely subordinate to God's purpose."[24] *This* dilemma (different from that expressed in Romans 3 and Romans 5) "requires a different solution." "The law *cannot* produce sin, since 'sin' is outside God's overall plan."[25] The law, consequently, is absent from this alternative-dilemma scenario.

Third, when we arrive at Romans 7:7–13, Paul "still holds that God gave the law; that the law and sin are connected," but their interrelationships change. The law is affirmed to be "good" (7:12). The law is "used . . . not by God himself, but by sin (7:8, 11, 13), "which produced a situation *contrary* to the will of God."[26] Rather than give the law to produce bondage to sin (as in Romans 3 and 5), here God has given it to save, and God's "intention . . . was frustrated," since he did *not* intend bondage to sin. The scenario that emerges in these verses, then, is that God has given the law (God → law), but sin has taken hold of the law (contrary to God's intention), the result of which is human transgression (sin → law → transgression). Why has Paul introduced these changes into his argument in Romans 7:7–13? He has done so because of the new and independent role that Paul has assigned to sin in the previous chapter.

Fourth, when we come to Romans 7:14–25, Paul introduces an entirely new scheme, with two parallel concepts. First, God gives the law (God's will → law). Second, there is "another law" or "sin" that inevitably yields human transgressions ("another law" = sin [7:23, 17, 20 RSV] → transgression). The "connection between the law and sin" that Paul maintained in Romans 7:7–13 has now been severed. Paul faults the law because "it does not bear within itself the power to enable people to observe it."[27] Paul positively roots the problem in "the flesh in the sense of human nature," *viz.*, "humans are fleshly (7:14), governed by a principle which causes them to act against the good which the law commands (7:15–23)."[28] In telling words, Sanders indicates that Paul resolves this crisis by "praising God for offering the possibility of redemption through Christ, not to criticize him for creating humans, who, fleshly, are sold under sin, nor even to criticize him for not sending a law strong enough to do the job in the first place."[29]

How do we explain such significant shifts that occur within a relatively brief argument, Sanders asks?

> We [must] think of them as arising from an organic development with a momentum towards more and more negative statements until there is a recoil in Romans 7, a recoil which produces other problems. Paul's problems with the law do not start with Romans 7. It is the continuing theological problem of how to hold together both his native belief that God gave the law and his new conviction that salvation is only by faith in Christ (which leads him to give the law a negative role) which largely accounts for the torment and passion which are so marked in Romans 7.[30]

In other words, it is because Paul's conception of plight is not his logical starting point, and because Paul's foundational commitments to the law and to Christ are fundamentally in tension, that we have the "torment and passion" of Romans 7.

While we will not return in our critique below to Sanders's exposition of this passage (he is not followed by all scholars on this point), we may register the following criticisms of Sanders's accounts of plight in Romans 7. In so doing, we may see that Paul's statements in Romans 7 are entirely consistent with one another. (1) That sin, to Paul, is a power independent of God, as Sanders maintains, is an argument from silence. Sanders's discussion overlooks Paul's personification of man's sinful nature. Sin, to Paul, is not a substance, nor is it properly conceived apart from the state or actions of a sinning agent. (2) Paul never affirms that the law *causes* or *produces* sin—its relationship to sin is consistently stated to be an instrumental one (cf. Rom. 3:20, "for *through* the Law comes the knowledge of sin"). (3) Paul consistently maintains that the problem with the law is not with the law itself; it is with those commanded to observe it. Hence the two purposes of the law (intention to save/intention to bring all into bondage) are not at all contrary, but part of one multifaceted divine purpose. Paul quotes Leviticus 18:5 to show that life results from obedience to the law (see Gal. 3:12; Rom. 10:5). The fact that no mere man experiences life in this way does not mean that one can charge God with some miscalculation. That is why Paul can state that the law "came in so that the transgression would increase" (Rom. 5:20). In other words, when God gives the law to a sinful people, the necessary effect is transgression.

The second example that Sanders cites in order to show inconsistencies in Paul's plight formulations is Romans 1:18–3:20. Bultmann had commented that "the view that all men are sinners, which [Paul] develops at length in Rom 1.18–3.20, is a basic one for his doctrine of salvation."[31] Sanders, however, argues that Paul's "doctrine of salvation led to the necessary conclusion that all men required salvation, with the result that his description of the human plight varies, remaining constant only in the assertion of its universality."[32] How does it vary here? Sanders outlines his understanding of Romans 1:18–2:29:

> I think that in 1:18–2:29 Paul takes over to an unusual degree homiletical material from Diaspora Judaism, that he alters it in only insubstantial ways, and that consequently the treatment of the law in chapter 2 cannot be harmonized with any of the diverse things which Paul says about the law elsewhere.[33]

What particular instances does Sanders have in mind? In Romans 1:18–32, the Gentiles are universally condemned. But in Romans 2:15–16, 26, Paul "entertains the possibility that some will be saved by works" in the context of an argument intended to condemn the Jews. Paul, at Romans 3:9, 20, returns to his main point (1:18–32), that all are "under sin" (3:9). At Romans 2:17–24, furthermore, Paul will condemn the Jews for "flagrant disobedience."[34] But at Romans

10:2, he "characterizes his kin as zealous for the law"; and at Galatians 2:15, he contrasts them with "Gentile sinners."[35]

We have, then, "a case for universal sinfulness [that] is internally inconsistent and rests on gross exaggeration."[36] It is *not* intended to be "an objective, or even a consistent, description of Jews and Gentiles"; rather, "Paul knows what conclusion he wants to draw . . . since universal sinfulness is necessary if Christ is to be the universal savior."[37]

In brief response to Sanders's comments on Romans 1–3, we may observe that Sanders has glossed over some important questions. When Paul speaks of justification in Romans 2, does he use this term in precisely the same manner as he does elsewhere in this letter, or in Galatians? Does Paul have a particular group of people in mind in Romans 2:13, or is this a hypothetical statement? We will return to these and other questions posed by Romans 2 in chapter 8. It is, furthermore, difficult to see how disobedience to the law and zeal for the law are necessarily incompatible—we have both things affirmed of the Pharisees in the same discourse in the Gospels (Matt. 23:15, 23). Paul, in like fashion, speaks of Jews who have zeal, but he qualifies this zeal as not "in accordance with knowledge" (Rom. 10:2).

A third line of evidence that Sanders mounts to show the inconsistencies of Paul's plight statements is from Romans 1–4. Sanders will argue that Paul's argument in Romans 1–4 reasons from solution to plight. "It is clear [from these chapters] that one of Paul's major concerns is to assert that salvation is for both Jews and Gentiles and that it must be *based on the same ground*."[38] How and where, according to Sanders, do we see this? At Romans 1:5, Paul tells us that as an apostle, he has been called to "bring about the obedience of faith among all the Gentiles." At Romans 1:16, he tells us that the gospel's power is "to the Jew first and also to the Greek"—*not*, of course, to maintain the Jew's "superiority," *but* to maintain "equality" of Jew and Greek.[39] Romans 2:11 ("for there is no partiality with God") serves to introduce and summarize the remainder of the argument in chapter 2 (2:12–29). At Romans 2:14–16 and 2:27, Paul in particular will attempt to establish the equality of Jew and Gentile by arguing against the superiority of the Jew.

Paul then asks, "What advantage has the Jew?" (3:1), a question to which he will return in chapters 9 and 11. He concludes in 3:9, "What then? Are we better than they? Not at all; for we have already charged that both Jews and Greeks are all under sin." Then, in 3:20, Paul will *deny* the law's efficacy for salvation, pointing rather (3:21–26) to the equality of Jew and Gentile through Christ, a point summarized at 3:29: "Or is God the God of Jews only? Is He not the God of Gentiles also? Yes, of Gentiles also." In chapter 4, Paul will point to Abraham as the " 'father of all who believe,' whether circumcised or not." He stresses, at 4:13 ("For the promise to Abraham or to his descendants that he would be heir of the world was not through the Law, but through the righteousness of faith"), once again that salvation is *not by law*. Positively, he'll affirm at 4:16 ("For this reason it is by faith, in order that it may be in accordance with grace, so that the promise will be guaranteed to all the descendants, not only to those who are of the Law, but also to those who are of the faith of Abraham, who is the father of us all") just why it is that salvation cannot come by law.

In summary, Sanders concludes, there are two reasons why, in Romans 1–4, Paul denies salvation by law. First, if the promise were to be received by law, then Gentiles would be excluded. "But Gentiles cannot be excluded" (because Christ is "Lord of the whole world and is savior of all who believe, and has especially called and appointed Paul as apostle to the Gentiles"), and therefore the promise must be received by some other means, *viz.*, faith. Second, if salvation were by law, then "Christ died in vain." Both of these arguments, Sanders tells us (i.e., "the inclusion of the Gentiles and the death of Christ"), "stand together, as we see, in Romans 3.21–26."[40]

A fourth line of evidence that Sanders adduces to prove that Paul moves from solution to plight and is therefore *not* concerned with the keep-ability of the law, but is primarily concerned to argue "against the necessity of keeping the law," regards the instability of the terms "faith" and "righteousness" in Romans.[41]

Faith

At Romans 3:25 ("whom God displayed publicly as a propitiation in His blood through faith"), Sanders claims that the term "faith" "means accepting the gratuity of salvation." But at 4:16–23, the term comes to mean "trust that God will do what he promises" (citing 4:18, 20), with faith's opposite (*apistia*, v. 20) meaning essentially "distrust." Sanders concludes that this instability of definition is significant:

> The argument about "faith" in Romans 1–4 is not *for* some one definite definition of faith, but primarily *against* the requirement of salvation by the law. The positive argument of Romans 1–4 is that Jews and Gentiles stand on an equal footing, and this requires the negative argument against the law, which is contrasted with faith. But no one positive definition of faith emerges from the argument.[42]

In other words, "Faith excludes boasting, but it is not defined simply as the opposite of boasting; faith involves trust, but it is not precisely trust; faith involves accepting salvation as a gift, but it is not just that either. Faith represents man's entire response to the salvation offered in Jesus Christ, apart from law; and the argument for faith is really an argument against the law."[43]

Righteousness

At points, Sanders argues that "righteousness" means the "power and action of God which are manifest in both wrath and grace (1.16–18; 3:21)"; at others, "his rightness and fidelity to what he promised and intended (3.1–7)." With respect to men, the term "justified" or "made righteous" can mean "the acquittal achieved by Christ's death (5.9ff., 18) or the possibility of salvation achieved by Christ's resurrection in contrast to the acquittal of trespasses achieved by his death (4.25)." But it can also mean one's "uprightness before God with regard to his works (2.13), or the right relationship with God that is received by faith and *not* by law (4.11)."[44] In other words, when applied to men, it can be either forensic or transformative. Righteousness, then, like faith, is a "negative category, directed against the view that obedience to the law is either the necessary or sufficient condition of salvation."[45]

Summary

Sanders argues that Paul's two fundamental convictions are laid down explicitly in Paul at two places, Galatians 2:21 ("if righteousness comes through the Law, then Christ died needlessly") and Galatians 3:21 ("for if a law had been given which was able to impart life, then righteousness would indeed have been based on law").

> The reasoning apparently is that Christ did not die in vain; he died and lived again "that he might be Lord both of the dead and of the living" (Romans 14.9) and so that "whether we wake or sleep we might live with him" (I Thessalonians 5.10). If his death was *necessary* for man's salvation, it follows that salvation cannot come in any other way and consequently that all were, prior to the death and resurrection, in need of a saviour. There is no reason to think that Paul felt the need of a universal saviour prior to his conviction that Jesus was such.[46]

It is because of such convictions that Paul developed two non-systematic "conceptions of man's plight": one juridical and the other participatory.[47] Sanders will cite 2 Corinthians 5:14–21 as a place where Paul can hold both of these conceptions together without any apparent awareness of tension among them. Here, Christ is said to die *for* believers ("He made Him who knew no sin to be sin on our behalf . . ." [v. 21]). This expresses the juridical line of man's plight. Believers are also said to participate in Christ in such a way that his "death provide[s] the means by which believers could participate in a death to the power of sin." Paul's phrase "that we might become the righteousness of God in Him" (v. 21) expresses the participationist line of man's plight.[48]

Transfer Terminology: *Righteousness* and *Justification*

One particular area where Sanders finds a significant difference between Paul and his Jewish contemporaries concerns the language of righteousness. Jews tended to use righteousness language as terminology describing those who were already in the covenant. It was, in other words, *maintenance* terminology. For Paul, Sanders argues, righteousness language is *transfer* terminology. It describes how one gets into the community of the saved.[49]

Justification in Paul

One way in which Sanders attempts to show this distinction is by offering a generic definition of the verb "justify" in Paul. He argues that at 1 Corinthians 6:9–11 (especially verse 11, "Such were some of you; but you were washed, but you were sanctified, but you were *justified* in the name of the Lord Jesus Christ and in the Spirit of our God"), the verb "justified" is a way of saying that "Christians were cleansed of the sins just enumerated."[50] All the verbs in this passage communicate the same thing ("the point of all the verbs here is that Christians were cleansed . . ."). Consequently, we do not have distinct acts of grace, but several modes of communicating the same salvific reality.

Concerning Romans 5:6–9 (especially verse 9, "Much more then, having now been justified by His blood, we shall be saved from the wrath of God through Him"), Sanders maintains that "the meaning of 'justified' is the same as 'reconciled,' " a word mentioned twice later in verse 10, and is that "past transgressions have been overlooked or atoned for," a meaning also found at Romans 8:30.[51]

In summarizing these distinct uses, Sanders comments that

> being justified refers to being cleansed of or forgiven for past trans-
> gressions and is an intermediate step between the former state of
> being an enemy of God and a transgressor and the future state of
> being glorified. . . . Thus far it appears, then, that "justify" as a "trans-
> fer" term can be paralleled either with "sanctify" and "reconcile"
> (referring to past transgressions) or with "set free" (referring to sin
> as an enslaving power).[52]

The Relationship of Participatory and Forensic Language in Paul

Sanders, then, regards Paul's verbal use of "justify" *not* to be exclusively forensic, but forensic *and* transformative. Sanders is aware that, while the distinction between participatory and juristic categories was not one used by Paul, it is one that the scholar must nevertheless settle.[53] Because Paul did not take human transgression as a psychological or anthropological starting point (as we saw Sanders argue above), then we ought not be surprised that Paul developed two con-

ceptions of man's plight—one juridical and the other participatory—
both outworkings of his doctrine of "being-in-Christ." This raises the
question of whether Paul has assigned priority to either juristic or participatory language in giving expression to his central conviction of
"being-in-Christ."

Sanders argues that Paul's participatory language and not his juridical language is fundamental to his thought because the latter is
solely an offshoot of his central, participatory conviction. First, Paul's
participationist language is "more frequent and typical" than his juridical language.[54] Furthermore, the former appears in his "discussion
of the sacraments and in his paranesis," while the latter does not.[55]
Second, Paul's juridical language is "defective, lacking a discussion of
repentance and forgiveness, and guilt."[56]

Sanders does concede that 2 Corinthians 12:21 is an exception ("I
am afraid that . . . I may mourn over many of those who have sinned
in the past and not repented of the impurity, immorality and sensual-
ity which they have practiced"), but this statement contains not *transfer*, but *maintenance* language.[57] It is the exception that, to Sanders,
proves the rule, for the solution in Paul is never phrased in terms of forgiveness and the removal of guilt.[58] We have, then, no movement from
plight to solution at the level of Paul's *thought*. He notes in this connection that 1 Corinthians 11:27 contains the only appearance of the
word "guilt" in the Pauline corpus ("*guilty* of the body and the blood
of the Lord"), but its solitary appearance simply "reinforces the point
that Paul did not characteristically think in terms of sin as transgression which incurs guilt, which is removed by repentance and forgiveness."[59] What about Romans 3:9? Paul says not that we are under *guilt*
but under *sin*[60]—consequently, Paul is not concerned with guilt. In similar fashion, at Romans 3:25 (RSV), God is said to have "passed over
former sins" but not to have forgiven them or removed guilt.

A third argument that Sanders mounts to show that participatory language is fundamental to Paul's thought is that in Paul it is not
"transgressions *qua* transgressions which exclude one . . . from the
Kingdom," but only transgressions that establish unions with others
than with Christ (1 Cor. 6:12–20; 10:6–14).

A fourth and final argument that Sanders mounts to show the

priority of participation in Paul is that Paul's " 'juristic' language is sometimes pressed into the service of 'participationist' categories, but never vice versa."[61] Sanders points to four passages as evidence for this claim.

At Romans 6:7, Paul will use juridical language ("is freed," *lit.* "is justified") to speak of one being set free from sin's power. Sanders comments that "the general context [in Romans 6] of participation in Christ's death so that one may participate in life determines the meaning of *dikaoumai*. It *cannot* mean 'justified' in the sense of 1 Corinthians 6.9–11, where one is justified from sins." Consequently, when one compares Paul's statement at Romans 6:7 and his statement at Romans 6:11 ("Even so consider yourselves to be dead to sin, but alive to God in Christ Jesus"), one must affirm that "there is no doubt in Romans 6 that the 'dies to' terminology better expresses his real meaning."[62]

At Galatians 3:25–29 (a passage that Stendahl had both isolated and stressed as a specimen of traditional misunderstandings of the apostle), Sanders observes that these verses "are the conclusion to the argument about whether righteousness comes by the law or by faith (although the discussion of slavery and sonship continues into chapter 4)." Nevertheless, when we arrive at the conclusion of the argument (i.e., in these verses), we find that righteousness has disappeared. Rather, we have affirmations that faith receives "sonship . . . in Christ Jesus," *viz.*, "the language immediately becomes completely 'participationist': baptized into, put on, all one person, Christ's."[63]

In Galatians 2:15–21, we have a parallel situation. Paul initially speaks of righteousness and faith ("nevertheless knowing that a man is not justified by the works of the Law but through faith in Christ Jesus . . ." [v. 16]). He will conclude, however, his discussion with participationist language ("and it is no longer I who live, but Christ lives in me; and the life which I now life in the flesh I live by faith in the Son of God . . ." [v. 20]). This movement within Galatians 2:15–21 tells us that Paul's *real* thought lies in participationist categories.

Concerning Philippians 3:4–12, Sanders concedes that we have "the righteousness/faith correspondence . . . but here that correspondence hardly determines the meaning of this passage."[64] For this righteousness is given "to one who is 'found in him' (Christ)."[65] Unlike

Romans, we are told, where righteousness dealing with one's past transgressions *precedes* (i.e., "leads to or makes possible") life in Christ Jesus,
in Philippians they "simply stand together." Furthermore, Sanders argues, righteousness language in this passage is clearly subordinate to
Paul's participationist language: the latter provides the "whole thrust
and point of the passage," and the passage "could have been written
without the term 'righteousness' at all" without compromising its soteriology. If this is so, why did Paul introduce this righteousness language at all? Sanders responds that Paul has included this language
because of his opponents, against whom he has begun his attack at 3:3
("for we are the true circumcision, who worship in the Spirit of God
and glory in Christ Jesus and put no confidence in the flesh").[66]

Sanders also tells us that Paul in Philippians 3 "was aware of his
own shift in the meaning of the term righteousness." Paul concedes that
"there is a righteousness under the law" (presumably Sanders has in
mind Philippians 3:6, 9), but his argument in Philippians is that it is not
"true righteousness or the right kind of righteousness."[67] Analogously,
Paul, in speaking of the true circumcision in verse 3, does not deny the
reality of the false circumcision presupposed by it (i.e., the literal, physical act). Consequently, "the only proper righteousness is Christian righteousness, which must be based on something else . . . the point is that
any true religious goal, in Paul's view, can come only through Christ."[68]

We find, then, for Paul, that "righteousness by faith and participation in Christ ultimately amount to the same thing."[69] The term
"righteousness" simply did not have "the same 'forensic-eschatological'
meaning which it is supposed to have in Judaism."[70] Righteousness to
Paul is not a (forensic) "gateway to life."[71] Paul uses forensic language
because it affords him yet another way to say that "man apart from
Christ is condemned."[72] Paul's thought, then, is properly and essentially participationistic.

The Law in Paul

When Paul engages in polemics or conflict with his opponents,
he frequently uses the terminology of law or works of the law. Sanders
addresses the traditional understanding of Paul that says that Paul's

disagreement with Judaism was not only soteriological but also focused on man's inability to keep the law. Sanders devotes his most concerted attention to this subject in *Paul, the Law, and the Jewish People*.

He returns first to a point that had been drawn in *Paul and Palestinian Judaism*, namely, that Paul does not conceive the law to be an
"entrance requirement" into the body of the Christian saved. Rather,
Paul uses righteousness language (including the language of justification) to speak of this transition. After examining a number of passages
in this connection (Gal. 2–3; 5:3; Rom. 3:27–4:24; 9:30–10:13; Phil.
3:9), he draws some conclusions:[73] (1) Paul did not view the law as an
entrance requirement. (2) Paul's polemical target, as seen in Galatians
and Philippians, is not Jews *simpliciter*, but rival Christian teachers.
(3) Paul's polemic against the works of the law is essentially a critique
of the Mosaic Law as such.

> The application to Judaism, however, is not against a supposed Jew-
> ish position that enough good works earn righteousness. In the phrase
> "not by works of law" the emphasis is not on *works* abstractly con-
> ceived but on *law*, that is, the Mosaic law. The argument is that one
> need not be Jewish to be "righteous" and is thus against the stan-
> dard Jewish view that accepting and living by the law is a sign and
> condition of favored status. *This is both the position which, inde-
> pendently of Paul, we can know to have characterized Judaism and
> the position which Paul attacks.*[74]

Paul, according to Sanders, has no objection against or even concern with the keep-ability of the law. What about passages that appear
to the contrary?

Galatians 3:10–13

Traditional readings of these verses have pointed to Galatians
3:10 and 3:13 in particular as evidence of Paul's belief that man is unable to keep the law. Sanders responds in *Paul, the Law, and the Jewish People* first by dissenting from these readings (thereby departing
from his earlier position in *Paul and Palestinian Judaism*) and second
by relegating these verses to a subordinate position in the argument of
this chapter.

Paul has carefully chosen his quotations from the Old Testament in order to support his argument. "Deuteronomy 27:26 is the only passage in the Septuagint" that pairs the word *nomos* (Greek "law") with the word "curse."[75] Paul was consequently drawn to this verse for obvious polemical reasons. The appearance of the word "all," in Paul's quotation of Deuteronomy 27:26 ("cursed is everyone who does not abide by *all* things written in the book of the Law, to perform them"), then, is incidental to Paul's argument. Paul certainly did not intend to communicate that law-keeping was impossible, as many traditional readings of this verse have maintained.

As to verse 13 in particular ("Christ redeemed us from the curse of the Law, having become a curse for us—for it is written, 'Cursed is everyone who hangs on a tree' "), Sanders argues that Paul was drawn to this verse because it provided a reply to the view that one who is crucified could not be Messiah.[76] But, as such, it does not supply an "argument against the requirement to keep the law."[77]

Sanders also argues that Galatians 3:10–13 is "subsidiary" in the argument of this chapter. It "consist[s] of a chain of assertions which are stated by Paul in his own words and which are proved by the citation of proof-texts which contain one or more of the key words in his argument."[78] Paul states his main proposition at Galatians 3:8: "God . . . justif[ies] the Gentiles by faith," a statement that Paul "prove[s] by citing Genesis 18:18," which uses the word "bless." The appearance of the word "blessed" naturally leads to its opposite, "cursed." Hence, at Galatians 3:10, he quotes Deuteronomy 27:26, which, as Sanders has observed, is the only passage in the Septuagint that pairs the words "law" and "curse."

Paul argues in 3:11–12 "that righteousness is by faith and that the law is not by faith." In doing so, Paul simply repeats the argument of verse 8, *viz.*, that "faith, not obeying the law, is the condition for being righteous." In Galatians 3:13 Paul states "how God has provided for the removal of the curse of the law," summarizing in Galatians 3:14 the argument begun at the outset of the chapter. By means of this analysis of Galatians 3:1–14, Sanders relegates verses 10–13 to a subordinate position in the argument. Paul's *real* view is said to be stated at Galatians 3:8. In other words, "the argument seems to be clearly wrong that Paul, in Galatians 3, holds the view that *since* the law cannot be entirely fulfilled, *therefore* righteousness is by faith."[79] In summary, we have in 3:6–18 a string of "Jewish exegetical argument" but no *reasons* supplied for excluding righteousness by the law.[80]

(·?L Chr B1

Galatians 5:3

Sanders acknowledges that there is a connection between this verse ("and I testify again to every man who receives circumcision, that he is under obligation to keep the whole Law") and Paul's affirmation in Galatians 3:10. Here we have a "threat" but not a statement of human inability to keep the law.[81] In other words, Paul is arguing that "if you start [the law] it *must* be all kept," *not* "the law should not be accepted because all of it *cannot* be kept."[82] In response to those who argue that Galatians 3:10 and Galatians 5:3 contain an implied, middle premise of human inability to keep the law, Sanders reasons that inability would have been an impossible doctrine for Paul to formulate:

> It would, in short, be extraordinarily un-Pharisaic and even un-Jewish of Paul to insist that obedience of the law, once undertaken, must be perfect. Such a position would directly imply that the means of atonement specified in Scripture itself were of no avail. . . . Now to have Paul's argument stem from his pre-Christian views about the law, one must have him . . . hold that the law is too hard to do adequately and that there is no atonement. Yet it is granted on all hands that, in the extant correspondence, he never states either view explicitly. . . . My argument is that none of this would have been obvious to someone of Paul's background. In fact, it would be unheard of.[83]

Why, then, does Paul speak as he does? Why does Paul make *this* threat (i.e., that "if you start it, all of it must be kept")?

> Although observing the law was not burdensome to Jews, it appeared onerous and inconvenient to Gentiles. Paul's opponents may have adopted a policy of gradualism, requiring first some of the major commandments (circumcision, food, days), a policy which was probably not unique among Jewish missionaries. Paul may very well sim-

ply have been reminding his converts that, if they accepted circumcision, the consequence would be that they have to begin living their
lives according to a new set of rules for daily living.[84]

While we are not yet engaging Sanders's arguments in criticism
here, we may observe that this is precisely what Paul does *not* say in
Galatians 5:3. Paul says that if the Galatians submit to circumcision,
then the whole of the law must be kept, not that they would have to
adopt a new and inconvenient code *simpliciter.*

Galatians 6:13

In this verse ("For those who are circumcised do not even keep
the Law themselves, but they desire to have you circumcised so that
they may boast in your flesh"), Paul simply observes the fact that the
Judaizers do not "observe the law with entire strictness" when they
"meet with the Gentile converts and argue their case," and this is due
to the sheer necessity of the case.[85] He uses the "dilemma" of the in-
evitability of human disobedience to the law to his own advantage in
his conflict with the Judaizers (cf. Gal. 2:14).

Romans 3:27–4:25

What does "works of the Law" in this passage mean? Is it "boasting in one's own meritorious achievement," or is it simply "immoral
behavior"?[86] We may note parenthetically that the way in which
Sanders engages the traditional reading of Romans 3:27–4:25 is
through Bultmann's exegesis of this passage. Paul, on this reading, is
said to have "opposed the law because following it leads to pride."[87]
This interpretation, of course, truncates what Protestants have traditionally argued from this passage.

Sanders lays out a case that boasting (3:27) does not refer to activity, but to status. (1) This is clearly the meaning of the term at Romans 2:17, 23, where Paul speaks of the Jew boasting in his status and
privilege as a Jew. (2) This is what Paul will go on to argue against in
this particular argument (3:29–30). God is the God of Jews *and* Gentiles (v. 29), and he justifies all "on the same basis" (v. 30). Earlier in
the argument (Rom. 3:21–25), Paul had put forward "faith" as that

"which is available to *all*, which excludes boasting in privileged status."[88] (3) The example of Abraham explains Paul's meaning at Romans 3:27. Paul is not trying to argue against a view that "Abraham *tried* to be righteous before God by works, and certainly not . . . that the effort to merit righteousness by following the law is what constitutes human sin and is why Paul objects to the law."[89] Rather, he is simply trying to argue that God has always justified by faith—it has never been otherwise. Hence, it would never have even occurred to Abraham to boast. The overall point is stated at Romans 4:9–12—God receives the circumcised and uncircumcised "on the same ground." Paul's concern is not achievement, but status. He argues that faith is the way to righteousness and that "this had nothing to do with the law." He is not at all concerned to establish that the law had been misused "by boasting about fulfilling it."[90]

What about Romans 4:4–5 ("Now to the one who works, his wage is not credited as a favor, but as what is due. But to the one who does not work, but believes in Him who justifies the ungodly, his faith is credited as righteousness.")? If Paul's overall concern is status (3.29–30, 4.9, 12, 14, 16), then this must shape the way that we interpret Romans 4:4. Sanders concedes that "Paul was against claiming the 'reward' as if God owed it and in favor of accepting righteousness as a gracious gift."[91] But this is not to say that Paul is impugning the law as having "failed because keeping it leads to the wrong attitude," nor that "his opposition to boasting *accounts* for his saying that righteousness is not by law."[92] The overall argument, which concerns Paul's fundamental view that "salvation . . . is now made available to those who have faith in Christ, without distinction," must shape our view of this verse.[93]

Romans 1–3

We have observed above Sanders's contention that Paul reasons from solution to plight in these chapters of Romans. We have also observed above that, for Paul, there are varying conceptions of the human plight, and that these diverse conceptions are evident in Romans 1–3. These variations, Sanders contends, are proof that they are subsidiary to and derivative of the more fundamental solution. Although these chapters, in the sequence of argument, *seem* to suggest that universal transgression lies behind "Paul's objection to righteousness by law," Paul is inconsistent in these chapters. In Romans 2, Paul "holds out the possibility" of perfect obedience to the law as a "real one" against other statements in Romans 1–3. He also holds in Romans 2 that "the same law judges everyone," contrary to Romans 5:12–14, where "from Adam to Moses, sin led to death even without the law."[94] The impossibility of harmonizing Romans 2 with other parts of Paul's thought is due in part to Paul's having borrowed Romans 1:18—2:29 as "homiletical material from Diaspora Judaism." Paul's reasons demanded an argument supporting universal sinfulness, and so he took hold of the nearest available argument. This is proof not only that Paul's argument in Romans 1–3 stems from his conclusion (not vice versa), but also that these chapters do not prove, in the end, Paul's argument that man is unable to keep the law.

Romans 9:30–10:13

The central issue in these verses swirls around Paul's affirmation at Romans 9:30–31: "What shall we say then? That Gentiles, who did not pursue righteousness, attained righteousness, even the righteousness which is by faith; but Israel, pursuing a law of righteousness, did not arrive at that law." Sanders admits that "at first blush [this passage] offers the best proof that Paul's argument against the law is really against a legalistic way of observing it."[95] This state of affairs is bolstered especially in view of what Paul mentions in Romans 9:32: "Why? Because they did not pursue it by faith, but as though it were by works." Sanders admits that this question may be answered by solving one exegetical uncertainty: to what does the second *nomos* (law) of Romans 9:31 refer? Sanders observes and dismisses two prior solutions: (1) Traditionally, it has been taken to mean a "law *of righteousness*," an interpretation that has found its way into the Textus Receptus (cf. KJV). (2) Sanders rejects C. E. B. Cranfield's translation of the Greek verb *ephthasen* as "fulfill." The verb is best translated, Sanders argues, as "attain."

How does Sanders attempt to answer this question? (1) Sanders first observes that the contrast between faith and works in Romans

9:32 means simply (in view of the quotation in Romans 9:33) "they did not believe in Christ," not "they incorrectly tried for righteousness and by trying achieved only self-righteousness." In other words, "Israel's failure is not that they do not obey the law in the correct way, but that they do not have faith in Christ."[96]

(2) Sanders regards Romans 10:4 ("for Christ is the end of the law for righteousness to everyone who believes") as crucial to our understanding of this portion of the argument. In the verses immediately preceding Romans 10:4, Sanders argues, Paul will exculpate the Jews for their misdirected zeal, and will attribute their pursuit of righteousness to "ignorance" (Rom. 10:3). Their zeal, then, Sanders stresses, is not sinful in character. This brings us, Sanders reminds us, to Paul's primary theme of Romans 3–4, *viz.*, "that God's righteousness is available on the basis of faith to all on equal footing."[97] This is seen in Romans by observing the contrast that Paul draws between the "righteousness" of 10:4 and "their own righteousness" of 10:3. The former is by faith, but the latter is not. The former is "available to all," but the latter is not. The force of "their own" in Romans 10:3 is not "self-righteousness" (i.e., works that one has personally amassed), but "limited to followers of the law" in an ethnocentric sense. In view of these observations, Sanders concludes that "their own righteousness" in Romans 10:3 must mean "that righteousness which the Jews alone are privileged to obtain" rather than a "self-righteousness which consists in individuals' presenting their merits as a claim upon God."[98]

(3) In Romans 10:5ff., Paul once again contrasts the two righteousnesses: the righteousness of which Moses spoke (v. 5) and the righteousness by faith (v. 6ff.). Sanders points to Romans 10:11 ("*Whoever* believes in Him will not be disappointed") and Romans 10:12 ("For *there is no distinction between Jew and Greek*; for the same Lord is Lord of all . . .") as evidence that the contrast in 10:5–6 is precisely the same as that observed throughout this section. Sanders summarizes the argument of this section, then, through the following three propositions: (a) "Israel has failed because, being ignorant of the righteousness of God, they sought the righteousness which is available only to those who do the law"; (b) "the righteousness of God is available to all on an equal basis"; and (c) "that basis is faith in Christ."[99]

(4) To return to our main question, to what does the second instance of the word *nomos* (law) in Romans 9:31 refer? Sanders says that "Paul did not say precisely what he meant"—it must be "more general" than the first appearance of the word *nomos*, and *really* mean "righteousness of God which comes by faith in Christ."[100] Sanders proposes to emend the text in the absence of external textual evidence because elsewhere in the passage Paul has no concern with "Israel's manner or success in fulfilling the law."[101] Paul faults Israel because they do not turn to Christ and so "attain . . . the one thing that would produce true righteousness."[102]

Philippians 3:9

In this verse ("and may be found in Him, not having a righteousness of my own derived from the Law, but that which is through faith in Christ, the righteousness which comes from God on the basis of faith . . ."), traditionalists have found support for their position. We have here the "two righteousnesses—one by law and the other by faith."[103] As examples of the latter, Sanders concedes that Paul points to both "status" and "activity" (Phil. 3:3ff.). Sanders, however, argues that we do not have an affirmation that "righteousness by law is a meritorious achievement which allows one to demand reward from God and is thus a denial of grace" or that "such righteousness is self-evidently a bad thing."[104] Rather, following Stendahl, Sanders observes that

> Paul does not say that boasting in status and achievement was wrong because boasting is the wrong attitude, but that he boasted in things that *were gain*. They *became loss* because, in his black and white world, there is no second best. His criticism of his own former life is not that he was guilty of the attitudinal sin of self-righteousness, but that he put confidence in something other than faith in Jesus Christ.[105]

In other words, this former righteousness was "in and of itself a good thing" but "shown to be 'wrong' ('loss,' 3:7f.) by the revelation of 'God's righteousness,' which comes by faith in Christ."[106]

Having reread passages traditionally mustered in support of human inability to keep the law, Sanders argues that there is positive evidence that Paul believed that the law could be kept by Christians and Jews alike. In Philippians 3:6, Paul claims that he once possessed the "righteousness which is in the law" and was "blameless." He furthermore calls Christians to be "blameless" or "without blame" in 1 Thessalonians 3:13, 5:23, and 1 Corinthians 1:8. Pauline passages that speak of universal sinfulness (e.g., Rom. 5:12–21) do not counter the above conclusions for Sanders. The rabbis could pair similar statements and not sense or be concerned with the tension among them, he reminds us. This must be true of Paul also.

Summary

If righteousness is by faith and not by law, why then did God give the law?

> Since all the world can be saved only through Christ, all the world must have stood condemned, and it was the law's role to condemn. It is for this reason that Paul can link the law with sin, "the flesh" and death and equate being under the law with being enslaved by the fundamental spirits of the universe (Romans 6.15–20; 7.4–6; Galatians 4.1–11). Apart from this, however, Paul has only good things to say about the law. Its requirement is just, in itself it aims aright. But the requirement is fulfilled only in Christ (Romans 8.4), and the aim, life, is accomplished only in Christ (Romans 7.10; 8.1–4).[107]

Because Paul's objections to the law stem from his central conviction that salvation comes only in Christ, his affirmations about the law are not necessarily consistent. Paul's inconsistent statements regarding the law evidence attempts to work out "his native belief that God gave the law and his new conviction that salvation is only by faith in Christ (which leads him to give the law a negative role)." This, Sanders avers, "largely accounts for the torment and passion which are so marked in Romans 7."[108]

Coherence and Consistency

It is now appropriate, in view of Sanders's comments on the law, to raise the question of whether Paul was a systematic thinker. Sanders, focusing on the question of the law, dissents from two prior propos-

als: Bultmann's insistence that Paul's statements on the law are consistent, but must be "seen from different perspective[s]"; and Hans
Hübner's argument that Paul's view of the law changed between the
composition of Galatians and Romans.[109]

Sanders contends that Paul's statements on the law cannot be reconciled into a systematic whole. Such inconsistencies are seen when
Paul attempts to relate God('s purpose), the law, and sin in Romans
7. This passage shows Paul recoiling again and again from the implications of his formulations (i.e., sin becomes autonomous, the flesh
becomes autonomous, the law and the flesh don't relate, the law fails
to produce good).

Such inconsistencies, however, are also seen when Paul contends
that the law cannot make righteous and that those in the Spirit are to
fulfill the very same law. Both these statements stem, Sanders argues,
from one of Paul's different central convictions, *viz.*, entry and maintenance. Such inconsistencies show us that Paul "held a limited number of basic convictions which, when applied to different problems,
led him to say different things about the law."[110] He was a *coherent*,
but not a *consistent* or *systematic*, thinker.

The Death of Christ—Forgiveness and Guilt in Paul

Before we depart consideration of Sanders, we want to ask what
role the death of Christ plays in Sanders's Paul. Sanders argues that
Paul "inherited the view that Christ died for trespasses."[111] It is a common supposition in New Testament scholarship that Paul received language concerning Christ's sacrificial death from earlier Christian
tradition, and that he "repeats without hesitation" this tradition.[112]
We will find this tradition surfacing, Sanders informs us, in Romans
2–3 and especially in 1 Corinthians 6:9–11, where man's plight is defined in terms of transgression and Christ's death is articulated as the
means by which those past transgressions were cleansed.[113] This way
of explaining the presence in Paul of the language of Christ's sacrificial death suits Sanders's general contention that forensic or juridical
categories play a relatively minor role in Paul's thought.

Sanders also notes that there are places where the believer is said to participate in the death of Christ in such a way that "one dies to the *power* of sin, and does not just have trespasses atoned for," citing 2 Corinthians 5:14; Galatians 1:4; and Romans 14:8ff.[114] Consequently, while Paul may have inherited an expiatory understanding of Christ's death, the primary "significance of Christ's death in Paul's thought" is participatory, *viz.*, death to sin as *power*, a "change of lordship which guarantees future salvation," in support of which Sanders cites Romans 6:3–11; 7:4; Galatians 2:19ff.; 5:24; 6:14; and Philippians 3:10ff.[115]

It is for this reason, Sanders contends, that Paul makes no mention of the system of atonement in Judaism (inclusive of repentance) and forgiveness. Paul "came to the conclusion that all men were enslaved to sin and could be saved only by Christ" only as a consequence of the prior conviction (by revelation) of "Christ the saviour of all."[116] As a result of the priority of this latter conviction (Christ the savior of all) he had a ready-made remedy for men's sins. The system of atonement offered by Judaism could be discarded—not because of intrinsic defects within it, but because it was not Christ, or, as Sanders puts it, "they do not respond to the real plight of man." "Repentance," Sanders continues, "no matter how fervent, will not result in a change of lordships. Men's transgressions do have to be accounted for; God must overlook them or Christ must die to expiate them; but they do not *constitute* the problem. Man's problem is not being under Christ's lordship."[117] The priority placed upon the change of lordship in connection with Christ's death also explains the paucity of two Christian concepts in Paul's letters, namely, Christ's death as cleansing the believer from past transgressions, and discussions of transgression.[118]

Summary and Conclusions

We are now prepared to draw some summary observations concerning Sanders's scholarship of Paul.

(1) Sanders, on the basis of his construct of Judaism, argues that Paul could not possibly have disagreed with Judaism on soteriological grounds. Paul never believed that Judaism was inherently faulty in its capacity to provide salvation to its participants. Paul had no prior

or present dissatisfaction with the ability of Judaism to function on its own terms.

(2) Paul is explicable if we understand four things: (a) We have, in Paul, a modified covenantal nomism. (b) These modifications have been made according to Paul's two prior, central, and organizing convictions: Jesus is the Christ, Lord of all, and Paul has been called as apostle to the Gentiles. (c) Paul in many respects is still a Jew—it is this prior set of convictions (above) that renders him distinct from his people. We may assume continuity in all other circumstances. (d) Paul has redefined the boundary markers for the people of God. He has a different answer from his Jewish contemporaries to the question of what constitutes a true member of the people of God.

(3) Paul faults Judaism *because it is not Christianity.* (a) His conception of the plight of the Jew or the plight of the Gentile stems from his *prior* conviction that being in Christ is the only way to ensure salvation at the judgment. (b) Consequently, Paul's depictions of man's plight are not consistent with one another—their inconsistency proves that they were not underlying reasons, but arguments advanced to prove these prior convictions. (c) We saw illustrations of this in Sanders's interpretation of the conflicting accounts of plight in Romans 7 and Romans 1:18–3:20, and in the (purportedly) unstable Pauline definitions of "faith" and "righteousness." (d) We also saw Sanders defend his view as respecting the rhetorical structure of Romans 1–4.

(4) Specifically, Paul is distinct from Judaism with respect to the use of "righteousness" terminology. (a) He uses this terminology not as *maintenance* terminology (as Judaism did), but as *entry* terminology. (b) In surveying Paul's uses, Sanders notes that Paul is not careful to distinguish juristic from participationist uses of righteousness language. The former are put in service of the latter, we saw Sanders argue, at Romans 6:7; Galatians 2:15–21; 3:25–29; and Philippians 3:4–12. (c) It is participationist language that is more fundamental and most accurately reflects Paul's thought: "righteousness by faith and participation in Christ ultimately amount to the same thing."[119]

(5) We have also seen that Sanders vigorously resists the notion that Paul believed in any person's inherent inability to keep the law.

(a) We have seen how he interprets passages that others have regarded as teaching the contrary—Galatians 3:10–13; 5:3; 6:13; Romans 3:27–4:25; Romans 1–3; Romans 9:30–10:13; Philippians 3:9. (b) In attempting to formulate a "Pauline theology of the law," Sanders reminds us that Paul's statements on the law are *consequent upon* his prior conviction that God had given the law, and his new conviction about Christ. Because these two convictions are ultimately irreconcilable, so will his arguments stemming from these convictions necessarily be contradictory.

(6) On the basis of Paul's statements regarding the law, Sanders concludes that Paul is not a *consistent or systematic* but a *coherent* thinker. This has become an increasingly common distinction employed by New Testament scholars.

(7) Christ's death was not fundamentally expiatory to Paul, but entailed the believer's deliverance from the power of sin by participation in his death. The prior and fundamental conviction that Christ is savior of all explains why Paul rejected the atonement system of Judaism, and why repentance and forgiveness play so little a role in his thought. Their absence is not due to inherent dissatisfaction with Judaism's ability to function on its own terms.

After Sanders:
Räisänen and Dunn

t has rightly been said that E. P. Sanders's work is a watershed in the critical study of Paul and of Second Temple Judaism. Notwithstanding the proliferation of alternative viewpoints,[1] many New Testament scholars have accepted Sanders's construct of Judaism and, consequently, its implications for the study of Paul. We turn in this and the next chapter to three prominent "post-Sanders" interpreters of Paul: James D. G. Dunn, Heikki Räisänen, and N. T. Wright. These three interpreters follow two different paths. the path of sheer inconsistency (Heikki Räisänen), and the path of coherence and some form of consistency (James D. G. Dunn and N. T. Wright). We turn to Heikki Räisänen first because he takes certain components of Sanders's proposal to their logical conclusion, and because his influence (whether in the academy or in the church) has been relatively limited compared to that of Dunn and Wright.

Heikki Räisänen

Heikki Räisänen, in good critical fashion, dismisses without argument what he terms both "patent harmonization" and "the dialectical approach" as valid approaches to bringing coherence to Pauline thought.[2] With little more argument, he dismisses the following approaches as well: (1) the existentializing of Paul's teaching on the law, notwithstanding the recognition of Paul's "absurd conclusions" (Hans Conzelmann); (2) interpolation theories for Romans and Galatians wherein these "letters started out coherent, but later interpolations have rendered the argument incoherent" (J. C. O'Neill);[3] and (3) the positing of development in Paul's theology of the law, especially from Galatians to Romans (C. H. Dodd, John Drane, Hans Hübner). Setting aside these proposals, Räisänen tells us that we must "call a spade a spade": Paul is inconsistent, and, what's more, his arguments are not even persuasive. Paul, in other words, works with "invalid premises."[4] It is by means of these two criteria (inconsistency and invalid premises) that Räisänen will investigate Paul's writings on the law.

Paul and the Law

Räisänen argues that there are several lines of inconsistency in Paul's theology of the law. First, Paul, according to Räisänen, never defines "law." Rather, he equivocates the term. Usually, and "with few exceptions," law for Paul is the Torah.[5] But elsewhere, notwithstanding statements that Gentiles are said to be "without the Law" (Rom. 2:12ff.; 1 Cor. 9:20ff.), Paul will say that Gentiles are subject to the Mosaic Law (Gal. 3:10–14; 4:5–6; 5:1).[6] The apostle gives us texts and arguments that make a distinction between cultic and moral laws impossible (many of Paul's references to the law in Galatians address "circumcision, food laws, and calendar").[7] Elsewhere, however, Paul "tacitly reduces the Torah to a moral law" (e.g., Gal. 5:14 ["For the whole Law is fulfilled in one word, in the statement, 'You shall love your neighbor as yourself' "]; Rom. 13:8–10).[8] Räisänen argues that Paul was probably not conscious of his "looseness of speech" and that it was precisely this looseness that "makes it more possible for Paul to impress his Christian readers on the emotional level."[9]

Second, Paul is not consistent concerning whether the law has continuing force or not. He states unambiguously that the law has been abolished (Gal. 3:15–20; 2 Cor. 3; Rom. 7:1–6). But he will also state that the law has been "fulfilled" (Gal. 5:14; Rom. 3:31; 8:4; 13:8–10). In other words, Paul will at times regard the law as having a "permanently normative character."[10] Paul will, therefore, in his actual moral teaching, ignore his abolition statements. Räisänen maintains that this language "could only have deceived those who were already convinced."[11] When Paul speaks of the law of Christ, he is not advocating a new law to replace the old; rather, this way of speaking "refers simply to the way of life characteristic of the church of Christ."[12] In practice, "rather than being an outspoken antinomian, Paul, in his practice, was selective about the law. He regarded it as an *adiaphoron*, and he treated it as such, too. In Jewish eyes such an attitude amounted, of course, to a rejection of the law."[13]

Third, Paul is inconsistent regarding the question of whether one can fulfill the law. At places, Paul states that no one can fulfill the law. Romans 7:14–25 was self-evidently "not intended by Paul as a description of the Christian," but rather as an account of "man's existence under the law."[14] Romans 1:18–3:20 is another passage that expresses Paul's view that no one can fulfill the law.[15] Some Gentiles, however, are said to do the law (Rom. 2:14–15, 26–27). These latter passages, Räisänen stresses, "stand in flat contradiction to the main thesis of the section [1:18–3:20]."[16] Paul will furthermore speak of Christians fulfilling the law (Gal. 5:14ff.; Rom. 8:4; 13:8–10). In summary, "Paul's mind is divided."[17]

How do we explain these inconsistencies concerning the fulfillment of the law? Agreeing in principle with Sanders, Räisänen tells us that Paul's

> point of departure is the conviction that the law must not be fulfilled outside of the Christian community, for otherwise Christ would have died in vain. Among Christians, on the other hand, the law must be fulfilled; otherwise Christ would be as weak as the law was (Rom. 8:3). That the law is neither fulfilled by Jews nor Gentiles, Paul "proves" by way of denigrating generalizations. Another device is to radicalize the claim of the law ad absurdum: only 100 per cent fulfillment of the law will hold (Gal. 3.10).

In other words, "Paul's theological theory pushes him in his thinking about the law into a direction in which he would apparently not go spontaneously."[18]

Fourth, Paul is inconsistent concerning the origin of the law: is it divine or angelic? This, moreover, occasions a second and related inconsistency: the purpose of the law. Paul generally holds to the divine origin of the law, but at Galatians 3:19, he argues contradictorily that the law was given by angels. He says this because "in the course of a polemical discussion" he "suggest[s] something radical about the law," rendering an "*ad hoc* adaptation" of a "Jewish tradition about the presence of angels on Sinai." But he never develops this idea and even appears to recoil from it elsewhere. This may, Räisänen conjectures, "express a latent resentment towards the law of which Paul was normally not conscious."[19] At points, Paul will argue that the law's purpose was negative (Gal. 3:19; Rom. 3:20; 5:20). Why does Paul do this? His "aprioristic theological thesis (Christ has superseded the law)" has compelled him to speak negatively about the law's function. And yet Paul will also ascribe to the law a less negative purpose (e.g., Rom. 7:10). Räisänen explains that "there are thus two lines of thought in Paul. . . . Either God did not want the law to be a way to salvation, or the actual law did not suit that purpose and another means had to be provided. Clearly these two lines contradict each other."[20] This contradiction again is to be explained by recourse to Paul's "aprioristic (Christological) conviction."[21]

In addition to pursuing these purported inconsistencies in Paul's thought, Räisänen argues that Paul sees the law as a "rival principle" of salvation in Judaism. He therefore misconstrued Jewish soteriology. Räisänen understands Paul to teach that "the Jews err in imagining that they can be saved by keeping the law rather than by believing in Christ. The root of evil lies in a Christological failure, not in an anthropological one."[22] Räisänen agrees with Sanders that "works of the law" are "simply the works demanded by Torah" (and not " 'self-chosen' works accomplished with the purpose of acquiring a reason for boasting").[23] Consequently, when Paul attacks Judaism, it is for its insistence that the law was "the Jewish gateway to righteousness."[24]

Räisänen asks whether the Jews really looked for " 'righteousness' (in anything like the Pauline sense of the word) in the Torah" and answers a "clear 'No.' "[25] Rather, "one went to the Torah, because one wanted to live his life as a member of an elect community under God, in thankful acceptance of the guidance shown by him."[26] Paul, then, has intentionally ignored the role of grace in Judaism: "He drives a wedge between law and grace, limiting 'grace' to the Christ event. He pays no attention to the central place of God's free pardon to the penitent and the role thus accorded to repentance in Judaism. It should not have been possible to do away with the 'law as the way to salvation' for the simple reason that the law never was that way."[27] Paul has disagreed, then, with a "distorted or uncharacteristic Judaism."[28] Sanders has argued that Paul actually passed over the concepts of grace and election in Judaism because of his prior conviction that salvation could come only in Christ.[29] In other words, his fundamental conviction (salvation for all in Christ alone) predetermined the matter for him: "the Jewish covenant [cannot] be effective for salvation, thus [he] consciously den[ies] the basis for Judaism."[30] But Räisänen argues that Paul has *deliberately misrepresented Judaism's soteriology* by representing Judaism to teach that the law is the means to righteousness. What has prompted Paul to such distortions? It was, Räisänen answers, because of his experience on the mission field, especially the pressures resulting from his "conflict with the Judaizers."[31]

Exceedingly Inconsistent

Far more than Sanders does, Räisänen stresses the incompatibility of Paul's two fundamental commitments: the Christ-event (perceived by Paul as of divine origin) and the law as a divine institution. To deny any part of the law, Räisänen maintains, is to deny a fundamental principle: a "divine thing can't be abrogated."[32] Paul is therefore inconsistent. His two fundamental commitments cannot be harmonized, and yet he is unable to discard either of them. Why, then, did Paul not dispense with the law altogether? He was "bound to pay lip service (surely never realized as such by himself) to the tradition in order not to undercut the unity of the divine purpose and will."[33] But Paul's modern critic can discern that the apostle's "actual attitude to the Torah . . . amounts to its abrogation."[34]

Aside from the above general explanation, what explains the specific contradictory statements about the law that Paul makes? Paul was

driven to these statements in controversy, especially the conflict at Antioch, as reflected in the epistle to the Galatians. In the heat of polemic,
Paul chose several "*ad hoc*" and contradictory arguments to serve his
immediate interests, even to the point of arguing "more radically than
his natural reasoning would suggest."[35]

James D. G. Dunn

Dunn presently serves as the Lightfoot Professor of Divinity at
the University of Durham. He is responsible for coining the term "New
Perspective" with respect to the study of Paul. He has taken up Sanders's
project, but we must note some important differences. One of the most
important is that Dunn perceives a fundamental coherence *and* consistency to Paul's thought. As a result, we have one of the most exegetically and theologically thorough NPP readings of Paul. Dunn,
furthermore, argues that Sanders's and Räisänen's formulations of justification suffer from an "individualizing exegesis"; they have "still
failed to grasp the full significance of the social function of the law at
the time of Paul and how that determines and influences both the issues confronting Paul and Paul's responses."[36] We will first examine
Dunn's landmark article, "The New Perspective on Paul: Paul and the
Law."[37] We'll then turn to his most recent (and comprehensive) study,
Theology of Paul the Apostle, as well as to his commentaries on Romans and Galatians, to observe what Dunn has to say about certain
topics and passages we examined above in our study of Sanders.[38]

The New Perspective on Paul

Dunn hails the arrival of Sanders's work as a powerful response
to the "typically Lutheran emphasis on justification by faith," which
has "impose[d] a hermeneutical grid on the text of Romans."[39] Dunn
does not balk at the emphasis on justification *simpliciter*, but at that
to which that emphasis was directed, *viz.*, a conception of Judaism as
a "system whereby salvation is *earned* through the *merit of good
works*,"[40] a religion that was "coldly legalistic, teaching a system of
earning salvation by the merit of good works, with little or no room
for the free forgiveness and grace of God."[41] Dunn agrees with Sanders

that the traditional portrait of Judaism is a "gross caricature" that helped to "feed an evil strain of Christian anti-Semitism."[42]

Dunn proceeds to commend Sanders's construct of covenantal nomism, but argues that Sanders did not "follow through this insight far enough or with sufficient consistency."[43] He argues that the question "What, then, can it be to which Paul is objecting?" was not sufficiently answered by Sanders.[44] Dunn understands Sanders to say that Paul's leap from a Jewish to a Christian covenantal nomism was "arbitrary" and left his "theology," especially regarding the "law," "incoherent and contradictory."[45]

Dunn prepares to answer that question with some preliminary considerations. He first argues that the word *nomos* (Greek "law") in Paul is to be translated "Torah." Hence, the term does not refer narrowly to the precepts of the Old Testament, but includes the whole of the Pentateuch, including the passages in Genesis, Exodus, and Deuteronomy that address the establishment and maintenance of the covenant. Dunn, then, establishes a link between the covenantal nomism of the Old Testament and of Paul. Citing "Ezra's reforms in the post-exilic period" and the Maccabean crisis of the second century B.C., Dunn argues that the law came to be a "basic expression of Israel's *distinctiveness* as the people specially chosen by (the one) God to be his people. In sociological terms the Law functioned as an identity marker and boundary, reinforcing Israel's sense of distinctiveness and distinguishing Israel from the surrounding nations."[46]

Now Dunn is prepared to answer the question "Against what is Paul arguing?" Dunn argues that a "natural and more or less inevitable converse of this sense of distinctiveness was the sense of *privilege*, precisely in being the nation specially chosen by the one God and favored by gift of covenant and law."[47] He concludes:

> Conviction of privileged election and the practice of covenantal nomism almost inevitably comes to expression in focal points of distinctiveness, particular laws and especially ritual practices which reinforced the sense of distinctive identity and marked Israel off most clearly from the other nations. In this case three of Israel's laws gained particular prominence as being especially distinctive—circumcision, food laws, and Sabbath.[48]

These laws, Dunn argues, were not thought to be "intrinsically more important," simply "points of particular sensitivity in Jewish national understanding," or "test cases of covenant loyalty."[49]

The "works of the law," then, are not "good works in general or any attempt by the individual to amass merit for himself, but . . . that pattern of obedience by which 'the righteous' maintain their status within the people of the covenant, as evidenced not least by their dedication on such sensitive 'test' issues as Sabbath and food laws."[50]

Paul's critique of the law is a critique of the "law as taken over too completely by Israel, . . . misunderstood by a misplaced emphasis on boundary-marking ritual, . . . a tool of sin in its too close identification with matters of the flesh, . . . a focus for nationalistic zeal."[51]

Righteousness

In view of the above, what does Dunn say about Paul's language of "righteousness"? First, righteousness, Dunn says, must be understood not as a Greek concept, but as a Hebraic concept: the former sees the term as "an idea or ideal against which the individual and individual action can be measured," the latter as "a more relational concept . . . the meeting of obligations laid upon the individual by the relationship of which he or she is a part."[52] This definition, of course, precludes any distinction between forensic and transformative uses of the term: the former must be subsumed into the latter.

Second, the righteousness of God, then, is "God's fulfillment of the obligations he took upon himself in creating humankind and particularly in the calling of Abraham and the choosing of Israel to be his people."[53] In other words, it is "God's *faithfulness* to his people."[54] The goal of Romans, then, is to "explain and vindicate the faithfulness of God."[55]

We see Dunn's conception of righteousness illustrated in his interpretation of three important passages in Romans.

Romans 1:17. Dunn observes that too often the West has read this phrase as "an ideal or absolute ethical norm against which particular claims and duties could be measured." If, however, we understand it in the context of "Hebrew thought," we have "essentially a concept of relation."[56] In other words, "people are righteous when they meet the claims which others have on them by virtue of their relationship."[57] The background of the language of righteousness in the Old Testament is the "covenant." God, therefore, is said to be "righteous" when "he fulfills the obligations he took upon himself to be Israel's God, that is, to rescue Israel and punish Israel's enemies," or when God "act[s] to restores his own and to sustain them within the covenant."[58]

That Paul inherits this particular concept of righteousness is evident in his use of this phrase to explicate "the power of God for salvation" (Rom. 1:16). The virtue of this interpretation, Dunn argues, is that it delivers readers from between the horns of two dilemmas: (1) Which genitive is represented in the phrase "the righteousness of God"? Do we have in this phrase an objective genitive (something that God does) or a subjective genitive (an attitude or attribute of God)? We have, Dunn argues, "not a strict either-or, but both-and, with the emphasis on the latter"—the "dynamism of relationship . . . can embrace both senses: God's activity in drawing into and sustaining within covenant relationship." (2) Is the verb "to justify" defined "to make righteous" or "to count righteous"? Once again, the answer is both. Ernst Käsemann was correct to see "divine righteousness as a gift which has the character of power, because God is savingly active in it."[59] This is why Paul has appended his comments in Romans 1:17 to his comments in 1:16. Righteousness gives definition and expression to the "power of God for salvation."

We see in these verses how Paul uses this concept of righteousness in a manner different "from that given to him in his Jewish heritage." "The covenantal framework of God's righteousness must be understood afresh in terms of faith—'to all who believe, Jew first but also Gentile.' "[60] Dunn elaborates on this difference between Paul and his heritage:

> It is the fact that man's righteousness is always to be understood as faith which explains why man's righteousness is nothing other than God's righteousness. . . . And it is his fellow Jews' forgetfulness of this fact which, in Paul's view, has resulted in a distorted under-

standing of their part within the covenant ("their own righteousness") and so in a missing of "God's righteousness" (cf. 10:3).[61]

In other words, it is not simply, as Sanders argues, that Paul now has
two central and orienting convictions that cause him to reevaluate
covenantal nomism. Rather, Paul is calling his fellow Jews to understand (as they once did) the true bounds of covenantal relationship
with God, and to turn from a profound misconception of that
relationship.

> Paul will go on to analyze the plight of man as his failure to accept
> this status of complete dependence on God (1:21, 25, 28), including
> his fellow Jews whose narrower definition of covenant righteousness
> in terms of ethnic identity and "works" (9:6–13) in Paul's view in-
> volved a departure from the fundamental recognition that faith on
> man's side is the only possible and sufficient basis to sustain a rela-
> tion with God, as exemplified above all in Abraham's unconditional
> trust and total dependence on God and his promise.[62]

We may conclude our survey of Dunn's reading of this verse by asking
one further question. When Paul says that this "righteousness" is "from
faith to faith," what does he mean? This, Dunn says, is a "play on the
ambiguity of the word faith/faithfulness, in the sense 'from *God's* faithfulness (to his covenant promises) to man's response of faith.' "[63]

Romans 3:21–26. A second important passage in Paul addressing "righteousness" is Romans 3:21–26. Dunn observes that the "righteousness of God" (3:21–22) means precisely the same thing that it did
at 1:16–17. In what sense is this "righteousness" said to be "apart
from the law"? This latter phrase, Dunn explains, means "apart from
the law understood as a badge of Jewishness, understood as the chief
identifying characteristic of covenant membership by those 'within the
law.' "[64] Insofar as this "righteousness" is "witnessed by the law and
the prophets," Paul is communicating that "the gospel is the continuation or completion or fulfillment of the law properly understood
within the scriptures as a whole."[65]

But what about the uses of this phrase in Romans 3:25–26, where the possessor of the righteousness in both instances is clearly said to be God, and where Paul draws a connection between "righteousness" and the sacrificial death of Christ? Dunn first reminds us that, with a few notable exceptions, most Pauline scholars regard 3:25–26a to be a pre-Pauline formula.[66] He summarizes these verses as speaking of "Christ's death [as] a sacrifice for sin provided by God in accordance with the law, (and) God's means of extending his righteousness to all who believe (including those outside the law)."[67] The absence of any defense of this assertion also establishes its pre-Pauline origin (i.e., no one in the church would have disputed it). This, we may note, also excuses Dunn from having to establish a necessary relationship in Paul between righteousness and the death of Christ.

Dunn nevertheless sees Paul's phrase at verse 25 ("this was to demonstrate His righteousness") as in full keeping with previous Pauline uses.[68] Paul merely asserts that God's righteousness is demonstrated by "providing a sacrifice which fulfills the terms laid down in his covenant with Israel;" it is an "expression of God's saving grace."[69] In similar fashion, Paul's phrase at verse 26 ("for the demonstration, I say, of His righteousness at the present time") is an "obviously deliberate . . . repetition" of verse 25b. How does this show that "God is just" (v. 26)? "Not because he acts in accordance with some abstract ideal of justice, but because he has acted in fulfillment of the obligation he took upon himself as covenant God of Israel," *viz.*, "Jesus' sacrificial death was God's effective way of dealing with his people's sin (had he simply disregarded it, he would not have acted in accord with the covenant and would not have been just)."[70] Dunn will elaborate concerning Paul's understanding of the relationship between "righteousness" and the death of Christ:

> God's righteousness is indeed God's fulfilling of his covenant obligation to be Israel's God, to save and sustain Israel, as the devout Jew would well understand. The sacrificial system demonstrates this: that God provided a way for dealing with failure, for Israel's breach of the covenant. And now Christ's death demonstrates God's righteousness in the same way, for both past and present; that is to say,

Christ's death demonstrates God's righteousness *precisely by being a sacrifice*, by doing with effective finality what the sacrificial system had done only in part (that is only for some sins, or only for Israel's sins). Once again, then, the very important emphasis comes through that God's saving action for and to faith is *not* a departure from the covenant with Israel, but is continuous with it and in accordance with it; God's righteousness is not an arbitrary choosing of Israel and then dropping of Israel, but his choice of Israel is always with the *all* in view, the extension of his saving purpose to all in accordance with his covenant obligation to Israel.[71]

In conclusion, we may observe that Dunn, even though he concedes that Paul frames Christ's death as a sacrifice, leaves certain questions unanswered regarding Christ's death. What does it mean, for instance, that God dealt with his people's sin in accord with the covenant (although not in terms of "some abstract ideal of justice")? Undoubtedly this vagueness stems from Dunn's unwillingness to view divine righteousness in traditional categories.

Romans 10:3. A third important passage addressing righteousness is Romans 10:3 ("For not knowing about God's righteousness and seeking to establish their own, they did not subject themselves to the righteousness of God."). About what is Israel ignorant? Dunn comments that there is a "basic misunderstanding of how God deals with his people and what he requires of his people—that is, God's righteousness as God's gracious accepting and sustaining power to faith, therefore open to all and not the special prerogative of Israel to be defended by the sword."[72] They are not "ignorant [of] God's righteousness in general, but the *character* of that saving power, the terms on which it can be received and known."[73] This definition is seen against what is contrasted in this verse ("their own"), which term Dunn defines as "Israel's claim to a righteousness which was theirs exclusively, shared by no other people, possessed by them alone."[74] What of the term "establish"? This is not referring to "an act of creation, a bringing about of something which previously did not exist, but a setting or establishing or confirming of something which is already in existence. . . . They sought to establish and confirm what God had already given them."[75] How then did they fail to subject themselves to it? "It was *not* that they had misunderstood righteousness by understanding it in terms of law, by understanding that the covenant relation with God required obedience."[76] Rather, they "so misunderstood what that obedience entailed that their zealous obedience had actually become disobedience, a zeal attested more by sword than by love of neighbor. By pursuing obedience at the level of the flesh (cf. 8:7), in terms of ethnic and particular rituals, they showed their misunderstanding of God's righteousness. . . ."[77]

Justification, Faith, and the Works of the Law

Paul ties together the concepts of "justification" and "righteousness." How does Dunn understand the language of "justification" and the related concepts "faith" and "works of the law"? Dunn says that the options of "*make* righteous" and "*declare* righteous" are a false dichotomy: "So once again the answer is not one or the other but both. The covenant God counts the covenant partner as still in partnership, despite the latter's continued failure. But the covenant partner could hardly fail to be transformed by a living relationship with the life-giving God."[78] He concedes, in a comment on Galatians 2:16, that "the one thus 'justified' or acquitted was thereby found to be 'righteous'; the ground of a favourable judgement was the 'righteousness' of the one judged . . . , to be 'justified' was to be formally recognized as 'righteous.' "[79] But, Dunn continues, we must not read our Greek categories into this term. "In Hebrew thought 'righteousness' was more a concept of relation. People were 'righteous' when they met the claims which others had on them by virtue of their relationship." Consequently, "to be righteous was to live within the covenant and within the terms it laid down (the law); to be acquitted, recognized as righteous, was to be counted as one of God's own people who had proved faithful to the covenant."[80] Elsewhere, Dunn elaborates precisely what Paul means by "justification" at Galatians 2:15–16:

In talking of "being justified" here [i.e., Gal. 2:15–16] Paul is not thinking of a distinctively *initiatory* act of God. God's justification is not his act in first *making* covenant with Israel, or in initially accepting someone into the covenant people. God's justification is rather God's acknowledgement that someone is in the covenant—whether that is an *initial* acknowledgement, or a *repeated* action of God (God's saving acts), or his *final* vindication of his people . . . "To be justified" in Paul cannot, therefore, be treated simply as an entry or initiation formula; nor is it possible to draw a clear line of distinction between Paul's usage and the typically Jewish covenant usage.[81]

We have, therefore, a clear difference with Sanders. Sanders sees Pauline "justification" language as a transfer term, thereby effecting a break from its predominant uses in Judaism. Dunn sees the language of justification as an acknowledgment or declaration that one is *already in* the community of the saved, thereby establishing continuity with the use of this term in Judaism.

Why, then, did Paul take this doctrine [a "restatement of the first principles of his own ancestral faith"][82] and frame it polemically? This, Dunn argues, raises two further questions: How and why did Paul perceive his doctrine of justification to distinguish Christianity from Judaism? How does Paul define those "works of the law" by which he categorically denies justification to take place?

In answering this cluster of questions, Dunn first addresses his conception of Paul's transition from Judaism to Christianity. Dunn argues that this transition is to be identified with what he calls Paul's conversion, "a turning from his 'way of life previously in Judaism.' "[83] How is this Judaism to be defined? Dunn argues that the background of this word in the Second Temple literature militates against a definition of "the religion of the Jews."[84] Rather, the term is used in contradistinction with "Hellenism" and therefore involves a consciousness of "separating [oneself] from the wider world" and an understanding of "the Torah in part at least as reinforcing and protecting that separateness."[85] This definition is borne out by Paul's own self-description as a Jew in Philippians 3:3–6. Paul will focus on his "physical and ethnic identity as a Jew" by pointing to "four identifying features" (circumcision, racial identity, tribal identity, and language).[86] When Paul cites his blamelessness (Phil. 3:3–6) and zeal (Gal. 1:14) as a Jew, we learn that Paul "converted from measuring righteousness primarily in terms of covenant distinctiveness, and from a competitive practice within Judaism which sought to outdo other Jews in the degree and quality of its Torah-keeping."[87] Furthermore, Paul's zeal, in the Second Temple Period, was conceived "as an unconditional commitment to maintain Israel's distinctiveness, to prevent the purity of its covenant set-apartness to God from being adulterated or defiled, to defend its religious and national boundaries"—something that was to be done "by force" and even against "fellow Jews."[88] Dunn reminds us that when Paul converted, he did not convert from Judaism *simpliciter* so much as "from 'Judaism' as it called forth this zeal," *viz.*, a zeal to preserve Israel's integrity and purity by ensuring that this "particular expression of Jewish religion and tradition" (i.e., Christianity) did not "open the door . . . to the Gentiles."[89]

This background helps us to understand what Paul's polemic concerning works of the law entails. Dunn stresses that "works of the law" does not mean "good works done as an attempt to gain or achieve righteousness," although he concedes that this "interpretation is wholly understandable, particularly in the light of Romans 4.4–5"; and that "the post-Pauline Ephesians 2.8–9 looks very much like a confirmation of this (cf. 2 Timothy 1.9 and Titus 3.5)."[90] The definition of works "in terms of human acceptability before God . . . may have happened already in Ephesians 2.8–9, where the issue does seem to have moved from one of works of law to one of human effort."[91] When we turn to the undisputed epistles, our working definition of "works of the law" will be "what the law required *of Israel as God's people.*" The phrase "works of the law" is the "Pauline term for 'covenantal nomism,' "[92] although Dunn grants that Paul will speak of this latter concept positively using "obedience of faith," *not* "works of the law," language.

How do we account, then, for the consistently negative way in which Paul uses the phrase "works of the law"? Paul is highlighting these works' tendency among his contemporaries to "protect Israel's privileged status and restricted prerogative."[93] Dunn will cite the Qumran text *Some of the Works of the Torah* (4QMMT) as evidence of such an understanding among the Qumran community.[94]

In summary, "works of the law" "refer[s] to all or whatever the law requires, covenantal nomism as a whole. But in a context where the relationship of Israel with other nations is at issue, certain laws would naturally come more into focus than others. We have instanced circumcision and food laws in particular."[95] It is for this reason that, while Paul embraces ancient Israelite covenantal nomism, he rejects the works of the law (so understood) as a perversion of that traditional pattern.

By way of contrast, Paul stresses faith, not works of the law, as the means by which justification is effected: Dunn sees the contrast between faith and works not simply as an "argument" to promote "Gentile acceptance"; rather, he "presses beyond to provide a fundamental statement of human dependence on God."[96] Dunn explains the significance of the contrast in Paul's thought:

> It was a profound conception of the relation between God and humankind—a relation of utter dependence, of unconditional trust. Human dependence on divine grace had to be unqualified. . . . God would not justify, could not sustain in relationship with him, those who did not rely wholly on him. . . . [Hence] Paul was so fiercely hostile to the qualification which he saw confronting him all the time in any attempt to insist on works of the law as a necessary accompaniment of or addition to faith.[97]

It becomes clear, however, that Dunn cannot and does not maintain faith in its office in justification in the same sense that the Reformers understood it. Concerning Romans 3:28 ("For we maintain that a man is justified by faith apart from works of the Law"), Dunn observes that the narrower definition of "works of the Law" (see above) that is employed in this passage "means that there is no real contradiction with [Romans] 2:13 ('for it is not the hearers of the Law who are just before God, but the doers of the Law will be justified')." How, then, does Dunn understand Romans 2:13? Observing that "acquit" is the appropriate translation of the Greek verb *dikaioō*, Dunn comments that "like his fellow Jews and the whole prophetic tradition, Paul is ready to insist that a doing of the law is necessary for final acquittal before God; but that doing is neither synonymous with nor dependent upon maintaining a loyal membership of the covenant people," that is, in the sense of hearing divorced from doing. The Jew ought not look to covenantal obedience (*qua* boundary markers) to vindicate his membership in God's people.[98] What is necessary for his justification at the last day is his obedience to the law. Dunn, then, does not regard Paul's statement at Romans 2:13 to be either hypothetical or indicative of works evidencing a final and unchangeable verdict of justification issued prior to the Judgment Day. Rather, Dunn sees Paul in Romans 2:13 as describing an imminent state of affairs that is in keeping with the believer's present justification. With respect to the believer's future and present justification(s), Dunn argues that the two are best conceived as distinct stages in a process. "The 'righteousness of God' is nowhere conceived as a single, once-for-all action of God, but as his accepting, sustaining, and finally vindicating grace."[99] Dunn elsewhere explains this point at greater length:

> As the whole conception of God's righteousness has indicated, justification is not a once-for-all act of God. It is rather the initial acceptance by God into restored relationship. But thereafter the relationship could not be sustained without God continuing to exercise his justifying righteousness with a view to the final act of judgment and acquittal. . . . Throughout this life the human partner will ever be dependent on God justifying the ungodly.[100]

We may now draw three conclusions from our discussion of Dunn's understanding of justification in Paul. (1) For Dunn, justification is less a single act or declaration than a *series* of declarations or acts for the believer. These declarations extend from initiation to the Day of Judgment. (2) Further, for Dunn, Romans 2:13 teaches that the doing of good works is necessary for the believer's justification at the last day; and this "justification" does not appear to be of a different kind or order from the justification mentioned elsewhere in this epistle. (3) Faith in justification, for Dunn, is predominantly defined as "trust" in the sense of trusting in God's promises (cf. Rom. 4). Faith in justification, however, cannot be said to exclude the covenantal obedience that identifies someone as properly belonging to the people of God.

In view of these arguments, how does Dunn's conception of justification relate to both the death and the resurrection of Christ in

Paul's thought? In relating justification and the death of Christ, Dunn appears to reject the traditional Protestant relationship between these two concepts. He observes that justification may be cleared from "the charge of legal fiction" because

> God's sentence of death on sin is carried through in the death of Christ. Were Paul's doctrine of atonement one of substitution (Jesus died and the sinner went scot-free) that would be more open to such a charge. But . . . Paul's teaching is of Christ's death as a representative death, the death of all, of sinful flesh. . . . The cancer of sin in the human body is destroyed in the destruction of the cancerous flesh.[101]

Dunn also does not believe that Romans 3:25 should read "whom God set forth as an expiation, through faith in his blood . . ." but "whom God set forth as an expiation, through faith, in his blood" (notice the comma inserted between "faith" and "in"). Dunn rejects the former rendering because it would be "without parallel in the New Testament."[102] He argues that Paul has inserted "through faith" into a traditional formulation perhaps "in order to provide a balance to the (Jewish) emphasis on God's provision of the sacrificial cult," *viz.*, to preclude a Jewish "presumption" with respect to the "cult."[103] "Paul insists on a faith which is not tied into a continued practice of the cult (faithfulness) but which can only be an acceptance of the decisive sacrifice already provided by God."[104] We, of course, need to stress that, for Dunn, what is accepted by faith is not a sacrifice that Paul conceives to be a substitutionary atonement.

In relating justification and the resurrection, Dunn considers Romans 4:25 ("He was handed over because of our transgressions, and was raised for our vindication" ["justification," NASB]). Dunn informs us that the "distinction between Jesus' death and resurrection . . . is purely rhetorical." We should not see the two acts of death and resurrection as "effecting quite separate results."[105] He goes on to say that "the justifying grace of God is all of a piece with his creative, life-giving power."[106] To understand this latter statement and other statements made above, we will need to have a clearer understanding of what Dunn understands Paul to mean by the death of Christ, already adumbrated above and detailed below.

Dunn Responds to Traditional Arguments

Before we proceed to examine Dunn's views on the death of Christ, we need to consider how he responds to traditionalist defenses of justification and works of the law and traditionalist understandings of Paul's relationship to (his past life in) Judaism. We do so by turning to six representative passages that pose problems for Dunn's synthesis.

Galatians 3:10–13 (5:3; 6:13). The law, Dunn argues, never required perfection. The theory that there is an implied premise of human inability to keep the law in Galatians 3:10–13 is mistaken. Rather, "obedience was considered practicable." The law did, after all, come "within the terms of the covenant" and had "the provision of atonement by covenant law."[107] Note here that Dunn is in fundamental agreement with Sanders. Neither Jews nor Paul believed that the law required perfect obedience or that one was bound to render it perfect obedience. Dunn, in his commentary on Galatians, will explicitly say so, pointing not only to Deuteronomy 30:11–14 (the passage that lies behind Romans 10:6–8), but also to Romans 8:4.[108]

When Paul speaks in Galatians 3:10 (RSV) of "all who rely on the works of the law" [NASB: "as many as are of the works of the Law"], he speaks of "those who were putting too much weight on the distinctiveness of Jews from Gentiles, and on the special laws which formed the boundary markers between them, those who rested their confidence in Israel's 'favoured nation' status."[109] Dunn assumes, here, of course, that we have accepted his definition of "works of the law," which "involved 'shutting out' Gentiles, even believing Gentiles ([Galatians] 4.17)."[110] In other words, the problem that Paul raises in Galatians 3:10–13 is one of identity or status, not of activity: the debate is ecclesiological, not soteriological, in nature.

With this explanation in mind, we might quickly turn to Galatians 5:3 ("And I testify again to every man who receives circumcision, that he is under obligation to keep the whole Law"), and Galatians 6:13 ("For those who are circumcised do not even keep the Law themselves, but they desire to have you circumcised so that they may boast in your flesh"). Commenting on 5:3, Dunn observes that "under obligation to keep the whole Law" is not a recognition that the law requires perfect obedience, *but* another way of saying "the obligation of those within the covenant people, as that which marked out the covenant people, as the way to live within the covenant."[111] Paul stresses, then, not the "perfect life, . . . without any sin or failure," but the "total way of life, which, through the cult, its sacrifices and atonement, provided a means of dealing with sin and failure."[112] In similar fashion, Galatians 6:13 means simply that "those who rely on their practice as Jews (covenantal nomism, 'works of the law') are not in fact doing what the law demands." Such persons' "pride and presumption" are what in fact the law "undermines."[113]

   Romans 9:30–32. Dunn argues that Israel's failure to attain the law (Rom. 9:31) because they pursued it by works (Rom. 9:32) restates Paul's argument at Galatians 3:10. By having a truncated view of the law (works of the law), Israel failed to attain the whole of what the law required.[114] But to what does the second "law" of Romans 9:31 ("but Israel, pursuing a law of righteousness, did not arrive *at that law*") refer? We may recall that Sanders had said that Paul did not say what he meant. Dunn tells us that the second law must mean the "Jewish law" and "not 'norm' or 'rule.' "[115] When Paul says that Israel has not "reached the law" (Rom. 9:31), he refers not to "moral perfection" but "to responsible covenant membership." The language of pursuit does not mean "a frantic striving to achieve a claim on God"; nor does the faith/works contrast mean "self-accomplishment or self-assertion."[116] Rather, Paul's use of "works" and "faith" in Romans 9:32 reminds us of his customary use of these two terms: "the law defining righteousness understood too narrowly in terms of the requirements of the law which mark off Jew from Gentile" and "the law defining righteousness understood in terms of the obedience of faith which a Gentile can offer *as Gentile*."[117]

   Romans 11:5–6. How does Dunn address the contraposition of grace and works in these verses ("But if it [i.e., "a remnant according to God's gracious choice," v. 5] is by grace, it is no longer on the basis of works, otherwise grace is no longer grace")? Works, Dunn reminds us, are "a way of understanding election which Paul firmly rejects . . . —works understood as the hallmark of election, as that which marks out the elect as such."[118] When Paul declares that the election rather is by grace, he is saying that "the remnant is not constituted as a group within Israel by their faithfulness to the law, but as a group sustained by God's grace."[119] What we do *not* have is "Paul's objecting to a belief that justification can be earned by good works."[120]

Romans 4:4–5. This passage ("Now to the one who works, his wage is not credited as a favor, but as what is due. But to the one who does not work, but believes in Him who justifies the ungodly, his faith is credited as righteousness") raises two issues. The first issue raised is that Paul's "wage" language seems to exclude the strict "status" view that Dunn has been promoting. Dunn argues, however, that Paul here simply states a principle, with which none of his Jewish readers would disagree, simply to "remind [his audience] of the fundamental character of all God's dealings with human beings."[121]

How does Dunn respond to the charge that "works" in this passage does not admit of the exclusive concern with "status" that he has maintained defines Pauline usage of this word? He tells us that "the language used here (working, reckoning, reward) should not be taken as a description of the Judaism of Paul's day. In particular, Paul is not castigating contemporary Judaism for a theology of (self-achieved) merit and reward."[122] Paul's point, rather,

> is simply that in the case of Genesis 15:6 the whole language of "payment due" is inappropriate. . . . Here he simply poses the alternatives, work → reckon → debt / faith → reckon → favor, as a way of setting up the exposition which is about to follow and as a way of shaking his Jewish interlocutor out of a too ready equation of Abraham's believing with his covenant loyalty. Where (Abraham's) faith is in view, the righteousness is surely reckoned in terms of grace, not of payment due.[123]

But Dunn seems to evade the obvious question: if there is no disagreement between Paul and Judaism on this point ("Nor is it necessary to assume that Paul was accusing his fellow Jews of making that equation [*viz.*, 'between works of law and the payment-earning work of day-to-day life']"),[124] *then why does Paul need to raise this question at all? Is this strictly academic?* Dunn suggests so. "He simply points out that to interpret Genesis 15:6 in terms of Abraham's acts (works) of covenant loyalty, leaves no room in the common-sense logic of the work-a-day world for grace."[125]

The second issue raised is that Paul's doctrine of the justification of the ungodly seems to exclude Dunn's conception of Pauline justification as God making a declaration concerning one who is already in the covenant. Dunn defines "ungodly" not in moral terms but as "one who is outside the covenant, that is, outside the sphere of God's saving righteousness."[126] Consequently, the offense posed by Paul's argument in Romans 4:4–5 "to Jewish ears" would have consisted of the assertion that God "justifies (that is, through the covenant)" one who is "ungodly," that is, one who is "outside the covenant."[127] Paul, citing Abraham as the example referenced in Romans 4:5, would have had ample precedent in Second Temple thought, which conceived Abraham "as the type of the proselyte, the Gentile who turns away from his idolatry to the one true God."[128]

Philippians 3:6. Dunn comments that when Paul speaks of himself as "blameless" with respect to the "righteousness within the law" (3:6), he is not claiming "to have been sinless or never to have transgressed the law."[129] Rather, the language of blamelessness simply meant that one "live[d] within the terms of the covenant," inclusive, of course, of "the provision of atonement for sin through repentance and sacrifice."[130] Paul rejects, then, his "confidence in his covenant righteousness"—that 'separatism' which would have marked his life as a Pharisee and "ensured that in the terms of covenant obligation ('righteousness') he was 'without reproach.' "[131]

Verses 7–9. By "righteousness" as a Jew, Paul is not referring to "a righteousness attained by his own efforts," but rather "the practice of the devout within the covenant."[132] "My own" does not mean "my own (and no one else's)," as though Paul had achieved a private stock of gain. Rather, "all it need mean is 'my own' as 'belonging to me,' forgetful of its essentially gracious character ('from God'). Further, the *primary* contrast is between 'from the law' and 'through faith in Christ.' "[133] In support of this interpretation, Dunn will point to Paul's list of the privileges he had enjoyed as a Jew (Phil. 3:4–6). All the items enumerated in this list are headed by "confidence . . . in the flesh" (Phil. 3:4), which shows that Paul's concern is not with self-achievement but zeal and pride for Israel's covenantal privileges. Paul is opposing the notion that "God's righteousness was only for Israel, and only for Gentiles, if they became Jews and took on the distinctive obligations of God's covenant with Israel."[134]

Romans 7:7–25. Dunn dissents from the critical orthodoxy that, since W. G. Kümmel's 1929 monograph, had argued that Romans 7:7–25 describes "man under the law" and therefore belongs to the "convert's past."[135] We have, rather, an "existential anguish" in 7:14–24 especially that "sounds like an experience Paul knew only too well,"[136] and continues into the present.[137] Consequently, Dunn will not look at this passage to speak of Paul's interaction with his Jewish past.

Romans 7:7–13 (and other plight passages) is a reversion to the "Adam narratives." Paul has offered us here a "semi-allegorical reading of Genesis 2–3," into which he may possibly "have been deliberately meshing in the story of Israel."[138] The command of Genesis 2.17 is "a particular expression of" the tenth commandment; the "serpent is identified as the representation of sin"; and "the 'I' is an existential self-identification with Adam."[139] Dunn grounds this connection between Romans 7 and Genesis 2–3 in "Jewish theological reflection on Adam's disobedience," which saw "wrong desire, lust, or covetousness" to be the "root of all sin." Paul is said to acknowledge this tradition by citing the tenth commandment and by recognizing with other Jews that "the serpent appealed to . . . Adam's coveting of divine status."[140] Incidentally, Dunn gives no particular texts (biblical, apocryphal, or noncanonical) that evidence a parallel allegorization of Genesis 2–3 in this way.

We may also observe parenthetically that Dunn sees Romans 1:18–32; 3:23; and 8:19–22 as Pauline retellings of the Adamic narrative of Genesis 1–3. The whole point of 7:7–13 is "to defend the law from any implication that the law should bear primary responsibility for the experience of death."[141] What Dunn appears resistant to is interpreting this passage in terms of individual experience, or as a commentary on the apostle's personal transition from Judaism to Christianity, a transition centered on a reevaluation of the law.

Salvation as Metaphor in Paul

One consideration that we will want to bear in mind as we conclude our study of righteousness, justification, and works of the law is the way in which Dunn conceives of these terms—they are metaphors.[142] "Justification is a legal metaphor," for example. Paul also uses redemption, liberation, freedom, reconciliation, citizenship, kingdom-transfer, salvation, and inheritance as some of the other metaphors in his letters.[143] For Dunn, "these metaphors bring out the *reality* of the experience of the new beginning for Paul. Evidently they all described something in the experience of his readers with which they could identify."[144]

Why is metaphor important to the study of Paul? Dunn tells us that these metaphors "were presumably attempts to express as fully as possible a reality which defied a simple or uniform or uni-faceted description."[145] They are attempts to put into words that which was "so rich and real in the various experiences of conversion which Paul's gospel brought about."[146] Analogously, "the impact of a piece of music or the distinctions among different wines can often be so intensely personal and intangible as to be beyond communication in terms of logic. Still more so with regard to experiences which are so life-transforming."[147] Dunn cautions us not to privilege one metaphor over another: "many of Paul's first readers experienced the gospel as acceptance, liberation, or rescue, as cleansing and new dedication, as a dying to an old life and beginning of a new."[148] Incidentally, we are told, "there is little evidence that Paul preached for conviction of sin or to stir up feelings of guilt."[149] We ought not "take any one of Paul's metaphors and exalt it into some primary or normative status so that all the others must be fitted into its mould."[150] Protestant theology has done this with justification; popular evangelism has done this with salvation and new birth.[151] But such efforts are "dangerous" because they assume that "the experience of individuals must conform to the language which describes it" when the Pauline pattern was vice versa. For Paul, "the crucial transition was a many-sided event, and not necessarily the same for any two people."[152] The three metaphors that Dunn sees as "bring[ing] out the central features of the new beginning for Paul" and "significan[t] in the history of Christian theology" are justification by faith, participation in Christ, and the gift of the Spirit.[153] As with Sanders, then, justification and participation may be resolved into essentially the same reality. Their difference is, for Dunn, purely a nominal one.

Christ's Death

Where does the death of Christ, so prominent in Paul's letters, fall in Dunn's scheme? Dunn concedes that Paul saw Christ's death as an atoning sacrifice.[154] It is an "image" that Paul drew from the "cultic sacrifice," specifically the "sin offering"[155] (cf. Lev. 4) and the "annual Day of Atonement sacrifices."[156] Paul will speak of Christ's death as expiatory, but not as propitiatory ("the imagery is more of the removal of a corrosive stain or the neutralization of a life-threatening virus than of anger appeased by punishment"[157]).

How does Christ's death become effectual to the believer? Dunn has already intimated in the passage quoted immediately above that Paul addresses Christ's death in terms of nullifying sin's power. Commenting on Galatians 3:13, he observes that "here the plight of humankind is put in terms of curse rather than of being under the power of sin and death. But it comes to the same thing."[158]

Underlying these differences, "Paul uses a rich and varied range of metaphors in his attempt to spell out the significance of Christ's death," including "representation, sacrifice, curse, redemption, reconciliation, conquest of the powers."[159] But, Dunn says, they are strictly "imagery and metaphor. As with all metaphors, the metaphor is not the thing itself but a means of expressing its meaning. It would be unwise, then, to translate these metaphors into literal facts, as though, for example, Christ's death were literally a sacrifice provided by God (as priest?) in the cosmos, conceived as a temple."[160] Further, citing

Colossians 2:11–15 as an example, he notes that these metaphors "do not always fit well together."[161]

All the metaphors, however, can be resolved into one thing: the "initiative of God" (but in such a way that "the cross of Jesus does not constitute the basis of a religion different from that of Israel"[162]). We can't dispense even with the "outdated metaphor" of sacrifice; it "has to be remetaphored rather than simply discarded if the potency of its message for Paul and the first Christians is not to be lost."[163]

In sum, Dunn's views of Paul on Christ's death, as with his views on soteriology, are nominalistic. The biblical language that Paul uses does not correspond to any reality outside itself (i.e., a judicial transaction, a genuine sacrifice). When Paul *does* speak about the nexus of the cross and sin, Dunn notes, Paul tends to focus on sin *qua* power, almost never sin *qua* guilt.[164]

Summary

We may now offer a brief summary of our conclusions regarding Dunn's study of Paul.

1. Dunn regards "works of the law" to have been the whole pattern of Jewish obedience to the Mosaic Law, as that pattern came to expression in certain boundary-marking ordinances: circumcision, Sabbath, dietary laws. In this respect, Dunn differs from Sanders.

2. Paul's critique, then, is directed at individuals who would, in pride, cling to certain boundary markers to the exclusion, e.g., of Gentile believers. He is not concerned to address persons who by striving to obey the Mosaic Law are attempting to meet a divine moral standard in order to be justified before God.

3. Paul converted from his zeal for Judaism, but did not change religions. In stressing faith as the boundary marker of the covenant community, he is proposing nothing new, but restoring true and ancient Judaism from a contemporary truncation (i.e., works of the law) of it. Dunn concedes, however, that the traditional Protestant interpretation of Paul (works as activity, not status) has warrant in the post-Paulines, *viz.*, Ephesians, 2 Timothy, Titus.

4. Paul's "righteousness" language is not fundamentally forensic (i.e., Greek)—it is primarily relational and transformative (i.e., Hebrew), pointing us to the initiative of God. Dunn, against Sanders, does *not* see "righteousness" language as transfer terminology.

5. Justification is conceived as a series of declarations that one is *already in* the covenant people of God. Consequently, the justified person is contemplated as one who is (admittedly imperfectly) faithful to the terms of the covenant.

6. Salvation and the death of Christ are not conceived realistically, but nominalistically. Metaphor or image in Paul is a sub-adequate attempt to verbalize the diversity of many individuals' experiences of God through the Pauline gospel. The various Pauline images and metaphors resolve into the initiative of God.

Enter the Church:
N. T. Wright

hile he does not presently hold an academic position, N. T. Wright has grown in influence among New Testament scholars, especially evangelicals. Why does Wright's understanding of Paul merit a close study? One important reason to do so is that the leading NPP proponents that we have thus far considered have all restricted their literary activity to the academy. E. P. Sanders and Heikki Räisänen, especially, have little interest in engaging in anything further than a descriptive project. Räisänen in particular, taking up Wilhelm Wrede's mantle, has vehemently rejected the legitimacy of academic attempts to undertake questions of normativity in the study of the New Testament.[1] Wright, on the other hand, has actively promoted pursuing questions of normativity within New Testament scholarship. Wright, then, lends a practical dimension to the NPP that merits careful attention.

A second reason that one should study Wright is that he has done more than any other single individual to mediate NPP exegesis into the mainline and evangelical churches. This, in part, is due to the fact that he has long served as an officer within the Church of England. In so doing, he has never intentionally segregated his scholarship and his parish ministry. Wright's popularity among evangelicals is also due to his general respect for the integrity of the New Testament. His scholarship on Jesus stands out from contemporary lives of Jesus and theologies of the Gospels in at least one respect. Wright purposefully approaches the Gospels as credible historical records, sidestepping many of the source-critical and redactional-critical concerns that New Testament scholars often bring to the text. His interest in engaging the text as it stands has won him the respect of many younger evangelicals in the academy. Another reason for Wright's popularity among evangelicals is his conception of each part of his scholarship as part of a greater whole. His as yet unfinished New Testament theology is unique in New Testament studies not only in its scope but also in its attempt to treat the New Testament synthetically.

It is tempting to begin with Wright's specific views on Paul, but we need first to ask two prior questions: How does Wright conceive the theological task? How does Wright conceive Second Temple Judaism and Paul's relationship to it?

"Theology" Proper in N. T. Wright

Wright treats this subject in his *New Testament and the People of God*, the first installment in his ongoing New Testament theology.[2] Wright begins with an interest in blazing past the impasse caused by "post-Enlightenment rationalism" and "anti-Enlightenment supernaturalism,"[3] that is, by reading the New Testament as "story" and not as "declaring unstoried ideas."[4] Epistemologically, he advances a "critical-realist theory of knowledge and verification," one that "acknowledges the essentially 'storied' nature of human knowing, thinking and living, within the larger model of worldviews and their component parts."[5] Such an approach, Wright is confident, will bypass both naïve objectivism and skeptical phenomenalism. With Michael Polanyi and Nicholas Wolterstorff, Wright defines a worldview as a "tacit and pre-theoretical point of view" that is a "necessary condition for any perception and knowledge to occur at all."[6] Wright argues that "story" plays a vital role in the formation and expression of a worldview:

> Stories are a basic constituent of human life; they are, in fact, one key
> element within the total construction of a worldview . . . All world-
> views contain an irreducible element, which stands alongside the other
> worldview elements (symbol, praxis, and basic questions and answers),
> none of which can be simply "reduced" to terms of the others . . .
> Worldviews, the grid through which humans perceive reality, emerge
> into explicit consciousness in terms of human *beliefs* and *aims*, which
> function as in principle debatable expressions of the worldviews. The
> stories which characterize the worldview itself are thus located, on
> the map of human knowing, at a more fundamental level than ex-
> plicitly formulated beliefs, including theological beliefs.[7]

For Wright, then, "story" lies back of theological propositions, which
are the expression of that particular narrative. Consequently, when,
for example, we speak of monotheism and election, we "summon into
the mind's eye an entire worldview," which is fundamentally storied.
The words ("monotheism," "election") themselves are "late constructs,
convenient shorthands for sentences with verbs in them . . . not mere
childish expressions of a 'purer' abstract truth."[8] Wright contrasts the
"Jewish story-theology" with "the rarefied territory of abstract Hellenistic speculation"[9] (recall our consideration of this distinction in
our study of J. D. G. Dunn). Paul is decidedly to be found in the camp
of the former: his "statements and arguments are in fact expressions
of *the essentially Jewish story now redrawn around Jesus*."[10] We have,
then, in Wright's thought, an inherent bias against doctrinal formulation and linear, logical reasoning, a predisposition against conceiving
of the relationship of God and man in *vertical* terms. Rather, Wright
is inclined to understand that relationship in essentially *horizontal*
categories.

The Jewish Story: Second Temple Judaism

Having established the necessity of "worldview" and "narrative"
to understanding biblical, Hebraic thought, Wright then moves to the
task of constructing Israel's story as Jews conceived that story in the
biblical and post-biblical periods. Wright argues that there was a basic
story common to all Judaism. This story is given expression by means

of four distinct categories: a common story; variations upon this story; symbols of this story; and praxis grounded on this story.

First, Wright argues, there was a story common to all ancient Jews. The creator formed the world, and his covenant people, Israel, played a central role in that world. Israel's story moved forward in stages: this "God has given Israel her Torah," by which she would have "rescue" from her "pagan enemies," would be "his people," and would be "confirmed as ruler in her own land."[11]

Second, by the first century A.D., Wright argues, Israel had reached the apex of a crisis that had been in place since the exile. All first-century Jews were consumed with the question, "From what quarter would come the 'full liberation of Israel'?" Although Cyrus had restored Israel to the land in the sixth century B.C., all Jews continued to believe that they were still in exile. Various Jewish groups wrote their own disparate ending(s) to the common story, *viz.*, their restoration stories. For the author of 1 Maccabees, deliverance had come through the Hasmoneans; to Josephus, deliverance had and would come through submission to Rome. Notwithstanding this diversity of restoration narratives, Jewish groups in the meantime had unanimously resolved "to remain faithful to god [*sic*] and his Torah," awaiting vindication and God's enthronement over the nations.[12]

Third, Temple, land, Torah, and racial identity were "key symbols which anchored the 1st c. Jewish worldview in everyday life."[13] They themselves were, of course, closely integrated into the story.

Fourth, Jewish praxis synthesized "story" and "symbol," and was in the first century expressed in two main ways: (1) worship and festivals (whereby Israel's story was publicly retold) and (2) study and learning. Jewish praxis in the first century came to focus on "three badges . . . which marked out the Jew from the pagan: circumcision, Sabbath, and the kosher laws."[14]

In summary, Wright distills the narrative of first-century Judaism into four questions and answers:

1. Who are we? We are Israel, the chosen people of the creator god [*sic*]. 2. Where are we? We are in the holy Land, focused on the Temple; but, paradoxically, we are in exile. 3. What is wrong? We have the

wrong rulers: pagans . . . [and] compromised Jews. . . . 4. What is the
solution? Our god [*sic*] must act again to give us the true sort of rule . . . ;
in mean time Israel must be faithful to his covenant charter.[15]

According to Wright, the basic beliefs stemming from this worldview were monotheism, election, and covenant/eschatology. The consequent beliefs were those divergent solutions posed to the problem of
exile by diverse Jewish groups.

The Early Christian Worldview

The early Christian worldview, Wright argues, was conceived
from the matrix of the Jewish worldview. In company with other Jewish groups, the early Christians created an alternative solution to the
problem of exile posed by the basic story of Israel. Correspondingly,
Jewish praxis and symbols were either discarded or reformulated in
accordance with the terms of the early Christian story. For example,
church as family replaced ethnic identity; church ethics replaced the
Torah; creedal belief replaced the Jewish badges of circumcision, Sabbath, and dietary laws.

Wright argues that early Christians saw themselves as a "new
group . . . yet not new." They were the "true people" of the God of
Israel. They argued that their problem was that we live in a world
made by God, but in bondage to idols, though those idols' "absolute
power" has ended. Believers have enemies both within ("heresies and
schisms") and without ("persecutions"). The solution that the early
Christians posed to this problem was that God in Jesus' death and resurrection has "defeat[ed] the pagan gods," has "create[d] a new people, through whom he is to rescue the world from evil." This process
"is not yet complete." "The King will return to judge the world," erect
a new kingdom, and raise dead Christians "to a new physical life."[16]
The genius of Christianity, then, Wright argues, is not in its soteriologically proffering something that contemporary Judaism opposed
(faith in Christ versus works of the law), but in *reconfiguring the community of God's people*. Wright does, however, admit a broad soteriological difference between Judaism and Christianity (notwithstanding
fundamental similarities):

In particular, the Jewish doctrines of salvation and justification are reflected across early Christianity, even where those terms are not necessarily used. The church appropriated for itself the Jewish belief that the creator god would rescue his people at the last, and interpreted that rescue in terms of a great law-court scene. This is the doctrine of the "righteousness of God," which is best seen in terms of the divine covenant faithfulness, and which comes to major expression in Paul's letter to Rome. The major underlying difference between the Christian and the Jewish views at this point was that the early Christians believed that *the verdict had already been announced* in the death and resurrection of Jesus. Israel's god had at last acted decisively, to demonstrate his covenant faithfulness, to deliver his people from their sins, and to usher in the inaugurated new covenant. . . . To the Jewish formulation ("how can we tell, in the present, who will be justified in the future?") the Christians added a second question: how can we tell in the present, who is included in the death and resurrection of Jesus? . . . [Answer: they] are circumscribed not by race, geography, or ancestral code, but by Jesus, and hence by faith.[17]

We now turn to consider precisely how Wright conceives Paul's understanding of the similarities among ancient Jews and Christians.

Paul and the Righteousness of God

We still await Wright's fullest treatment of Pauline theology, but we do possess several loose articles (scholarly and popular), his *What Saint Paul Really Said*, and his recently published commentary on Romans in the *NIB* series. [18] Consequently, we have sufficient material from which to draw informed judgments concerning Wright's views on Paul. In an important sense, Wright's understanding of the phrase "the righteousness of God" is central to understanding his synthesis of Paul. Wright argues that the term "the righteousness of God" has three distinct backgrounds: covenant, the law court, and eschatology. Wright argues that "for a reader of the Septuagint . . . the 'righteousness of God' would have one obvious meaning: God's own faithfulness to his promises, to the covenant."[19] Similarly, Wright maintains that this phrase "summed up sharply and conveniently, for a first-century Jew such as Paul, the expectation that the God of Israel . . . would be faithful to the promises made to the patriarchs."[20] Wright elaborates on the import of the Jewish background to Paul's use of this phrase:

> God's "righteousness," especially in Isaiah 40–55, is that aspect of God's character because of which he saves Israel, despite Israel's perversity and lostness. God has made promises; Israel can trust those promises. God's righteousness is thus cognate with his trustworthiness on the one hand, and Israel's salvation on the other. . . .[21]

The phrase "the righteousness of God" stems not only from the covenant but also from the law court, back of which, Wright tells us, was a Jewish view that "the covenant between God and Israel was established in the first place in order to deal with the problem of the world as a whole."[22]

What is this problem, and in what way will God deal with it? Wright contends that "in biblical thought, sin and evil are seen in terms of injustice—that is, of a fracturing of the social and human fabric." Consequently, what is needed "is that justice be done, not so much in the punitive sense that phrase often carries [though punishment comes into it] but in the fuller sense of setting to rights that which is out of joint, restoring things as they should be."[23] God's righteousness then is "seen in terms of covenant faithfulness" as the "instrument of putting the world to rights—of what we might call cosmic restorative justice."[24] Wright (against Sanders) argues that righteousness in Paul has been drawn from the "law court."[25] It has, then, a specifically forensic sense. Righteousness, to anticipate a point on which we will elaborate below, speaks to "the status [the plaintiff and the defendant] have when the court finds in their favour."[26] Interestingly, Wright argues that this use precludes either of the traditional conceptions of righteousness imputed/infused to the believer:

> If we use the language of the law court, it makes no sense whatever to say that the judge imputes, imparts, bequeaths, conveys or otherwise transfers his righteousness to either the plaintiff or the defendant. Righteousness is not an object, a substance or a gas which can

be passed across the courtroom. . . . To imagine the defendant somehow receiving the judge's righteousness is simply a category mistake.
That is not how the language works.[27]

If righteousness in Paul denotes God's covenantal faithfulness, and
specifically that covenantal faithfulness as engaged on behalf of his people in a forensic context, and specifically imputation of any sort is denied, then how are God's people said to be righteous? Wright asserts
that "if and when God does act to vindicate his people, his people will
then, metaphorically speaking, have a status of 'righteousness.' "[28]
Wright is vague, however, precisely why God's people enter such a status in consequence of the divine vindication.

There is a third element to Paul's language of righteousness: eschatology. This Wright draws from Paul's use of the phrase "is revealed" (*apokalyptetai*) in Romans 1:17. Clearly, there is here a
"coded way of saying that God would at last act within history to
vindicate Israel."[29] To anticipate our discussion on justification in
Wright, we find Wright arguing that the Jews had said that their
works of the law were certain indications that "one can tell in the
present who precisely will be vindicated when God finally acts in fulfillment of his righteousness, of his covenant obligations."[30] Justification by works, then, amounts to the view that "the present sign of
our future vindication consists in our present loyalty to the covenant
obligations laid upon us by our God," *viz.*, our "works of the law."[31]
It would be with *this* view of the law and of God's righteousness that
Paul would disagree.

If the preceding provides a general background to the Pauline language, then how did Paul himself take up the righteousness of God?
Wright reminds us that "Paul's world of thought was a variation on
the Second Temple Jewish worldview."[32] After his call on the Damascus Road, he "quickly came to regard the events of Jesus' death and
resurrection as the apocalyptic moment for which he and others had
longed, and he rethought his previous way of viewing the story of Israel and the world as a result."[33] In so doing, he affirmed that "Israel's
God had been true to the covenant and the promise," specifically the
Abrahamic promises. In this light, Wright reminds us, the righteous-

ness of God in Paul is not a "status people have from God" but "God's own righteousness."[34]

In other words, this phrase, which constitutes the chief theme of the epistle, is "about God and God's covenant faithfulness and justice, rather than simply . . . 'justification.'"[35] This puts Romans 9–11, the chapters of Romans where Paul is said to address these concerns most thoroughly, in its proper place: not as an "appendix" but as the "intended major climax of the whole letter."[36] It is this concern, therefore, that gives structure to Romans. Wright tells us that the doctrine of justification by faith as the great concern of Romans is a "half-truth." The letter's "stated theme," rather, is "the revelation of God's righteousness, God's covenant faithfulness, God's justice, in and through the gospel proclamation of the crucified and risen Messiah."[37]

The Centrality of the Righteousness of God in Romans

We may look briefly at how Wright understands Romans 1–8, the portion of the letter traditionally understood to lay out Paul's soteriology most comprehensively. In doing so, we see the influence of Wright's understanding of the centrality of the righteousness of God (so defined) in Romans in shaping his reading of these important chapters.

> *Chapters 1–4:* God's gospel unveils the fact that in the Messiah, Jesus of Nazareth, the God of Israel has been true to the covenant established with Abraham and has thereby brought saving order to the whole world. In the face of a world in rebellion and a chosen people unfaithful to their commission, God has, through the surrogate faithfulness of Jesus the Messiah, created a worldwide—that is, a Jewish and Gentile—family for Abraham, marked out by the covenant sign of faith.
>
> *Chapters 5–8:* God has thereby done what the covenant was set up to do: to address and solve the problem expressed in biblical terms as the sin of Adam. In the Messiah, Jesus, God has done for this new people what was done for Israel of old in fulfillment of the promise to Abraham: Redeemed from the Egypt of enslavement to sin, they are led through the wilderness of the present life by the Spirit

(not by the Torah), and they look forward to their inheritance, which will consist of the entire redeemed creation. This is how the creator will finally put the whole world to rights. All this is the result of God's astonishing, unchanging, self-giving covenant love expressed completely and finally in the death of Jesus.[38]

Two Particular Passages

We can furthermore see illustrated in Wright's comments on two important passages of Romans his understanding of the centrality of this theme and its global implications for our understanding of Pauline theology.

Romans 3:21–4:25. In commenting on this passage, Wright insists that traditional readings of Paul have perverted the true Pauline understanding of the relationship between the righteousness of God and the death of Christ (the latter of which we'll examine in more detail below). Once we grasp the true definition of the righteousness of God, Wright tells us, then we will find that "Paul's purpose in 3:21–26 is not, then, to give a full doctrine of atonement, a complete account of how God dealt with the sins of the world through the death of Jesus."[39] Paul, rather, "is content to state, not completely *how*, but simply *that*" "on the cross the righteousness of God was unveiled."[40] Romans 3:22, furthermore, should be translated "even the righteousness of God through the faithfulness of Jesus the Messiah"[41]—the righteousness of God is something that is to be witnessed in Jesus' own life.[42]

Furthermore, when Paul speaks of Christ's obedience in this section (and 5:12–21), he is not

> suggesting that Jesus' "obedience" was somehow meritorious, so that by it he earned "righteousness" on behalf of others. That is an ingenious and far-reaching way of making Paul's language fit into a theological scheme very different from his own. Rather he is highlighting Jesus' faithful obedience, or perhaps we should say Jesus' obedient faithfulness, to the saving plan marked out for Israel, the plan by which God would save the world. On the cross Jesus ac-

complished what God had always intended the covenant to achieve. Where Israel as a whole had been faithless, he was faithful.[43]

Consequently, through Jesus' death, "sin and its results have been dealt with. Wrath has been turned away from God's people."[44] In this exposition, we see not only Wright's consistency of resistance to the language and concept of imputation in Romans 3, but also his positive understanding of the "righteousness of God" and its relationship to the work of Christ.

Romans 10:3. Regarding this verse ("For not knowing about God's righteousness and seeking to establish their own, they did not subject themselves to the righteousness of God."), Wright will comment that the first and third uses of "righteousness" in this verse are entirely in keeping with prior uses in this letter (e.g., 1:17; 3:1–8). One may paraphrase "the righteousness of God," then, as "God's own character and actions," or the "quality of equitable covenant faithfulness." The concept revolves "around the question, 'Has God been faithful to his promises?' "[45] When Israel is said to fail to "subject themselves to the righteousness of God," Paul is saying that the Jews "have attempted . . . to set up a status of covenant membership in which the principle of 9:6–29 would be quietly set aside; this would be a status for all Jews, and only for Jews. No pruning down to a remnant; no admission of Gentiles (except by becoming full Jews through proselyte initiation)."[46] Wright argues, therefore, that in view of Paul's definition of the righteousness of God, the apostle's central concern in Romans 9–10 is not moral activity but covenantal status.

Again, Wright is aware that his reading of these verses runs counter to traditional readings. He claims that Paul "does not regard his contemporaries as proto-Pelagians, trying to pull themselves up by their own moral bootstraps in order to be good enough for God and to earn 'works-righteousness' of that sort." Paul, in other words, is "not turning his back on Judaism and its traditions. He is claiming to interpret them in their own terms, through their own Scriptures, and around their own Messiah (9:4–5)."[47] Wright, then, stresses that Paul's primary concern here, as throughout Romans, is not soteriological but ecclesiological in nature.

Justification and the Believer's Faith in Justification

If this is what Paul means by the righteousness of God, then what does it mean to be justified? Wright distances himself from Albert Schweitzer and Sanders when he states that justification is not "secondary, . . . ad hoc, and polemical" to Pauline thought. Although justification "cannot be put right at the centre, since that place is already taken by the person of Jesus himself, and the gospel announcement of his sovereign kingship," it "does not mean that justification becomes a secondary, still less an inessential matter."[48] Despite Wright's protests that he does not see this doctrine as Paul's *ad hoc* response to a crisis in the church,[49] we nevertheless have within Wright's comments above *formal* agreement with Schweitzer and Sanders.

Wright frequently polemicizes the traditional Protestant doctrine. It "distorts" Paul and causes us to "lose sight of the heart of the Pauline gospel," although Wright grants that it is not "entirely misleading."[50] The traditional reading of Romans has "systematically done violence to that text for hundreds of years, and . . . it is time for the text itself to be heard again."[51] He concurs with Alister McGrath that "the 'doctrine of justification' has come to bear a meaning within dogmatic theology which is quite independent of its Pauline origins."[52]

One of Wright's crispest definitions of the believer's justification appears in his commentary on Romans. "The verdict of the last day has been brought forward into the present in Jesus the Messiah; in raising him from the dead, God declared that in him had been constituted the true, forgiven worldwide family. Justification, in Paul, is not the process or event whereby someone becomes, or grows, as a Christian; it is the declaration that someone is, in the present, a member of the people of God."[53] As with righteousness, justification, Wright avers, is covenant language, is forensic language, and is eschatological in nature.[54] "The covenantal declaration, seen through the metaphorical and vital lens of the law-court, is put into operation eschatologically. The verdict to be announced in the future has been brought forward into the present. Those who believe the gospel are declared to be 'in the right.' "[55] The book of Galatians, Wright argues, is concerned not with "how precisely someone becomes a Christian or attains to a relationship with God," but with "the question of how you *define the people of God*: are they to be defined by the badges of the Jewish race, or in some other way?"[56] It is the question of "how you can tell who is a member of the covenant family."[57] Put polemically, "Justification is not how someone *becomes* a Christian. It is the declaration that they *have* become a Christian."[58] Hence, the "question of justification" at Galatians 2:15–16 "is not 'how to become a Christian' but 'whether Jewish Christians and Gentile Christians can share table fellowship.' "[59]

Embedded within Wright's definition of justification is an understanding of justification as a two-staged event in the believer's experience. Primary for Paul, Wright argues, is the believer's *future* justification (see below on Romans 2:13), in view of which act the believer experiences *present* justification, *viz.*, the declaration that this person is a true member of God's covenant people. Wright, then, inverts the traditional ways of relating one's justification to the Day of Judgment. For Protestants, the Day of Judgment has been understood as an occasion when the believer's justification will become publicly manifest. Nothing, however, can or will be added then to his justification because the ground of that justification (the perfect obedience and full satisfaction of Christ) cannot be improved upon or found deficient. For Wright, however, it is the future verdict of justification that has primacy in Paul's thought. Excepting the doctrine of the imputation of Christ's righteousness to the believer (which Wright rejects), Wright's doctrine of *future* justification appears to play the role that the traditional Protestant doctrine of justification plays in the present experience of the believer. In order to understand Wright's views on what we have termed present and future justification, we turn now to consider his treatment of two verses, Romans 3:28 and Romans 2:13.

Romans 3:28. On this verse ("For we maintain that a man is justified by faith apart from works of the Law"), Wright argues that Paul's language does not have a resumptive function—that is, it does not recapitulate his argument in the preceding several verses (3:21ff.). Instead, "Paul is reporting on a calculation that has taken place, not in the present passage, but elsewhere, which he will shortly unveil."[60] Wright, then, can divorce Paul's affirmation of Romans 3:28 from his preceding discussion of Christ's death as sacrificial and propitiatory (Rom. 3:21–26). After Wright's reminder that he will be bound to no traditional *ordo salutis*, and that he is no mere NPP "company man," he tells us that we must "let Paul say what he means by his own key terms" (even if this "does violence to many such well-loved frameworks of thought").[61] Wright reminds us that present justification does not address the "event of 'conversion' or the process of Christian living"; it is, rather, "God's declaration that certain persons are members of the covenant people, that their sins have been dealt with."[62] How is justification by faith? "The badge of membership in God's people, the badge that enables all alike to stand on the same, flat ground at the foot of the cross, is faith."[63] Faith, so understood, is to be contrasted with works of the law (3:20; 9:32), which Wright takes to be especially "the works that marked out the Jews from their pagan neighbors."[64] Jews are faulted, then, for their claim "to possession of Torah as the badge of being God's special people."[65] Hence, Paul's faith/works dichotomy serves to communicate Paul's point "that all who attempted to legitimate their covenant status by appealing to possession of Torah would find that the Torah itself accused them of sin."[66] That Paul is concerned with the Jew/Gentile question in these verses is also borne out by what he says just below in Romans 3:29–30 ("Or is God the God of Jews only? . . . God who will justify the circumcised by faith and the uncircumcised through faith. . . ."). These verses also show why justification cannot be by the Torah (to which Wright appears to take "works of the Law" to refer)—"God's impartiality would be impugned (2:11), and the whole fabric of the righteousness of God, the justice and faithfulness of God, would start to unravel," since "God's faithfulness to the covenant with the Jewish patriarch, Abraham, and his descendants, can only be fulfilled through the creation of a worldwide, Jew-plus-Gentile, family."[67]

Romans 2:13. Wright, like Dunn, takes Romans 2:13 ("for it is not the hearers of the Law who are just before God, but the doers of the Law will be justified") to be a nonhypothetical affirmation of the justification of believers. Wright comments that the "force of verse 13 is to undergird God's impartiality," *viz.*, "it cannot be the case that mere possession of Torah, hearing it read in synagogue, will carry validity with God."[68] Rather, "what counts is doing Torah," and Wright regards 8:1–4 and 10:5–11 as explicating Paul's view of "doing Torah." At the very least, we see that in this verse (2:13), Wright has in mind the believer's obedience to the law. The significance of this verse, Wright continues, is that "Israel's ethnic privilege, backed up by possession of Torah, will be of no avail at the final judgment if Israel has not kept Torah. *Justification, at the last, will be on the basis of performance, not possession.*"[69] In point of principle, Wright is correct: the believer's justification must be grounded on *someone's* obedience to the law. The problem presented by Wright's formulation is that he has already rejected the imputation of Christ's righteousness (see above) as a Pauline doctrine. We are left, then, with no other alternative than that it is the *believer's* performance (and not *Christ's* performance) that is the ground of this verdict. That this is Wright's view may be seen from his comment at Romans 5:9–10: " 'justification,' when applied to the future, as in 2:13, [speaks] in terms of their acquittal in the final Assize";[70] and his comment on Romans 8:4: "What is spoken of here is the future verdict, that of the last day, the 'day' Paul described in 2:1–16. That verdict will correspond to the present one, and will follow from (though not, in that sense, be earned or merited by), the Spirit-led life of which Paul now speaks."[71]

As with Dunn, we appear to have a multistaged doctrine of the believer's justification. Wright's model, however, appears simpler than Dunn's, possessing only two stages (present and future). Present justification contemplates the believer as bearing the badge of covenantal membership, *viz.*, faith. Future justification contemplates the believer's covenantal obedience. When we turn below to Wright's comments on faith, we will see again that one's covenantal *faithfulness* is contemplated in the verdict(s) of justification.

Justification and the Death of Christ

Before we consider the office of faith in justification, let us examine what relationship Wright understands there to be between the verdict(s) of justification and the work of Christ. We'll consider first the role of the death of Christ in justification by studying Wright's treatment of three passages, Romans 3:25a; 5:9; and 5:18–19.

Romans 3:25a. In Romans 3:25a ("whom God displayed publicly as a propitiation in His blood through faith"), Wright, with Dunn, argues that we must conceptually separate "in His blood" and "through faith." Faith, furthermore, refers to the covenantal faithfulness of Jesus, not the believer's subjective appropriation of Christ's propitiatory death. We have already considered above how Wright balks at conceiving of justification as a soteriological doctrine—it is instead a declaration of who constitute the people of God. If justification is ecclesiological in nature and Paul nevertheless ties the doctrine (cf. Rom. 3:24) to Christ's death, how are we to understand this verse? Wright explains that there *is* a connection between the believer's justification and Christ's death. "Thus is God's righteousness revealed in the gospel events of Jesus' death and resurrection: God has been true to the covenant, has dealt properly with sin, has come to the rescue of the helpless and has done so with due impartiality between Jew and Gentile."[72] There exists, then, an oblique connection between one's justification and Christ's death, but certainly not in the manner that Protestants have traditionally conceived of the connection.

Romans 5:9. Wright has little to say in his "Romans" commentary about this important verse ("Much more then, having now been justified by His blood, we shall be saved from the wrath of God through Him."). Other than to speak of believers as "already justified by Jesus' sacrificial death," Wright unfortunately does not elaborate on the nature of the relationship between Christ's death and the believer's justification, except to take an opportunity to speak of the future of the believer, which will involve a future justification or acquittal (as at Rom. 2:13).[73]

Romans 5:18–19. Commenting on these verses ("So then as through one transgression there resulted condemnation to all men, even so through one act of righteousness there resulted justification of life to all men. For as through the one man's disobedience the many were made sinners, even so through the obedience of the One the many will be made righteous."), Wright paraphrases Romans 5:19 as "Christ's obedience has given 'the many' the status of being 'righteous.' " In other words, "Jesus . . . is the servant of YHWH, whose

obedient death has accomplished YHWH's saving purpose."[74] Wright
in his comments explicitly repudiates the traditional view that this
verse teaches that Christ's active and passive obedience are imputed
to those whom he represents.[75] The obedience mentioned in these
verses, rather, is the Messiah's faithfulness (as at Romans 3:22), his
"obedience to God's commission (as in 3:2), to the plan to bring salvation to the world, rather than his amassing a treasury of merit
through Torah obedience."[76]

How, then, are God's people "made righteous"? "Justification,
rooted in the cross and anticipating the verdict of the last .day, gives
people a new status, ahead of the performance of appropriate deeds."[77]
In other words, Paul is focusing on the "status" of the people of God
(although, for Paul, to be righteous is "more than simply status"; Paul
will not develop this theme, Wright says, until Romans 6). It is difficult, however, to reconcile Wright's claim above that "justification . . .
gives people a new status" with his repeated comments that justification is a declaration that one is *already* in the people of God.

Justification and the (Death and) Resurrection of Christ

How does Wright understand Romans 4:25 ("He . . . was delivered over because of our transgressions, and was raised because of our
justification")? Wright claims that the first half of the verse means that
"he was so identified with 'us' that he suffered the fate we deserved."[78]
As to the latter half of the verse, Wright understands justification and
resurrection to be virtual equivalents:

> Thus if faithful Jesus is demonstrated to be Messiah by the resurrec-
> tion, the resurrection also declares in principle that all those who be-
> long to Jesus, all those who respond in faith to God's faithfulness
> revealed in him, are themselves part of the true covenant family prom-
> ised to Abraham. In other words, the resurrection of Jesus can at this
> level be seen as the declaration of justification. And this can perfectly
> well be expressed as "He was raised because of our justification."[79]

The functional equivalency of justification and resurrection appears
to consist in their declarative value. As resurrection declares Jesus to

be Messiah, so justification declares God's people to be part of the true covenant family.

The Believer's Righteousness

We have above considered Wright's views on the righteousness of God, and have seen that it refers to God's faithfulness to his covenant promises, seen especially in his deliverance of his people. Paul, however, will also speak of other righteousnesses (of the law/ from God) that belong to the human beings. We have had occasion above to broach this question. Now we may ask more directly: of what, in Wright's view, do these two righteousnesses consist? The righteousness of the law against which Paul speaks is "a covenant status, which was his as a Jew by birth, marked with the covenant badge of circumcision, and claiming to be part of the inner circle of that people by being a zealous Pharisee."[80] Commenting on Romans 9:31 ("but Israel, pursuing a law of righteousness, did not arrive at that law"), Wright argues that Paul is saying that "the more Israel clung to the law, the more it found that evil lay close at hand, and that covenant membership could not be found that way."[81] But why did Paul append "of righteousness" to "law" in Romans 9:31 if he were fundamentally concerned with a question of status or covenant membership and not ethical activity? Wright claims that this addition was included in order to justify the law as "God's law, holy and just and good."[82] By a "law of righteousness," Wright claims, Paul means here not a law that demands righteous behavior so much as a law that is essentially good and right.

Paul's comment in 9:32 ("Why? Because they did not pursue it by faith, but as though it were by works.") continues the argument. Here the apostle claims that "the reason Israel did not attain Torah, the covenant charter, is because they were pursuing it, not by faith, but 'as though by works.' "[83] "Works of the law," then, means here "the works that marked out the Jews from their pagan neighbors"— Israel "has sought . . . an inalienable identity as God's people for all those who possess Torah, for (that is) ethnic Israel as a whole." We have, then, an exposition of 9:31–32 that very closely resembles Dunn's exposition considered in the previous chapter. Commenting on Romans 10:3, Wright argues that Israel's "own" righteousness is not the traditional " 'works-righteousness' resulting from keeping the law, or a more general effort," but "the covenant status that Israel according to the flesh had thought to set up for itself."[84] The "righteousness *from* God" (not the righteousness *of* God, which also appears in Romans 10:3) is, on the other hand, the "status of covenant *membership*," a "gift bestowed upon faith."[85] We may note that in both uses of the term "righteousness" as applied to human beings, Wright has advanced definitions that are framed *not* in moral categories, but in categories of status.

In passing, we may briefly observe Wright's inconsistency with his own formulations. Wright, in commenting on Romans 1:18–32, observes that God's "wrath" is revealed (1:18) and his "ordinance" is directed (1:32) against certain human behaviors. In other words, when Paul speaks of the unrighteous behavior of men in Romans 1:18–32, which he summarizes as "unrighteousness" (1:18), Wright understands this behavior not only in moral terms but also in terms of human activity, *not* status.[86] Nevertheless, when Wright interprets the language of righteousness elsewhere in Romans (as above), such interpretations are decidedly without reference to moral or behavioral categories. Such a disjunctive reading of Paul's language of righteousness and unrighteousness renders unlikely and implausible Wright's proposal that the language of the "righteousness from the law" and the "righteousness of God" is concerned exclusively with covenantal status.

Faith in Justification

What, then, is the office of faith in our justification? Faith in present justification is the "badge of covenant membership, not something one 'performs' as a kind of initiation test," nor a "surrogate 'work.' "[87] Is it more? Wright leaves us wondering when he says that "the place of faith in this picture has long been problematic within post-Reformation dogmatics."[88] In a concluding chapter to *What Saint Paul Really Said*, commenting on the phrase "the obedience of faith," Wright discusses the relationship of faith and obedience:

Faith and obedience are not antithetical. They belong exactly together. Indeed, very often the word "faith" itself could properly be
translated as "faithfulness," which makes the point just as well. Nor,
of course, does this then compromise the gospel or justification, smug-
gling in "works" by a back door. That would only be the case if the
realignment I have been arguing for throughout were not grasped.
Faith, even in this active sense, is never and in no way a qualification, provided from the human side, either for getting into God's
family or for staying there once in. It is the God-given badge of membership, neither more nor less.[89]

Similarly, in commenting on Romans 1:5, Wright argues that "the obedience of faith" should be rendered "the obedience which consists in
faith." But he notes that past interpreters have been concerned whether
such a reading "does not suggest the priority of good moral works
rather than pure faith."[90] Such a concern, Wright says, "misses the
point. . . . [Paul's] apostolic commission is not to offer people a new
religious option, but to summon them to allegiance to Jesus, which
will mean abandoning other loyalties. The gospel issues a command,
an imperial summons; the appropriate response is obedience."[91] It is
this obedience that in Paul is the content of faith.

The "obedience" which Paul seeks to evoke when he announces the
gospel is thus not a list of moral good works but faith. Faith, as Paul
explains later (10:9), consists in confessing Jesus as Lord (thereby re-
nouncing other lords) and in believing that God raised Jesus from the
dead (thereby abandoning other worldviews in which such things did
or could not happen, or not to Jesus; cf. too 4:23–25). This faith is actually the human faithfulness that answers to God's faithfulness. As
we will discover in chap. 3, that is why this "faith" is the only appropriate badge of membership within God's true, renewed people. . . .[92]

Faith and faithfulness, then, amount to the same thing. Faith, Wright
will protest, is not a work (in the classical sense of the word), since
works for Paul belong to a different discussion from that conducted by
the Reformers. In short, whereas faith in present justification is conceived as a badge without particular reference to its obedience, faith,

conceived as faithfulness or a life of covenantally faithful obedience, is the *ground* of the believer's future justification. "Present justification declares, on the basis of faith, what future justification will affirm publicly (according to 2:14–16 and 8:9–11) on the basis of the entire life."[93]

Paul and the Death of Christ

Given Wright's disagreement with the Reformers' conception of justification, righteousness (whether of God or of the believer), and faith, we may ask, "Why, then, did Jesus Christ die?" Unlike Dunn, Wright will not simply resolve Paul's language regarding Christ's death into one of a number of metaphors; nor, like Sanders, will he see Christ's expiatory death as Paul's obligatory nod to earlier Christian tradition. How, then, does Wright conceive the relationship between the atoning death of Christ and the believer's experience? Telling is Wright's gloss of Romans 3:24–26, in which he draws together the concepts of justification, righteousness, and faith:

> Within this context, "justification," as seen in 3:24–26, means that those who believe in Jesus Christ are declared to be members of the true covenant family; which of course means that their sins are forgiven, since that was the purpose of the covenant. They are given the status of being "righteous" in the metaphorical law court. When this is cashed out in terms of the underlying covenantal theme, it means that they are declared, in the present, to be what they will be seen to be in the future, namely the true people of God. Present justification declares, on the basis of faith, what future justification will affirm publicly . . . on the basis of the entire life. And in making this declaration (3:26), God himself is in the right, in that he has been faithful to the covenant; he has dealt with sin, and upheld the helpless; and in the crucified Christ he has done so impartially. The gospel— not "justification by faith," but the message about Jesus—thus reveals the righteousness, that is, the covenant faithfulness of God.[94]

In these comments, as in his comments surveyed above, Wright continues to speak in vague terms concerning the manner in which Christ's death results in believers' pardon.

Other crucial passages concerning the expiatory and propitiatory death of Christ are treated in a similarly imprecise way.

1 Corinthians 1:30. If understood in the traditional sense of teaching an imputed righteousness, this verse requires, Wright maintains, a doctrine of "the imputed wisdom of Christ; the imputed sanctification of Christ; and the imputed redemption of Christ." To assert the imputation of such things, however, is "certainly [to] make nonsense" of the way in which the righteousness of Christ has been traditionally conceived.[95]

2 Corinthians 5:20–21. This verse has been traditionally understood to teach the imputation of the believer's sin to Christ, and of Christ's righteousness to the believer. Wright disagrees and argues that this verse simply teaches that the apostles are the "living embodiment of the message they proclaim." They are an "incarnation of the covenant faithfulness of God."[96]

Romans 8:3–4. Wright has devoted attention to Romans 8:3–4 ("For what the Law could not do, weak as it was through the flesh, God did: sending His own Son in the likeness of sinful flesh and as an offering for sin, He condemned sin in the flesh, so that the requirement of the Law might be fulfilled in us, who do not walk according to the flesh but according to the Spirit."). The thrust of these two verses is that God had to "condemn sin in the flesh of Jesus, so that the life the law offered could rightly be given to those led by the Spirit."[97] Paul affirms that Jesus died as the representative of his people. Consequently, "what was true of him was true of them. His death could therefore be counted as theirs."[98]

How was Jesus a "sin offering" (Rom. 8:3)? Wright reminds us that the Levitical sin offering addressed only "sin that has been committed ignorantly or unwillingly."[99] By describing Jesus' death in this way, the "problem" of Romans 7 is thereby resolved: the *ego* or "I" of Romans 7 has committed sins in ignorance and against its will ("for what I am doing, I do not understand; for I am not practicing what I would like to do, but I am doing the very thing I hate" [7:15]). Wright, however, reminds us that "the sin-offering thus answers exactly, not indeed to any and every sin (that is not what this phrase was designed to do)." Wright, then, would not have us understand this verse as exhaustive of Paul's thought on the atonement. We may also observe that throughout his comments on this passage, Wright speaks vaguely concerning the *manner* in which Christ represented his people as sin-bearer. Wright simply affirms that it was in the Messiah that sin "might there be dealt with, be condemned, once and for all," or that "the death of Jesus [is] the means whereby the judicial punishment on sin itself was meted out."[100]

Romans 3:25–26. Wright frequently avers that God at the cross "dealt once and for all with the sin of the world."[101] A study of his comments on Christ's death (from 3:25–26) in his recent commentary on Romans shows Wright's consistent refusal to articulate Christ's death in terms of an imputed righteousness:

> [In referring to Jesus as *hilastērion*, Paul is] alluding to Jesus as the place where the holy God and sinful Israel meet, in such a way that Israel, rather than being judged, receives atonement. . . .[102]

> The significance of Isaiah 40–55 here lies in its ability to tie together and explain what otherwise is inexplicable, namely why Paul should imagine that the death of Jesus, described in sacrificial terms, should be supposed not only to reveal the righteousness of God but also to deal properly, i.e. punitively, with sins. The idea of punishment as a part of atonement is itself deeply controversial . . . But it is exactly this idea that Paul states.[103]

> Dealing with wrath or punishment is propitiation; with sin, expiation . . . Vehement rejection of the former idea in many quarters has led some to insist that only "expiation" is in view here. But the fact remains that in 1:18–3:20 Paul has declared that the wrath of God is revealed against all ungodliness and wickedness and that . . . those who are Christ's are rescued from wrath; and that the passage in which the reason for the change is stated is 3:25–26, where we find that God, though in forbearance allowing sins to go unpunished for a while, has now revealed that righteousness, that saving justice, that caused people to be declared "righteous" even though they were sinners.[104]

Wright elsewhere specifies Jesus' death to be "the decisive victory over the powers, sin and death included,"[105] the "means . . . of the liberating victory of the one true God, the creator of the world, over all the enslaving powers that have usurped his authority. That is why it is the heart of 'the gospel.' "[106]

While Christ's death may be said to be atoning, punitive, even propitiatory, Wright consistently refuses to detail the mechanism by which Christ's death comes to be applied to the individual believer in time and history. Having categorically and expressly denied imputation in Paul, Wright cannot mean that the righteousness of Christ is in any way credited to the believer forensically. He has, however, presented us with a predominantly *Christus victor* view of the atonement. On this construction, sin as *power* is treated, but sin as *guilt* is functionally neglected. It is in such a view of Christ's death that Wright's true views are likeliest to be found. Wright, to be sure, uses the language of "atonement" and "propitiation" to speak of Christ's death. Since Wright rejects imputation as a Pauline category, however, he cannot mean by "atonement" and "propitiation" what these terms have traditionally been understood to mean. Atonement and propitiation cannot, therefore, play a central role in Wright's real understanding of the significance of Christ's death to Paul.[107]

Paul, Conversion, and the Christian Life

In concluding our exposition of Wright, we may ask two final questions. What does Wright say about Paul and the transition from outside to inside Christianity? How does Wright understand Paul to speak of contemporary Christian experience? Recall that, for Wright, the gospel is "not, for Paul, a message about 'how one gets saved,' in an individual and a historical sense." Rather, it is an "announcement about Jesus" that embraces the death of Christ, the resurrection of Christ, the messiahship of Christ, and the universal lordship of Christ.[108]

Wright *will* use the word "conversion" to speak of Paul's transition from Judaism to Christianity,[109] but he is careful to underscore that this transition did not reflect a burdened conscience or discontent with the spirituality of his fathers.[110] It was, rather, the discovery of a "new vocation," *viz.*, as a "herald of the king."[111] It consisted of Paul's embracing the fact that "the one true God had done for Jesus of Nazareth, in the middle of time, what Saul had thought he was going to do for Israel at the end of time."[112]

Wright, with other proponents of the NPP, balks at seeing Paul's soteriological discontent with Judaism in passages to which traditionalists have pointed as evidence of that discontent. (1) Commenting on Philippians 3:3–6, Wright observes that Paul, in declaring his "blamelessness," meant only that "as a good Jew, he regularly used the means of forgiveness and purification that were on offer in the Temple and the sacrificial cult and took part in the great fasts and feasts through which the devout Jew was assured of God's forgiveness and favor."[113] He was not, of course, claiming "that he had always done what Torah prescribed," as though he were "so ignorant of his own motivation and behavior."[114]

(2) Commenting on Romans 7:7–25, Wright argues that the "I" of that passage is not the "normal Christian." In so doing, he breaks from the reading of Romans 7 adopted by C. E. B. Cranfield and Dunn. The "I" is not the "normal Christian" because of "repeated assertions" throughout Romans 6–8 that the believer is said to be not "in sin," "in the flesh," or "under the law."[115] Further, Paul has said at Romans 6:17, 18, 22, that believers are no longer "slaves of sin" but "slaves of righteousness." At this point Wright will fault a tendency in the "history of exegesis" to read Romans 5–8 as a "theology of the Christian life"—a tendency that has led to a slipshod pairing of general individual "moral struggle" and the description of the "I" in Romans 7. Conversely, others have dismissed Romans 7 as the "experience" of the "non-Christian" in order to defend a doctrine of sinless perfection.[116]

Back of both tendencies, Wright warns us, is a belief that Romans 7 is a "transcript of the 'experience' either of the non-Christian, or of the Christian who is still struggling to live a holy life by means of 'law' (not usually conceived, in such schemes, as the Torah, but rather as a more general moral law one tries to follow by one's own efforts instead of relying on the Spirit)."[117] These "debates," we are told, are "rendered beside the point when the passage is read in its full context within the ongoing argument of Romans, and with full attention to the meaning of 'the law' throughout the passage."[118] We are wrong to read this passage *experientially* (whether of Paul's pre-Christian or Christian experience). This passage *cannot* speak of Paul's own experience under Judaism—after all, in Philippians 3, Paul tells us that "in his pre-Christian life he had been 'blameless' in regard to 'righteousness under the law.' "[119] Romans 7:7–25 is a passage that addresses something that transcends individual experience. Rather, the "I" must be understood "within Paul's two main controlling narratives," *viz.*, the "story of Adam and the Messiah," and the "new exodus." Romans 7:7–12 therefore speaks of Israel "when Torah arrived," and Romans 7:14–25 speaks of Israel "continuing to live under Torah thereafter."[120]

What we have, in conclusion, is "a Christian theological analysis of what was in fact the case, and indeed what is still the case for those who live 'under the law,' not a description of how it felt or feels." Romans 7:7–25 is a recapitulation of Romans 2:17–29, *viz.*, "those who embrace Torah find that Torah turns and condemns them."[121]

Wright, consequently, agrees that the death of Christ provides a resolution to this plight described in Romans 7. The plight, however, is entirely different. Those who intentionally resolve to live under the Torah (i.e., as Jews) will find themselves in the flesh. The Torah "increases and exacerbates the plight of humankind 'in Adam.' "[122] The solution (as described in Romans 8) is assigned to "Christ and Spirit together," not in such a way as to replace the "covenant with Abraham" and the "covenant of the Torah," but in such a way as to "renew" them.[123] The Spirit effects the exodus of which Romans 6 has spoken, and which Paul's dilemma in Romans 7 has warranted. In the Spirit, believers have inaugurated a new exodus in which Spirit-given life is to be found in both the present and the future.[124]

What about Christians today? As the gospel (so conceived) is proclaimed, "through this means, God works by his Spirit upon their hearts; as a result, they come to believe the message; they join the Christian community through baptism, and begin to share in its common life and its common way of life. That is how people come into relationship with the living God."[125] Were one to inquire about the role and importance of justification to Christian experience, Wright would reply that justification is not an entry term and, furthermore, needn't be grasped for one to be a true Christian: "believing in Jesus—believing that Jesus is Lord, and the [*sic*] God raised him from the dead—is what counts."[126] One may even be "justified without knowing it."[127]

How, then, does one become and remain a Christian? Wright argues that there are at least three necessary components to the Christian life. First, one must assent to the gospel of the death, resurrection, messiahship, and lordship of Christ. Second, one must submit to the sacrament of baptism. Wright balks at "good Protestant reader[s]" who see "baptism simply as an outward expression of a believer's faith, and [are] anxious about any suggestion that the act itself, or indeed any outward act, might actually change the way things are in the spiritual realm." Such anxiety is said to be due to the Enlightenment, romanticism, existentialism, and the theology of the sixteenth century.[128]

What, in Wright's opinion, does baptism *do*? The sacrament, he contends, was not a "generalized sign of initiation" but "that which brought people into the historical narrative of the new exodus," *viz.*, "the larger story of God, Israel, and Jesus."[129] Of those who are baptized, "that which is true of the Messiah is therefore now true of them; that is, what happened to him happens to them *with him*, as in the famous string of words beginning with *syn* ([Gk.] with, vv. 4–8)."[130] Wright assures us, moreover, that there is no conflict between baptism "as a physical act" and faith "as an interior event":

> [Paul] was well aware of the problems that arose when baptized persons, regularly attending the eucharist, gave the lie to these symbols by the way they were living. . . . Yet he never draws back from his strong view of either baptism or the eucharist, never lapses back into treating them as secondary. Indeed, in the present passage one might actually say that he is urging faith on the basis of baptism: since you have been baptized, he writes, work out that what is true of Christ is true of you (v.11).[131]

Although he assures us in the above quote that Paul is not endeavoring to establish any "systematic *ordo salutis*,"[132] Wright is well aware of the pastoral implications of this doctrine:

We are all too aware that thousands, perhaps millions, of the baptized seem to have abandoned the practice of Christian faith and life;
but we are nevertheless called to allow the dying and rising of Christ
in which we have shared to have its force and way in our own lives.
If Jesus and his dying and rising are simply a great example, we remain without hope; who seriously thinks that they can live up to that
ideal in their own strength? But if the fact of the messianic events has
become part of our own story through the event of baptism, and the
prayer and faith that accompany it, and above all the gift of the Holy
Spirit . . . then we will indeed be able to make our own the victory
of grace, to present our members, and our whole selves, as instru-
ments of God's ongoing purposes.[133]

We may summarize our brief discussion of Wright's conception
of baptism in Paul in a few observations: (1) Paul has a strong view of
the sacrament of baptism. (2) The recipient of baptism must cooperate with the grace that is bestowed in the sacrament in order for that
grace to become effectual. (3) Baptism has a primacy even over faith
in Paul's thought. For Wright's Paul, faith, as a badge, occupies a role
that baptism has played in many traditional readings of Paul. Baptism,
in certain respects, appears to occupy the role that faith has played in
many traditional readings of Paul.

The third act necessary to the Christian life, according to Wright,
is participation in the inclusive life of the community, a community
that ought to transcend "our petty and culture-bound church group-
ings, and which declares that all who believe in Jesus belong together
in the one family."[134] For this reason, incidentally, Protestants and
Catholics ought to be in "eucharistic fellowship," "because what matters is believing in Jesus . . . , detailed agreement on justification itself,
properly conceived, isn't the only thing which should determine eucharistic fellowship."[135]

Wright and Traditional Arguments

At this point, as we did above with Dunn, we ask the question:
how does Wright respond to passages that appear to give his thesis difficulties? We have already consulted Romans 7:7–25. Wright has chas-

tised traditional Protestants for reading this passage experientially. It rather refers to the whole experience of Israel "under the law" and therefore gives us no evidence for Paul's discontent with his way of life in Judaism soteriologically prior to his conversion, or for his inability to keep the law aright after his conversion.

Concerning Romans 4:4–5 ("Now to the one who works, his wage is not credited as a favor, but as what is due. But to the one who does not work, but believes in Him who justifies the ungodly, his faith is credited as righteousness."), Wright concedes that Paul uses the "metaphorical field" of "employment and wage-earning" in a treatment of "justification."[136] He stresses, however, that this is simply one instance and that it ought not "to become the dominant note." He notes that it is a mistake to understand Romans 4:5 "as a straightforward reversal of v.4." He argues that Paul in the latter half of Romans 4:5 is "pull[ing] himself out of the bookkeeping metaphor" and returning "to his main points, the lawcourt and the covenant."[137] Wright, rather than explaining the significance of the "wage" language in Romans 4:4–5, appears concerned to discount it.

What about Paul's language of the justification of the ungodly in Romans 4:5? Wright reminds the reader that the Jew/Gentile concern is in the background, especially in Paul's radical move in calling Abraham "ungodly." Paul cites Abraham at this point in his argument, Wright says, because he is "actually *more like* believing Gentiles than he is like believing Jews."[138] Wright *appears* to understand the term "ungodly" in moral terms. Wright will speak of "moments of apparent disobedience" on Abraham's part in view of his general pattern of "worshipping and obeying God."[139] Wright's comments on this verse help us to further understand his definition of the term "ungodly":

> The covenant was always intended to be God's means of putting the world to rights; the key moment in this promised accomplishment comes when, because of the unveiling of God's righteousness in the death of Jesus, God not only can but must declare the ungodly to be set right, to be within the covenant . . . one who believes in this God, therefore, will discover that this "faith" will be regarded, not as a meritorious spiritual act (how could that be, for the "ungodly"?), but as the badge of covenant membership given by God in sheer grace.[140]

On the one hand, Wright appears to understand justification to be a declaration that the (morally) ungodly are within the covenant; on the other hand, justification contemplates faith as a presumably existing badge of covenant membership. It may be, then, that Wright considers "ungodly" to mean an imperfectly covenantally faithful person. Nevertheless, such a definition would certainly be a departure from the way that Paul has most recently employed the term "ungodly" (Rom. 1:18).

Summary of Wright

We are now in a position to draw some summary observations of our study of Wright.

1. Wright has self-consciously adopted the project of critical realism (which he sees as bypassing both Enlightenment phenomenalism and fundamentalist objectivism). Consequently, he argues that "story" lies back of all theological formulation and expression.
2. For Wright, the New Testament writers have reconfigured a basic Israelite story around Jesus: Jesus is the proposed solution to the abiding problem of Israel's exile. For this reason, one should see the early Christian movement as another species of Judaism (although distinct from other expressions of Judaism).
3. Wright sees "righteousness of God" language as referring to God's own faithfulness to his covenant promises. As such, this language finds its background in three areas: covenant, law court, and eschatology.
4. Concerning righteousness, Wright argues consistently that, when applied to Jews of Paul's day, this refers to a truncated covenant status focused on zeal, flesh, and ethnocentric exclusivity.
5. Wright sees present justification as God's declaration that one is already in the people of God. It is a doctrine touching ecclesiology, not soteriology. Present justification is declared on the basis of future justification, which will be grounded on the believer's faithful obedience to the covenant.

6. Wright sees faith in present justification as that which evidences one to be a true member of the people of God. In this context, it is counter to works of the law, which, with Dunn, Wright sees preeminently as circumcision, Sabbath, and food laws. With respect to future justification, Wright will argue that "faith" and "faithfulness" are to be understood synonymously.

7. Concerning the death of Christ and justification, Wright knowingly and explicitly repudiates imputation as an un-Pauline concept. Wright is fairly silent on the connection between these two concepts, other than that there *is* a connection that the apostle forges between them.

8. Concerning the death of Christ more generally considered, Wright concedes that we may speak of Christ's death as atoning and propitiatory. Nevertheless, in terms of expressing the mechanism whereby Christ's death is applied to the believer, Wright is consistently vague. Although Wright uses language of the law court to speak of Christ's death (Christ's death was judicial punishment; in Christ, sin was condemned[141]), Wright also rejects imputation as a Pauline doctrine. Consequently, one cannot speak in traditional terms of the pardon of the believer's sin by reason of imputation. Where Christ's death *does* connect with the believer's experience, in Wright's view, is as it defeats the powers of sin and death.

9. For Wright, Paul made a decisive transition from Judaism to Christianity, but this did not involve either a burdened conscience or discontent with his former life in Judaism. Romans 7 describes the corporate experience of Israel under the law, *not* the experience of Paul or any other individual believer. For believers today, being a Christian entails: (1) assent to four propositions (the death, resurrection, messiahship, and lordship of Christ); (2) submission to baptism, which Wright perceives to be far more realistic in Paul than traditional Protestants have taken it; and (3) participation in the inclusive life of the community, which participation is conceived largely in terms of social activism and ecumenism.

A Critique of the New Perspective

p to this point, our task has been largely descriptive. What have the proponents of the NPP (and their forebears) said? How have they said it? We, of course, have recognized diversity and divergences among the primary NPP proponents.

Nevertheless, there is enough held in common among them to group them as a school. We turn now to an extended critique of the NPP. We'll move in three directions. First, we will show that at a basic level the NPP is flawed hermeneutically; that is, its basic working principles of interpreting the Bible are problematic. Our concerns here will largely center on the way in which Judaism is constructed, and the way in which Paul is related to those constructions. Second, we will show that the exegesis propounded by the Reformers and their heirs is faithful to Paul, and that the revisionist exegesis of E. P. Sanders, J. D. G. Dunn, and N. T. Wright fails to render satisfactory readings of Paul. Third, we will show that the theological assumptions and implications of the NPP writings are contrary to good, sound biblical teaching.

The Hermeneutical Problems

Flawed Constructions of Judaism

The constructions of Judaism presented by Sanders and Wright are flawed and, at best, imbalanced.

151

1. *E. P. Sanders.* We have already engaged Sanders above in a critique. We observed that, according to Sanders's own evidence, ancient rabbinic Judaism is a semi-Pelagian religion. In this religion, to be sure, the language of the grace of God is not absent. We argued, nevertheless, that it is ultimately synergistic. Works occupy a fundamental or essential place in this religion. We might quote again the paradoxical statement attributed to R. Akiba—"the world is judged by grace, and yet all is according to the amount of work"[1]—as but one example of the fact that grace and merit are held together in the rabbinic literature in apparently unresolved tension. One shining example of merit in ancient Judaism was the notion that one can effect atonement by such extrabiblical means as one's repentance, suffering, or death. We have also seen that, at poignant moments, a leading rabbinic teacher despaired of the hope that his religion offered him.

Undoubtedly, Sanders has responded to the earlier scholarship of Judaism that had been mediated to modern New Testament scholars through Rudolf Bultmann, Joachim Jeremias, and others. Earlier scholarship had promoted what might fairly be termed a purely *Pelagian* portrait of Judaism. This portrait, of course, was a caricature that overlooked important pieces of the evidence. But Sanders, we may observe, has *over*reacted to this portrait. His own portrait of Judaism is liable not only to the charge of being selective in its reading of the evidence but also to the charge of dismissing evidence that problematizes his thesis.

More recent studies of Judaism have raised questions about the adequacy of Sanders's model of ancient Judaism to explain all the ancient evidence.[2] In one especially, we find D. A. Carson drawing several conclusions regarding the state of the current academic discussion of ancient Judaism.[3] Some of these conclusions are worth summarizing here: (1) Many scholars do not regard Sanders's *covenantal nomism* to apply evenly or equally to all the relevant primary (Second Temple Period) literature. (2) Some scholars charge that the construct of covenantal nomism is a "reductionistic category," that is, it does not capture the diversity of "balance" (or imbalance) that individual Second Temple writings have with respect to getting in and staying in the covenant community.[4] Some works, for instance, will be largely concerned with "staying in" and relatively unconcerned with "getting in" the community of the saved. (3) Some scholars charge that the category of covenantal nomism is "misleading," that is, it falsely leads the reader to assume "more uniformity in the literature than there is." Covenantal nomism also fails to provide a true "alternative" to the model of Second Temple Judaism that it was intended to replace (i.e., "merit theology"). The term is "so flexible that it includes and baptizes a great deal of merit theology."[5] (4) Some scholars believe that Sanders has overstated the role of covenant in the Second Temple literature. (5) It is impossible to discern to what degree the Jewish *literature* of this period reflected *popular* (i.e., local) theological awareness and understanding.

2. *N. T. Wright.* Wright's portrait of Second Temple Judaism is at best idiosyncratic. Especially objectionable is his hinge proposition that all Jews conceived themselves as being under exile. This idea is crucial to Wright's understanding that, for Paul and the rest of the New Testament authors, Jesus' death and resurrection was conceived as the solution to Israel's ongoing exile.

We may register three specific objections to the view that all Jews and early Christians conceived of themselves as under exile and awaiting restoration:

(1) The biblical chapters that Wright claims underlie his model (Deut. 27–32), when investigated, yield a pluriformity of interpretations in the Second Temple literature. This literature's engagement of these chapters does not produce the neat model of "sin-exile-restoration" that Wright posits.[6]

(2) There is no explicit indication that Paul was laboring under this model. In view of our criticism above, one certainly can't establish that he inherited such a model by virtue of his being a Jew: there was no such model for Paul to inherit from Judaism. When Paul speaks of his own experience as a Jew, or of the experience of Israel "according to the flesh," he never references the category of exile. As Mark Seifrid has rightly observed, Paul "interprets the history of salvation through the lens of Christ, not the reverse." Christ is not so much a solution to a felt-problem within Israel; rather, Christ creates a problem for Israel—there are those who believe and those who do not (Rom. 9–11).[7]

(3) There are indications within the New Testament that the apostles did not believe Christ to be the solution to a purported exile. Christians are *still* said to be in exile at 1 Peter 1:1 ("Peter, an apostle of Jesus Christ, *to those who reside as aliens, scattered throughout Pontus, Galatia, Cappadocia, Asia, and Bithynia. . . .*") and at James 1:1 ("James, a bond-servant of God and of the Lord Jesus Christ, *to the twelve tribes who are dispersed abroad. . . .*").[8]

Mistaken Reliance on Scholarly Reconstruction

The NPP operates with the mistaken principle that the interpretation of Paul is to be controlled by a scholarly reconstruction of Judaism. The logic of many proponents of the NPP in relating Paul to ancient Judaism might be summarized in the following way: We know that Paul did not oppose Judaism as a religion of works, and we all know anyway that Judaism was *not* a religion of works, but a religion of grace; therefore, Paul's opposition to Judaism must have been on some other grounds. This constrains proponents of the NPP to the following exegetically objectionable solutions: (1) Paul objects to Judaism because it is not Christianity (Sanders). (2) Paul objects to Judaism because its boundary markers are not sufficiently inclusive (Dunn, Wright). (3) Paul deliberately misrepresented Judaism as a religion of works, and we know this because Paul counters our secondary reconstruction of Jewish soteriology (Heikki Räisänen).

We can highlight three problems with the underlying logic behind these various explanations. First, even were we to grant the truth of this approach, we would still have a number of insuperable problems concerning the texts of ancient Judaism in question. It is simply impossible to know with certainty to which Second Temple texts Paul had access. It is in many cases (although not all) impossible to discern the sphere of influence that a given text or texts had within Judaism. We can say, for instance, that the Qumran texts probably had little influence beyond the sphere of their host communities. But what about a text such as *Joseph and Aseneth*, to take but one example—did a community or an individual produce this text? For what purposes was it produced? For what purposes was it later employed? What authority was ascribed to it? What was its reception beyond the bounds of that particular community? Did subsequent generations of the host community accept this document? How? Was its interpretation stable across communities and generations? In summary, the Jewish texts of the Second Temple Period often come to us with virtually no context—they are in many respects mute documents.

This raises a second problem. The Second Temple texts themselves need to be interpreted. One often gets the impression in reading the scholarly literature that the Second Temple texts (relative to Paul) are unencumbered with interpretative difficulty, that they themselves are somehow free of the difficulties thought to attend Paul's letters. But of course, these Jewish texts themselves require interpretation. They are not pure, pristine, and free from the difficulties of interpretation. This, you may recall, is precisely the objection that the Reformers and their heirs have raised against Rome's doctrine of the necessity of tradition for interpreting Scripture aright: tradition itself must be interpreted!

A third problem that we may identify with this logic is that the notion that a secondary reconstruction of one set of texts should control our reading of another set of primary texts is flawed. As Christians, we may raise objections against such a proposal by appealing to the biblical principle of Scripture interpreting Scripture. As readers generally, we may object that any author is best interpreted according to his own statements and according to the sense of his own words. Let us hear Paul, then, and listen openly and objectively to the statements and arguments that he has left us. Let us not predetermine what Paul is or is not permitted to teach and so miss what the apostle is communicating to us.

A Priesthood of Scholars?

The NPP proposes that a priesthood of scholars be established within the church. The Reformers rightly objected to Rome's insistence that the person in the pew could not interpret Scripture to the salvation of his soul. Such a person, Rome teaches, required the assistance of the church if such an interpretation were to materialize. Proponents of the NPP tell us that Paul will be understood only if Second Temple Judaism is rightly understood. But only a community of scholars, with knowledge of the original languages and of the proper methods of interpretation of texts very different from modern literature, can competently access and read these Second Temple texts. Students of the Bible without the benefit of such specialized training, if they are to understand what Paul taught, are therefore placed at the mercy of an academic elite. Further, it is of the nature of academic discourse to be indefinite, to resist closure, and to prize innovation over tradition. Our understanding of Paul, then, not only will be held hostage to what the consensus of scholarship holds at any given moment, but also will necessarily be fluid.

Such a model for reading Paul falls short of Paul's expectations of his own readers. First, Paul acknowledges the right of his readers' private judgment ("Judge for yourselves . . ." [1 Cor. 11:13]). No human institution, furthermore, was to interpose between the conscience and its Lord ("*Not that we lord it over your faith*, but are workers with you for your joy" [2 Cor. 1:24]). Second, Paul sets forth his teaching as authoritative ("If anyone thinks he is a prophet or spiritual, let him recognize that the things which I write to you are the Lord's commandment" [1 Cor. 14:37]). Persistent disobedience to his apostolic instruction results in excommunication ("If anyone does not obey our instruction in this letter, take special note of that person and do not associate with him, so that he will be put to shame" [2 Thess. 3:14]). If Paul mandates excommunication for sustained disobedience to his teaching, then this tells us that he assumed his audience would be competent to understand his writings! Paul, then, did not operate with the same principles of interpretation that many scholars apply to Paul today.

Old Testament versus Second Temple Literature?

Functionally, most New Testament scholars do not distinguish between the Old Testament and the literature of the Second Temple Period. This necessarily results in distortion in the interpretation of the New Testament.

For many scholars, the canon is an arbitrary imposition on a fluid and seamless literature composed (largely if not exclusively) during the Second Temple Period (515 B.C.–A.D. 70). The functional absence of such distinctions within this literature as the Old Testament, the Apocrypha, and noncanonical literature surfaces especially in Wright's construction of Judaism. One has the impression that Second Temple writings informed and constructed in an undifferentiated way Paul's worldview, a worldview that, to be sure, he reconfigured according to Christ. Such a conception of this literature does not do justice to those distinctions that Paul himself employed to speak of this literature. Paul accorded authority (and that of Scripture) only to the books of the Old Testament (2 Tim. 3:16). There is no indication that he regarded noncanonical books as having any comparable or intrinsic authority. Paul will speak, furthermore, of the "ancestral traditions" that he received from his forefathers in "Judaism" as something in the past tense (Gal. 1:14). To fail to recognize this crucial Pauline distinction between Scripture and tradition is necessarily to set our interpretation of Paul askew. The Scripture alone must control our readings of Paul.

The New Testament, furthermore, is clear that while there was a faithful remnant of Jews (Elizabeth and Zacharias, Anna, Simeon, and Mary and Joseph, for example), the majority of Jews (whether leadership or populace) rejected the teaching both of Jesus and of the apostles. It is simply not true (unless our narratives deceive us) that there is a virtually seamless continuity between the Judaism(s) of Paul's day and the specimen of religion that he adopted and promoted subsequent to his encounter on the Damascus Road.[9] To maintain such continuity is to distort (at best) or to overhaul (at worst) the historical and theological evidence that the New Testament provides us about Christianity's relationship to Judaism. Were we to inquire what is controlling this new hermeneutic, we might point both to the postwar ecumenical spirit and to the guilt borne by students of the New Testament writing in what has been termed a post-Holocaust era of scholarship. For many critical scholars, the fault for Christian violence perpetrated against Jews over the last two millennia, culminating in the Holocaust of the twentieth century, has been placed squarely at the feet of the New Testament. While such a belief may not be responsibly attributed to each proponent and argument of the NPP, it does help to explain the enthusiastic reception with which such "continuitarian" proposals have been received within mainstream biblical scholarship.

al Problems

ly, the NPP stands or falls on its ability to interpret Paul's a satisfactory way. In engaging the NPP exegetically, we the following four categories of crucial passages: the works justification and faith; the death of Christ; and the universal guilt of humanity and the conscience of Paul.

The "Works of the Law": Jewish Soteriology and Human Inability

We may briefly recall the diversity of opinion observed concerning the works of the law. Sanders sees "works of the law" as Paul's way of referring to the Torah or Judaism. The phrase is Paul's affirmation "that one need not be Jewish to be 'righteous.' " The emphasis is not on works, according to Sanders, but on law, *viz.*, the Mosaic Law.[10] Dunn sees the works of the law as preeminently demarcating those status markers (circumcision, Sabbath, dietary laws) that were representative of the whole pattern of law-keeping. Wright sees works of the law as indications that "one can tell in the present who precisely will be vindicated when God finally acts in fulfillment of his righteousness, of his covenant obligations."[11] Commenting on Romans 3:28, he takes "works of the Law" to mean "the works of Torah that demarcate ethnic Israel."[12] For all the diversity, each proponent considered is agreed on the fact that works of the law *cannot* refer to Jews' efforts to achieve a state of righteousness by the activity of obedience to the law.

We may observe, as Mark Seifrid has observed, that Qumran's use of the phrase "works of the law" cannot be used exclusively as a status marker—it connotes ethical precepts:[13]

> I must confess considerable puzzlement that both Dunn and Wright, who recognise that some Jews could regard other Jews as outside the community of the elect on the basis of *halakhah*, regard distinctive practices as simply "exclusivistic," borders without interior meaning. Insiders saw them as emblems of community values, especially fidelity to *Torah* and covenant.[14]

On their own merits, Seifrid rightly comments, Dunn's and Wright's proposals regarding the works of the law are overly refined. Both scholars attempt to distinguish status from behavior in a way that, practically, few Jews could or did.

Paul's "works of the law," however we might allow this phrase to embrace in certain instances questions of status or identity, must primarily encompass human activity. We will argue this point now by considering several passages that were addressed in previous chapters.

Romans 11:5–6. Paul, in a discussion of the ground of election ("there has also come to be at the present time a remnant according to God's gracious choice" [Rom. 11:5]), here contrasts grace and works in such a way that they are mutually exclusive ("but if it is by grace, it is no longer on the basis of works, otherwise grace is no longer grace" [v. 6]). Both Dunn and Wright take "works" in this passage to mean "works of the law" in an ethnic sense.[15] This, however, cannot be Paul's primary sense. This phrase must mean "anything that human beings do."[16] (1) Notice that the contrast between grace and works (Rom. 11:5–6) is carried over into the following verse (Rom. 11:7). Here a parallel contrast is drawn between "those who were chosen" and "Israel"/"the rest." Consequently, we are to see the contrast of Romans 11:7 as illuminating the contrast of Romans 11:6. (2) In Romans 11:7 ("What Israel is seeking, it has not obtained"), Paul, when he faults Israel, exclusively identifies human effort and not status. In other words, the contrast is framed squarely in terms of effort, not in terms of identity. The nature of this contrast in Romans 11:7, then, should inform the contrast drawn in the previous verse. "Works," therefore, should be understood as human striving or effort. (3) Why, then, is Israel mentioned if Paul is not specifically referencing questions of covenantal identity or works as boundary markers? Paul does so because Israel is a specimen of a *human* problem—the tendency to ground one's (here) election in human works, evidences of which we observed in our earlier discussion of Sanders's evaluation of Judaism.[17]

Romans 3:20. Sanders has argued (generally) that when Paul speaks of the works of the law, the stress is to be placed on the *Law of Moses*, not *works*. Paul is simply saying that "one need not be Jewish to be righteous."[18] Dunn has argued that "works of the Law" in Romans 3:20 "must denote the 'works' referred to" in Romans 2, specifically "circumcision."[19] They are different from "*doing* the law" (as in Rom. 2:13–14) or "*fulfilling* the law" (as in 2:27); neither are they "the work of the law written in the heart" (2:15). Rather, they should be seen as "something more superficial, at the level of 'the letter' (2:27, 29), an outward mark indicative of ethnic solidarity (2:28). . . ."[20] There is, Dunn says, a "hidden middle term" in this phrase, namely, that "works of the law" is "*a way of identifying the individual with* the people whom God has chosen and will vindicate and of *maintaining his status within* that people."[21] Throughout Romans 2:1–3:8, he concludes, "works of the law" means "doing what is necessary to be (become, or remain) within the covenant," *not* "a *means to achieving* righteousness and acquittal."[22] Wright substantially agrees with Dunn's reading. For Wright, "works of the law" are "the works that marked out the Jews from their pagan neighbors."[23] Jews are faulted, then, for their claim "to possession of Torah as the badge of being God's special people."[24] Hence, Paul's faith/works dichotomy serves to communicate Paul's point "that all who attempted to legitimate their covenant status by appealing to possession of Torah would find that the Torah itself accused them of sin."[25]

Are Sanders, Dunn, and Wright correct? Does Paul have in mind a question of status exclusively? We find upon examination of this verse and its context that he does not primarily have status in mind. Recall that Paul has just concluded a discussion comprehending Jew *and* Gentile. While the argument of Romans 2 substantially treats Jews, the argument of Romans 1:18–32 has included Gentiles. Paul will turn his attention at Romans 3:1 briefly to consider Jews before he concludes in Romans 3:9 that "we have already charged that both Jews and Greeks are all under sin" (followed by the supporting catena of Romans 3:10–18). We turn to his conclusion at Romans 3:19–20, where he reminds us that the law condemns (he has already affirmed this both of Jews *and* of Gentiles in Romans 2:14–15), and then concludes his argument with this verse ("because by the works of the Law no flesh will be justified in His sight"). It is gratuitous, therefore, to restrict Paul's concern to simply Jews. The fact that he includes Jews *and* Greeks means that "works of the Law" at Romans 3:20a must then comprehend more than simply being Jewish.[26] We find, then, that Dunn's hidden middle is not hidden at all—it is absent. NPP readings of this verse fall short of Paul's meaning.

Romans 4:4–5. These verses ("Now to the one who works, his wage is not credited as a favor, but as what is due. But to the one who does not work, but believes in Him who justifies the ungodly, his faith is credited as righteousness"), we observed, were recognized by Dunn as one of the most plausible objections against NPP readings of Paul. Dunn, following Sanders, argues that "the language used here (working, reckoning, reward) should not be taken as a description of the Judaism of Paul's day. In particular, Paul is not castigating contemporary Judaism for a theology of (self-achieved) merit and reward." Paul's point, rather,

> is simply that in the case of Genesis 15:6 the whole language of "payment due" is inappropriate. . . . Here he simply poses the alternatives, work → reckon → debt / faith → reckon → favor, as a way of setting up the exposition which is about to follow and as a way of shaking his Jewish interlocutor out of a too ready equation of Abraham's believing with his covenant loyalty. Where (Abraham's) faith is in view, the righteousness is surely reckoned in terms of grace, not of payment due.[27]

We observed that this explanation surely evades the point of Paul's argument.

Wright concedes that the metaphor of bookkeeping is in fact present in Romans 4:4–5. But he does not seem to recognize the way in which Paul's use of the language of labor and wage problematizes his reading of this verse or his entire synthesis of Paul. We see, rather, that these verses present insurmountable difficulties to the NPP hypothesis: (1) Paul here contrasts grace and works (as he will at 11:5–6), and Paul explicitly defines "working" not as status but as activity ("now to the one who works, his wage is not credited as a favor, but as what is due" [Rom. 4:4]).[28] (2) It is precisely against "working" so defined that Paul will counter faith ("but to the one who does not work, but believes in Him who justifies the ungodly, his faith is credited as righteousness" [Rom. 4:5]). (3) As Stephen Westerholm points out, the fact that Paul points to Abraham as an example of this principle is fatal to the NPP proposal: Abraham, of course, *did not have the Mosaic Law*. It is impossible, then, that Paul could have in mind, in the case of Abraham, questions of status pertaining to a legal administration given centuries after Abraham's death.[29]

Romans 9:30–32a. Concerning these verses ("What shall we say then? That Gentiles, who did not pursue righteousness, attained righteousness, even the righteousness which is by faith; but Israel, pursuing a law of righteousness, did not arrive at that law. Why? Because they did not pursue it by faith, but as though it were by works."), Sanders concludes that "Paul did not say precisely what he meant": Romans 9:31 *should* have read ". . . did not arrive at that *righteousness by faith.*"[30] Sanders resorts to emendation, then, in order to explain this verse which poses a great difficulty to his system. Dunn paraphrases the end of verse 31 ("did not arrive at that law") as "they did not attain to responsible covenant membership" because of a too-narrow understanding of the law.[31] Wright also takes "works" here to mean Israel's attempt to establish an identity as the people of God from the Torah.

None of these proposals adequately explains Paul's words. (1) If Paul is speaking strictly in terms of identity, why does he speak of the law (in *this* context) as a law of *righteousness*? In other words, why does he speak of the law in ethical or moral terms, if the issue at hand is not fundamentally ethical or moral in nature? Whether we take this phrase to mean "a law that promises righteousness, demands righteousness, results in righteousness, or a law that is falsely understood as a means of righteousness" or "for righteousness" (i.e., "for a right relationship with God"),[32] the point is the same: there is *some* connection with the law and righteousness in an ethical sense.

(2) Paul, as commentators observe, uses the metaphor of a race in these verses.[33] This is evidenced from his language of "pursue" and

"arrive." It is impossible, then, to escape the conclusion that Israel's failure to arrive at that law was a failure to reach a particular goal, *viz.*, the ethical standard of the law, or the righteousness that the law holds out to those who keep it.

(3) Dunn's argument (they failed to attain responsible covenant membership) fails to explain the way in which Paul uses his terms in these verses. Commenting on Romans 9:30, Dunn argues that "Paul shows that he understands 'righteousness' as a covenant word . . . [;] it is always something which depends ultimately on God, the power of God sustaining man in his creaturely dependence on the creator and enabling him to live through that relation." Paul faults Israel because she has somehow truncated the law's righteousness by shrinking its boundaries. But Paul does not say in these verses that Israel was following in effect a truncated standard, that is, a standard different from that which the Gentiles "attained" (v. 31). We have no warrant for understanding, as Dunn appears to do, "righteousness" in multiple senses in Romans 9:30–31. Paul pins the difference between Jews and Gentiles, rather, on the *manner* in which the goal was sought: by faith/by works (Rom. 9:32a). If the faith/works distinction means what Dunn would have it mean, then we expect equivocation in Paul's uses of "righteousness" in Romans 9:30–31. But we have no reason to posit anything other than consistency of meaning in these verses.

(4) This conclusion is borne out by a description of Israel immediately below as having "a zeal for God, but not in accordance with knowledge" (10:2). It would be special pleading to restrict this zeal to simply status. There is no way that one can reasonably exclude human activity (even if that activity is bound up in status) from the "zeal" of Romans 10:2.

Even further below, Israel is said to seek "to establish their own [righteousness]" (Rom. 10:3). Once again, if Paul had wanted to say that Israel's unique national identity were the object of this pursuit, he had words available to him better suited to this intention than the language of pursuit and effort. Rather, Paul is saying that Israel, in seeking to "establish their own righteousness" via Torah observance, "did not subject themselves to the righteousness of God," *viz.*, "they were ignorant of the fact that righteousness was a gift of God's grace and they mistakenly thought they could secure their own righteousness by observing the Torah."[34]

(5) In conclusion, then, we see three important things in these verses: (a) Paul discusses the law as holding out an ethical standard, which is righteousness. (b) Paul holds that the way this standard is attained is not by pursuit but by faith (e.g., 9:30). (c) Paul argues not only that Israel failed to attain this standard, but also that she pursued this standard, and that her failure was rooted in the manner of pursuit, *viz.*, works, an activity of striving and of effort.

Romans 10:5. When we come to this verse ("For Moses writes that the man who practices the righteousness which is based on law shall live by that righteousness."), we find it to have been shaped by a contrast (faith and works/faith and law/their own righteousness and God's righteousness) that extends back to Romans 9:30. Sanders recognizes that we have a contrast between 10:5 and 10:6–8. He argues that Paul pits Scripture against Scripture. Sanders paraphrases the argument of Romans 10:6ff.: "Moses was incorrect when he wrote that everyone who fulfills the law will 'live.' There is another righteousness, based on faith, available to all without distinction, and it is this righteousness which saves."[35]

While Dunn also sees a contrast between 10:5 and 10:6–8, he does not believe that Paul is setting Scripture against itself. He argues that we have "no thought of 'achieving righteousness' here" (in view of the verb of "doing" in the Leviticus 18:5 citation), nor do we have posited the law's "unfulfillability" from Leviticus 18:5;[36] rather, we have Paul speaking of "righteousness understood as marking out a relationship with God peculiar to the people of the law and documented and validated by their faithfulness to those ancestral customs in particular which gave them their distinctiveness among the nations."[37] By way of contrast, Paul in Romans 10:6 sets forth the true way of righteousness by faith. This way of righteousness by faith is preeminently true of *this* new epoch, but not, of course, absent from the old epoch.[38]

Wright argues that we do not have a contrast drawn between the righteousnesses of Romans 10:5 and Romans 10:6–8. This is so because the context of the chapters surrounding the verses quoted by

Paul from Deuteronomy at Romans 10:6–8 concentrates on the return or restoration of Israel from exile. Consequently, Romans 10:6–8 explicates Romans 10:5. Paul here "offers . . . a fresh explanation, granted exile and return, for what 'do the law and live' might actually mean."[39] This redefinition consists "not in terms of an impossible demand, but in terms of God's gift of God's own word; and this 'word is the word of faith, faith that Jesus is Lord and that God raised him from the dead.' "[40] We have, then, among Sanders, Dunn, and Wright three different readings—two of which posit a contrast (Sanders, Dunn), another continuity (Wright) between 10:5 and 10:6–8. All, however, are in agreement that the righteousness of 10:5 is *not* what traditional Protestants have taken it to mean.

In response, we may observe the following: First, in response to Wright, while the Greek particle at the outset of Romans 10:6 (*de*) *could* be translated "and" rather than "but," the context requires a contrast.[41] (1) We have seen how, from Rom 9:30ff., Paul is maintaining a contrast between two concepts: faith and a cluster of related concepts (works, law, their own righteousness).[42] It is special pleading to argue that Paul has suspended this running contrast in verses that are universally recognized to be of a piece with the argument of Romans 9:30ff. (2) Scholars have observed the similarity between Romans 10:5 and Philippians 3:9 ("not having a righteousness of my own derived from the law"), in the latter of which Paul is clearly *contrasting* that righteousness with the righteousness that is through faith in Christ.[43] (3) Paul also quotes Leviticus 18:5 (Rom. 10:5) at Galatians 3:12, in a context where Paul is speaking negatively of righteousness of the law.[44] Is it likely that Paul would switch gears and radically change his interpretation of this crucial Old Testament verse from Galatians to Romans?

Second, if a contrast is in view, what would prevent us from adopting Dunn's view? Dunn balks at the fact that the quotation from Leviticus 18:5 employs a verb of "doing" ("the man who practices the righteousness"). Had Paul simply wished to affirm *either* that the problem was a problem of identity or status, *or* that the problem concerned a question of truncated law obedience, he had ample opportunity and vocabulary to do so. The fact that Paul employs a verb of activity, as he has above in Romans 9:30–32 and Romans 10:3, militates against either of these alternative explanations.

Third, what is Paul really saying? Is he pitting Scripture against Scripture, as some critics have said? Does he believe that Moses promoted the very position of his legalistic opponents? We may answer both questions in the negative. Paul has in mind opponents who are arguing that one's righteousness in justification derives from one's obedience to the law. Paul's interest in Leviticus 18:5 at Romans 10:5 is simply to establish the connection between obedience and blessing (alternatively, disobedience and curse).[45] In this sense, we may paraphrase Paul's words as follows: "You who look to the Law for justification, listen to what the Law says: the only way you will find blessing is through obedience. If your obedience does not meet the standard of the Law, you will not find blessing." That Paul viewed his opponents' position (a position expressed, again, in the context of *justification*) to be impossible is seen in Romans 10:6–8, where we may again paraphrase: "All you need do for justification is hear and believe; you need not scale the heavens or plumb the depths."[46]

Philippians 3:2–11. Sanders argues that Paul does not find intrinsic fault with his "righteousness which is in the Law." This righteousness is faulty in comparison with the righteousness that he now has in Christ. Both Dunn and Wright, in explaining Paul's self-reflections on his life in Judaism, argue that Paul never believed that his blameless life in Judaism entailed sinless perfection. Rather, Dunn will say, Paul was distancing himself from the life of separatism that he had grown accustomed to embracing in Judaism. Dunn and Wright, however, do seem to overlook the importance of one element of Paul's understanding of righteousness in these verses. When Paul rejects his life under Judaism, he has rejected not just status, but activity ("as to zeal, a persecutor of the church"). Dunn will point to zeal as a common expression in the Second Temple Period of the kind of separatist mentality against which Paul contends in Galatians and Romans. But is it more likely that he reflected on that zeal strictly as something that would have promoted a separate identity from aberrant Jews, or that he would have conceived his activity of persecution in conjunction with any concerns of identity that he may have had? The latter is surely the likelier option. Consequently, when Paul follows that statement with "as to the righteousness which is in the Law, found blameless," it is likely that Paul, by pointing to his "righteousness which is of the law," intends to embrace not simply questions of identity, but also those of activity.

What about Sanders's comments that Paul has no inherent objection against this righteousness? If Paul is contrasting the two righteousnesses according to the criterion of effort or activity, then he must object on intrinsic grounds to "the righteousness which is in the Law." Paul's objection cannot be grounded exclusively in the relative inferiority of the "righteousness which is in the Law" to the "righteousness which is in Christ."

The Disputed Epistles. We have observed above that Dunn concedes that such passages as Titus 3:5 ("not on the basis of deeds which we have done in righteousness"), Ephesians 2:9 ("not as a result of works, so that no one may boast"), and 2 Timothy 1:9 ("who has saved us and called us with a holy calling, not according to our works, but according to His own purpose and grace which was granted us in Christ Jesus from all eternity") justify the traditional view. Sanders has conceded to me that Ephesians 2:9 teaches the traditional view. But to most NPP proponents, of course, these passages are post-Pauline. These verses, then, don't affect their argument.

This state of affairs raises two questions: (1) Students of Scripture who ascribe all thirteen epistles to Paul are faced *either* with two irreconcilable Pauline teachings of works (the one in the undisputed and the other in the disputed letters), *or* with a recognition that the view represented in Titus, Ephesians, and 2 Timothy should govern our view of the passages discussed in Galatians, Romans, and Philippians. (2) But there is also a problem for NPP proponents. How is it that these supposedly post-Pauline documents so quickly came to misunderstand what NPP proponents argue is a fundamental and organizing doctrine not only for Romans, but for Pauline thought as a whole? While some explanation of this misunderstanding is required, it has not been forthcoming.

Galatians 5:3–4; 3:10–13. Paul further believed that his opponents were teaching *not* a doctrine of status, but a doctrine of human activity. In speaking of "be[ing] justified by law" in Galatians 5:4, Paul argues that if one wishes to do this, he is "under obligation to keep the whole Law" (5:3). Dunn, of course, argues that Paul is attacking the truncated view of the law that attends his opponents' understanding of the law as a boundary-marking device. In response to Dunn, we may observe that it seems most natural to understand "to keep the whole Law" to mean to keep all its individual commandments rather than to keep the whole law *extensively* (i.e., not to omit any area from any particular individual's observance of it). This understanding is justified when we recall Paul's consistent contrast between those who do the law and those who believe, in which the former is never affirmed of Christians in a context of justification (provided we do not take the subjects of Romans 2:13–14 to be Christians). It is, rather, affirmed only of those under the law.[47] Paul, then, is not articulating a principle that every believer should follow (keep the whole law extensively). Rather, he is articulating a principle that his opponents, for consistency's sake, must observe, but cannot observe. In light of this, we find that Galatians 5:3 belongs to a cluster of verses in which not only is activity conceived, but also activity is conceived in a negative light—especially when we see that the question in dispute in the discussion is the means of justification.

In this light, Galatians 3:10–13 merits several observations. First, if we do not adopt the implied-premise view (i.e., that the unstated premise behind 3:10 is universal human inability to keep the law), then we make nonsense of the passage. If the implied-premise view is correct, then activity must be in view in Paul's reference to the works of the law.

Second, Sanders's view of this passage is that Paul's *stichwort* method of citing Scripture does not place the emphasis on "all" but on the words "curse" and "Law." But would this be a likely mode of citing and reading Scripture, given that just a few verses below, Paul is going to hang the whole of his interpretation on one word from Genesis ("Now the promises were spoken to Abraham and to his seed. He does not say, 'And to seeds,' as referring to many, but rather to one,

'And to your seed,' that is, Christ" [Gal. 3:16])? Third, Sanders will also tell us that no Jew contemporary to Paul (with the exception of the author of IV Ezra) understood the law to require perfect obedience, and that elsewhere, speaking of himself as a Jew and calling upon Christians to be blameless, Paul regarded the law to be keep-able.

We may reply that if one Jewish text (IV Ezra) understood the law to require perfect obedience, then it is certainly not implausible that Paul would have understood it in the same way. More to the point, however, is whether Paul must be bound by extant Jewish interpretations of Scripture, or whether Paul may speak for himself. Paul's language of "blamelessness" cited by Sanders is consistently used to speak of believers at the time that Christ appears (1 Cor. 1:8; 1 Thess. 3:13; 5:23). If we understand these verses to speak of sinless perfection, Paul's meaning is not that believers achieve a state of impeccable blamelessness antecedent to Christ's appearing; rather, it is that, at that day, believers will be made blameless (cf. Phil. 3:21). But we might understand these verses to speak of a kind of blamelessness that is frequently averred of Old Testament and New Testament saints (as Job, Zacharias, and Elizabeth), which, we will argue below, is entirely consistent with the view in Galatians 3:10 that the law requires perfect obedience and that no man can render that obedience.

Fourth, Dunn says that the issue at stake in Galatians 3:10–13 is not a question of human ability to keep the law. Paul's opponents, rather, had a deficient understanding of the law by "insist[ing] on Israel's privilege contrary to the gospel." Dunn concedes that this argument hinges on his interpretation of "works of the Law" as status.[48] Given the abiding presence of the language of activity in these verses ("abide," "perform" [3:10]; "practices them" [3:12]), it seems probable that Paul does not primarily have concerns of status in mind.

In summary, the verses that we have considered universally focus the problem with the works of the law upon human inability. That status is exclusively in Paul's mind by virtue of such language is therefore impossible. We may mention parenthetically that this understanding of the works of the law is not entirely without precedent in the history of interpretation. Turretin addresses those who would delimit works of the law to the specifically ceremonial (i.e., Jewish) prescriptions of

the Torah,[49] a view that was addressed and dismissed by Thomas
Aquinas. The innovation of Dunn and Wright with respect to this older
and overlapping view, is in driving a wedge between status and activity in regard to these works of the law and in refusing to restrict works
of the law to the ceremonial laws of the Mosaic administration. While
there have been sporadic attempts in the history of interpretation to
delimit Pauline works of the law, whether in the thirteenth or the
twenty-first century, interpreters throughout the church's history have
generally maintained the traditional view articulated and defended
above.

Justification and Faith

We have observed differences among NPP proponents concerning justification in Paul. Sanders sees "justification" as a transfer term,
but as peripheral to the center of Paul's thought, which is "being in
Christ." He argues that the instances of "justification" are fewer than
the instances of participatory language, *and* that Paul will use forensic terminology to communicate participationist concepts. Justification, consequently, is fundamentally transformative in nature. For Paul,
Sanders concludes, "righteousness by faith and participation in Christ
ultimately amount to the same thing."[50]

Dunn differs from Sanders. He does not see "justification" as a
transfer term, but as a word whereby Paul reminds his audience of the
covenant faithfulness of God. The *act* of justification is God's act in
counting the covenant partner as faithful despite the latter's previous
lapses. We might think, at first glance, that Dunn agrees with the Reformation in defining the term in a declaratory way. Dunn, however,
argues that justification is a series of acts, not simply at the beginning
stages of the believer's life, but throughout his existence even until the
Day of Judgment. Further, Dunn tells us, God justifies the covenant
partner as he looks and counts the covenant partner faithful—a declaration that, as he understands Romans 2:13 to teach, encompasses
(but is not exhausted by) the believer's covenantal obedience. Dunn
understands Romans 4:25 to teach that "the justifying grace of God
is all of a piece with his creative, life-giving power."[51]

Wright agrees in principle with Dunn. "Justification" is not transfer terminology (it is the declaration that one is already in the people of God), and it is forensic in nature. Wright, however, distinguishes present from future justification. Although both present and future justification are distinguished by time, they share faith as a central component in each act. Faith, however, has different roles in present and in future justification. Faith in present justification functions as a boundary-marking device. Faith in future justification is synonymous with the covenantal faithfulness that is the ground of that declaration.

All three of these scholars agree concerning the following statements. First, justification, although a polemical doctrine, was not Paul's soteriological rejection of Judaism as such. For Sanders, it was a polemical attempt to reflect Paul's underlying conviction that Judaism (by which Paul means "works of the law") was "not Christianity." For Dunn and Wright, the doctrine is more substantive and less *ad hominem*. It reflected a disagreement concerning the appropriate boundary markers for the people of God, and enabled Paul to restate the true principles of his ancestral faith (Dunn), or to tell the story of Christ as the solution to Israel's problem of exile (Wright). Second, justification does not involve the believer's appropriation of the imputed righteousness of Christ by faith alone. Wright and Dunn, notwithstanding their recognition of the declarative dimensions of justification terminology, see the ground of the believer's acceptance with God as the believer's covenantal faithfulness. This ground, then, consists of presumably infused but certainly not imputed grace. This is true of future justification in Wright, who claims that "justification, at the last, will be on the basis of performance, not possession,"[52] and that "future justification, acquittal at the last great Assize, always takes place on the basis of the totality of the life lived (e.g. Romans 14.11f.; 2 Corinthians 5.10)."[53] Sanders would also agree with Rome that the believer is never justified but by infused grace. Justification and participation, he argues, are functionally the same. Third, faith in justification, then, is not an instrument by which the righteousness of God in Christ is received. Faith is not entirely receptive in justification. Faith in justification, rather, may be properly translated "faithfulness" in many places in Paul's letters.

In response to these formulations of justification in Paul, we may make several observations. First, Paul never once says that we are justified *because of* faith—faith is always *instrumental* in nature. In theological parlance, faith is the sole *instrumental* cause of justification. This is an entirely Pauline formulation. We are said to be justified *dia pisteōs* (through faith), *ek pisteōs* (by faith), or *pistei* (by faith).[54] The apostle never says that believers are "justified *dia pistin* (on account of faith)."[55] This consideration is also vindicated by our discussion above that faith is everywhere in Paul contrasted with the striving or activity of the sinner. Pauline faith, in the act of justification, is consistently receptive in nature.

A second observation concerns what faith receives. Paul everywhere affirms that Christ's own righteousness is the sole *meritorious* cause of justification. This is seen from consistent Pauline affirmations that it is *Christ* who is our righteousness.

(1) In 2 Corinthians 5:21 ("He made Him who knew no sin to be sin on our behalf, so that we might become the righteousness of God in Him"), we read that Christ's righteousness is imputed to the believer. This righteousness cannot be said to be infused into the believer. Were this the case, the parallel structure of this verse would affirm that believers' sin is infused into Christ, something that Paul expressly denies ("Him who knew no sin").

(2) In 1 Corinthians 1:30, Christ is explicitly said to be "to us . . . righteousness." Immediately before this affirmation, Paul claims that "[Christ] became to us wisdom from God." We certainly are warranted in applying the phrase "from God" to apply to "our righteousness." In other words, Paul affirms Christ to be "our righteousness from God." In similar fashion, Paul elsewhere will affirm believers' righteousness to be from God, not our own (Phil. 3:9; Rom. 10:3).[56] The true contrast drawn by the apostle is not between one righteousness that is parochial and one that is inclusive, but between one righteousness that is of human origin and one that is of divine origin.

(3) In Romans 4:6 ("just as David also speaks of the blessing on the man to whom God credits righteousness apart from works"), Paul states the principle of imputation. God counts the sinner righteous quite apart from any activity of the sinner. In justification, then, the works of the sinner (of any kind) are simply not contemplated, whether

or not they are performed under the assistance of God's grace. What is received, furthermore, is not only pardon of sin, but the very "righteousness" of Christ.

(4) In Romans 5:18–19, Paul says that "through one act of righteousness there resulted justification of life to all men," and that "through the obedience of the One the many will be made righteous." This description of the relationship of Christ's work and those whom he represents is parallel to the relationship of Adam's one sin and his posterity ("so then as through one transgression there resulted condemnation to all men" [5:18]; "for as through the one man's disobedience the many were made sinners" [5:19]). Paul explicitly establishes this connection at Romans 5:16 ("for on the one hand the judgment arose from one transgression resulting in condemnation, but on the other hand the free gift arose from many transgressions resulting in justification"). We will return below to Paul's teaching in these verses regarding the doctrine of imputation. For the present, we may note that Paul explicitly ties the ground of the believer's justification solely to the righteousness of Christ. It is in this sense parallel to the "one" act of Adam that has grounded humanity's condemnation, and is said to be a "free gift" in contrast with our "many transgressions" (5:16). These verses in no way permit the believer's response (his "faithfulness") to be embraced in the act of justification. The ground of justification is, rather, entirely extrinsic to the believer.[57]

(5) Paul in several places affirms that believers are justified "through the redemption" of Christ (Rom. 3:24) "by His blood" (Rom. 5:9), and reconciled "through the death of His Son" (Rom. 5:10). Our justification, Paul consistently affirms, is grounded on the death of Christ and not on any act of the believer.

How do we know that redemption, blood, and death in Romans 3:24; 5:9; and 5:10 are not simply instrumental and so correlative to faith?[58] First, Paul elsewhere defines and delineates faith as *uniquely* instrumental in justification.[59] Second, Paul properly defines Christ's work as the sole ground of our acceptance before God (e.g., 2 Cor. 5:21; 1 Cor. 1:30; Rom. 5:18–19 above).[60] Third, Paul, having spoken this way in Romans 5:9 ("justified by His blood") and in 5:10 ("reconciled to God through the death of his Son"), speaks of "death through sin" at Romans 5:12, which he explicates as "so death spread to all men, because all sinned." Since Paul's affirmations in Romans 5:9–10 are grammatically parallel to those in Romans 5:12, then we ought to see Christ's blood and death as the ground of our justification and reconciliation.

We may now draw a third observation concerning justification. In view of what the NPP says about justification (that it is *either* essentially transformative [Sanders] *or* a series of declarations that contemplate in some measure the believer's covenantal faithfulness [Dunn, Wright]), it would seem that Paul's affirmation in Romans 5:1 ("Therefore, having been justified by faith, we have peace with God through our Lord Jesus Christ") is necessarily truncated. To the degree that justification both is a process and is grounded in some measure in the believer's obedience, whether explicitly (Sanders) or functionally (Dunn and Wright), peace simply cannot be the abiding possession of the believer. It will waver according to the degree and measure of transforming grace possessed by the believer at any given time.

Fourth, NPP teaching undercuts Paul's repeated affirmation that the doctrine of justification is one of "grace" (Rom. 4:4–5; 11:6) and that it precludes "boasting" (Eph. 2:9). If, as we have seen, Paul counterposes works and grace (Rom. 11:6; 4:4–6), and pairs works and boasting (Eph. 2:9), then the schemes of the NPP (which make faith in justification effectively faithfulness) are defective. In other words, the apostle and the NPP define grace in entirely different ways. For justification to be of grace to Paul, it must not embrace human activity (even the activity of the renewed) in any way. For the NPP, justification may still be gracious although it takes into consideration the labors of a believer assisted by grace. We might anachronistically speak of Paul as an Augustinian and his NPP interpreters as semi-Pelagians. However we define this difference, there is a theological divide between Paul and the proponents of the NPP.

Fifth, the NPP doctrines also counter Paul's statements that God "justifies the *ungodly*" (Rom. 4:5). Dunn, we observed, understands "ungodly" to mean one who is outside the covenant, *not* one who is a sinner before God. Wright seems to take the statement to be a reference to a sincere believer who experiences "moments of apparent disobedience."[61] NPP proponents, then, often appear to regard the justified subject as one who is *already* covenantally faithful.

When we turn to Romans 4:4–5, however, we find Paul arguing precisely the opposite. Paul's point is that the subject of justification is accepted or justified without *any* reference to his personal uprightness. We do *not* in these verses have a doctrine of justification that permits grace to be infused into the believer in the act. Nor do we have Paul grounding the declaration in any sense on the person's moral uprightness, whether we consider particular acts or his willingness to bear sincerely (albeit imperfectly) the yoke of the covenant. The justified subject is ungodly. We have no warrant to take this term in any other than a moral sense, as Paul has used it in Romans 1:18 ("For the wrath of God is revealed from heaven against all ungodliness and unrighteousness of men who suppress the truth in unrighteousness"). This is precisely why Paul will follow this affirmation in Romans 4:4–5 with the quotation from Psalm 32 in Romans 4:7–8. Justification occurs when "God credits righteousness [to a man] apart from works" (Rom. 4:6), Paul says by way of introduction to this quotation. The act of justification, then, can have no reference to the sinner's character, and can have reference only to what Christ has done.

Sixth, NPP proponents do not adequately explain why Paul affirms that believers "hav[e] now been justified by His [Jesus'] *blood*" (Rom. 5:9).

Justification, both Dunn and Wright argue, is an *ecclesiological* doctrine, that is, God's declaration that one is *already in* the people of God. It is not soteriological. While both Dunn and Wright argue that Christ's death procures the liberation of God's people from sin (especially considered as power), they generally seem unwilling to define "justification" in such terms. But Paul in Romans 5:9 views the act or declaration of justification to be grounded squarely and solely on Jesus' sacrificial and redemptive death.

A seventh and final observation regarding the NPP on justification is that NPP proponents also misinterpret Romans 2:1–29. Sanders, Dunn, and Wright all take Paul's statements in Romans 2:13–16 as proof that Paul teaches that justification is grounded on one's obedi-

ence to the law. Sanders argues that this is evidence of Paul's inconsistency: he (at 2:15–16) "entertains the possibility that some will be
saved by works."[62] Dunn and Wright both argue that in these verses
the believer is in view. In the justification that will transpire at the Day
of Judgment, the believer's works are clearly contemplated. In connection with Romans 2:10–16, they will appeal to Romans 2:25–29
as evidence that Paul has in mind Gentile Christians in Romans 2.

All three scholars reject two traditional explanations of Romans
2:13. The first is that Paul is establishing a standard (hypothetically
speaking) according to which God will judge, but that no man seeking justification by works can uphold. Charles Hodge summarizes this
position well: "He is not speaking of the method of justification available for sinners, as revealed in the gospel, but of the principles of justice which will be applied to all who look to the law for justification.
If men rely on works, they must have works; they must be doers of the
law; they must satisfy its demands, if they are to be justified by it."[63]
A second, although less likely, explanation of this verse is that Paul is
using the term "justify" in the sense that James uses the term in James
2:24. In other words, works have a *declarative* role concerning one's
justification. They will evidence that one is justified but not constitute
the ground of that declaration.

Sanders's view probably approaches most closely our critique: *If
Paul is teaching that works of the law justify, then we have a material
contradiction with his teaching on the doctrine elsewhere in this letter (Rom. 3, 5 et passim).* How should we respond to views that argue
that Gentile Christians are in view in Romans 2? There is no indication that Paul in Romans 2:1–16 has Christians in mind. Paul's burden seems to be to establish "the impartiality of God's judgment": *all*
(Jew and Gentile) must be assessed judicially according to the same
"standard of judgment."[64] The standard that Paul establishes in this
chapter ("[God] will render to each person according to his deeds"
[2:6]) is, then, that of obedience to all the demands of God's law. In
view of his arguments in this portion of the letter concerning human
inability, it seems unlikely that even works performed under the assistance of infused grace are in Paul's mind here.[65] Paul will later state
in his letter that "by works of the Law no flesh will be justified in His

sight" (Rom. 3:20). Given that this phrase concludes not only an important chapter (3:1–20) but also an entire section (1:18–3:20), the apostle's conclusion is more far-reaching than the Christian hypothesis would concede.[66] Paul is categorically excluding works as having any legitimate role in justification.

It is equally unlikely that Paul has Gentile Christians in mind at 2:25–29. Were this the case, then Paul's argument here has relaxed the standard of "perfect conformity" to God's law, a standard established earlier in the epistle.[67] Why, then, does Paul employ the flesh/spirit contrast in these verses if not to draw a contrast between believers under the Old Covenant and those under the New Covenant? Paul does so not to say that Gentile Christians will keep the law and so be justified by *this* obedience.[68] It is rather Paul's way of affirming that the strict standard established earlier (Rom. 2:6, 13) contemplates not only outward actions (Rom. 2:28), but also the very attitudes of the heart (Rom. 2:29).

The Death of Christ (2 Cor. 5:21; Rom. 3:24–26)

We have observed varying NPP attempts to account for the death of Christ. Sanders sees Paul's fundamental conception of Christ's death as being that act which effects the believer's participation with Christ. The connection of Christ's death with one's pardon has come to Paul largely by virtue of inheritance from earlier Christian teaching. In other words, there is no necessary connection in Paul's thought between pardon and the death of Christ. Sanders's primary interest in Christ's death is that it has effected a break (for those who participate in Christ) with the power of sin, and has enabled a change in lordship.

Dunn sees the death of Christ as communicated through a variety of nonharmonious metaphors, none of which is grounded in anything real. But he does seem to see as fundamental in Paul a view of Christ's death as that which effects a break (at least for the believer, perhaps for others) with sin as power. Wright is willing to speak of Christ's death as atoning and propitiatory, but he denies that Paul teaches a doctrine of the imputation of Christ's righteousness. In connecting the death of Christ and the experience of the believer, Wright is vague. Where Wright tends to be clearest is in his assertions that

Christ dealt with sin as power (not as guilt). What all three views have in common is that Paul conceived Christ's death primarily (if not exclusively) as a defeat of the powers of sin, and as something that was necessary to effect a change of lordships, *viz.*, the believer's transition from the realm of sin to the realm of obedience.

These views do not do justice to Paul's doctrine of the imputation of Christ's righteousness to the believer in justification, or to the grounding of the believer's justification in the sacrificial death of Christ. One passage where this may be seen is 2 Corinthians 5:21 ("He made Him who knew no sin to be sin on our behalf, so that we might become the righteousness of God in Him."). Sanders approves D. E. H. Whiteley's judgment that this verse is "primarily participationist" in outlook.[69] Wright sees these verses as referring exclusively to the labors of Christian ministers.[70] Dunn recognizes the double exchange expressed in this verse,[71] but gives no adequate explanation of how we are "the righteousness of God in Him." Dunn dwells, rather, on the sacrificial component of Christ's death.

What is Paul teaching in this verse? First, we must take the two halves to be parallel. What may we affirm of the first half? We know that Paul stresses here that Christ's being made sin is consistent with his "knowing no sin." Further, this act is said to be done "on our behalf." We have, then, the raw materials of an act of imputation. Our sins are counted to the account of one who is personally righteous, so that he is justly reckoned to be sin. Second, the first half ought, then, to structure our understanding of the second half, which is parallel to the three affirmations of the first half.[72] Believers, though remaining sinful (assumed in 5:21a, but proved by Paul's statement "in him" in 5:21b), yet become the "righteousness of God." Believers are said to become "the righteousness of God in Him." Believers are therefore reckoned righteous *not* by the infusion of grace, but by the imputation of Christ's righteousness, so that they are justly said to be "the righteousness of God in Him." Hodge's "summary" of Paul's teaching here cannot be improved:

> There is probably no passage in the Scriptures in which the doctrine of justification is more concisely or clearly stated than in [2 Corinthi-

ans 5:21]. Our sins were imputed to Christ, and his righteousness is imputed to us. He bore our sins; we are clothed in his righteousness. . . . Christ bearing our sins did not make him morally a sinner . . . nor does Christ's righteousness become subjectively ours, it is not the moral quality of our souls. . . . Our sins were the judicial ground of the sufferings of Christ, so that they were a satisfaction of justice; and his righteousness is the judicial ground of our acceptance with God, so that our pardon is an act of justice. . . . It is not mere pardon, but justification alone, that gives us peace with God.[73]

A second passage illustrating the deficient character of NPP conceptions of Christ's death in Paul is Romans 3:24–26 ("being justified as a gift by His grace through the redemption which is in Christ Jesus; whom God displayed publicly as a propitiation in His blood through faith. This was to demonstrate His righteousness, because in the forbearance of God He passed over the sins previously committed; for the demonstration, I say, of His righteousness at the present time, so that He would be just and the justifier of the one who has faith in Jesus."). In these verses, Paul will specify that righteousness which is the believer's; how Christ has procured it; and how it is that the believer is said to be justified.

First, we may say, by way of preface, that many New Testament scholars dismiss these verses as pre-Pauline and as therefore not a genuine expression of his thought. We might stress that it is by no means clear that these verses are pre-Pauline. Even were we to grant that they *are* pre-Pauline, we may observe that it is a dubious principle of interpretation to say that an author is not fully responsible for words that he cites or adapts.

Second, Paul stresses that justification has come "through the redemption which is in Christ Jesus" (cf. "redemption through His blood, the forgiveness of our trespasses" [Eph. 1:7]). Believers, then, are redeemed *from* "the wrath of God" *by* the sufferings of Christ.[74]

Third, Paul continues to unfold the nature and significance of Christ's death by affirming that God displayed Christ as "a propitiation in His blood through faith." Hodge rightly summarizes the import of this phrase:

The obvious meaning, therefore, of this important passage is that God has publicly set forth the Lord Jesus Christ, in the sight of the intelligent universe, as a propitiatory sacrifice for the sins of men. It is the essential idea of such a sacrifice, that it is a satisfaction to justice. It terminates on God. Its primary design is not to produce any subjective change in the offerer, but to appease God.[75]

Fourth, Paul stresses that Christ's redemptive and propitiatory death has served to "demonstrate His righteousness" (Rom. 3:25), *viz.*, "His righteousness at the present time" (Rom. 3:26). What has occasioned such a demonstration of God's righteousness, which in this context must refer to God's "inherent justice"?[76] It is the "pass[ing] over [of] the sins previously committed" (Rom. 3:25).[77]

Fifth, the consequence of this arrangement is that God is both "just" and the "justifier of the one who has faith in Jesus" (Rom. 3:26). In other words, we find Paul stressing that the death of Christ as redemptive and propitiatory was absolutely necessary to believers' justification. The arrangement is said to be a "gift" and "by His grace." Man's role is simply to receive what Christ has done by "faith in Jesus" (Rom. 3:24, 26). Such a state of affairs, Paul says in Romans 3:27, entirely excludes "boasting."

Sixth, having considered Paul's argument, we may see that we are far removed from a NPP model that tells us that Paul's language of righteousness has been drawn from Second Temple texts that looked forward to a Second Exodus, and that consequently defines righteousness as God's covenantal faithfulness to his people. This is the imposition of a foreign biblical-theological model upon the text of Paul.[78] A sounder and more textually faithful method of proceeding is to examine each instance of "righteousness" where it occurs and to allow the context to define this term for us. At Romans 3:25–26 (cf. 3:5), "righteousness" means God's inherent justice; at Romans 1:17; 3:21–22; 5:17; 10:3, the term means that "which God gives and which he approves."[79]

We may draw from our study of these verses the following conclusions: (1) Justification is an act that is essentially soteriological and not primarily ecclesiological in nature. (2) Justification is a forensic transaction and as such has absolutely no regard for the subjective condition of the sinner, who is conceived to be entirely receptive in this transaction. (3) The ground of this forensic transaction is the death of Jesus Christ as a substitute for those whom he represents, whereby pardon has been effected, the believer has been freed from the wrath of God and accepted as righteous in his sight, and God's inherent justice (his righteousness) is demonstrated to the watching world.

Universal Guilt (Rom. 5:12–21) and Paul's Conscience

1. *The Universal Guilt of Humanity.* Sadly neglected in most NPP writings is Paul's teaching that the guilt of Adam's sin has been imputed to his posterity, and that Christ's righteousness (passive or active) has been imputed to the elect. For Sanders, imputation is immaterial to considerations of Pauline soteriology. Questions of original sin (had the rabbis adopted them) are properly outside the purview of covenantal nomism. Sanders consequently says concerning imputation *either* that the doctrine does not fall within the realm of our comparative study of Paul and the rabbis *or* that "Paul was a good Jew and we have no reason to think that his views would have differed from the Rabbis' on this point."

Dunn explicitly denies that Paul taught the doctrine of imputation: "Nevertheless, guilt only enters into the reckoning with the individual's own transgression. Human beings are not held responsible for the state in which they are born. That is the starting point of their personal responsibility, a starting point for which they are not liable."[80]

Wright's exegesis of Romans 5 largely sidesteps questions of imputation, arguing rather that references to Adam in Romans 5:12–21 are the retelling of the story of Israel:

> Israel's obedience/faithfulness should have been the means of undoing the problem of Adam, of humanity as a whole. . . . the death of Christ (which is clearly the subject throughout this paragraph) functions as the true obedience/faithfulness of Israel through which this purpose is achieved. Romans 5:12–21 thus restates, in multiple and overlapping ways, what had been argued in 3:21–26.[81]

Wright also denies that Christ's active or passive obedience is at all said in Romans 5 to be imputed to the believer. Predictably absent in NPP views is any reference to the universal guilt of man through Adam.

In response, we turn briefly to Paul's argument in Romans 5:12–21, making a few observations.[82] Commentators recognize that Paul at Romans 5:12 ("Therefore, just as through one man sin entered into the world, and death through sin, and so death spread to all men, because all sinned—") introduces a digression and will not return to his main argument until Romans 5:18. Part of the reason for this argumentative pause is to avoid a certain misunderstanding, *viz.*, that by the statement "all sinned" (5:12) Paul means individual transgressions after the likeness of Adam's transgression.[83] First, this is evidenced by his argument that "death reigned from Adam until Moses, even over those who had not sinned in the likeness of the offense of Adam" (5:14). This condition of death, furthermore, did not come upon man willy-nilly. Paul states the principle that "sin is not imputed when there is no law" (5:13b), which is to say that "given that sin has been imputed, there has been sin and there has been transgression" ("for until the Law sin was in the world" [5:13a]).[84] How, then, was the connection between sin and death forged? This happened not by the individual sins of Adam's posterity, but by the sin of the "one man" (5:12). Second, this is seen in his conclusion in verse 18: "So then as through one transgression there resulted condemnation to all men. . . ." Paul presses this truth throughout this passage. From Adam's one sin has come "death" (5:15, 17), "condemnation" (5:16, 18), and the appointment of his posterity as sinners (5:19). This arrangement, Paul cannot stress enough, is entirely independent of any considerations of Adam's descendants' activities:[85]

1. "by the transgression of the one the many died" (v. 15)
2. "the judgment arose from one transgression resulting in condemnation" (v. 16)
3. "for if by the transgression of the one, death reigned through the one" (v. 17)
4. "as through one transgression there resulted condemnation to all men" (v. 18)

5. "for as through the one man's disobedience the many were made [*lit.* 'appointed' or 'constituted'] sinners" (v. 19)

Why is this understanding of Romans 5 important to our criticism of NPP readings of Paul? First, it evidences once again that Wright, in his reading of Romans 5, has unsuccessfully attempted to strain Paul through an imposed biblical-theological grid supposedly deduced from the Second Temple literature. Second, Paul's argument in Romans 5:12–21 renders comprehensible his empirically argued condemnation of Jew and Gentile in Romans 1–3. These verses answer the question, "How can Paul make such sweeping statements as he has in Romans 1:18–3:20?" Paul can affirm that all are "under sin" (Rom. 3:9) not only by empirical observation (Rom. 1:18–3:8) but also by virtue of man's relationship to Adam (Rom. 5:12–21). Third, Paul's argument helps us to see that just as man's *problem* is focused on the issue of the guilt of sin, so too the *solution* in Christ's death and resurrection is focused on the resolution of that guilt. Paul will not permit us to truncate the significance of Christ's death as pertaining only to the liberation of God's people from the power of sin. Fourth, Paul's argument renders comprehensible the traditional doctrine of Christ's representation of his people, the imputation of his righteousness in the act of justification. Adam and Christ, then, for all their differences, provide a vital parallel for Paul concerning these doctrines (Rom. 5:14c–19).

2. *Paul's Conscience.* In view of the preceding considerations, how may we respond to Krister Stendahl and others who stress that Paul possessed a robust conscience? First, we may observe that for Stendahl and others guilt has been conceived in a predominantly subjective sense (i.e., "I feel guilty"). The majority of Pauline teaching on the subject, however, treats guilt objectively (i.e., "I stand condemned; I bear obligation and accountability to justice"). It is primarily in *this* sense that Paul in his writings will address the problem of man's guilt (e.g., Rom. 3, 5).

Second, Stendahl's view that Paul in Romans 7 is simply attempting to vindicate the law from the charge of sin and to acquit his own ego is quite beside the point. Contrary to Stendahl, Paul most certainly recognizes his guilt with respect to the law. First, he concludes that he is "wretched" and requires liberation from "the body of this death" (7:24). Second, this affirmation in Romans 7:24 explains why he resolves his dilemma in 8:1 the way that he does ("Therefore there is now no condemnation for those who are in Christ Jesus" [8:1]). Hodge summarizes well the transition between these two verses:

> Those in Christ are not exposed to condemnation, not withstanding their imperfect sanctification, because Christ has died as a sacrifice for their sins. . . . Since men, being sinners, cannot be justified by works; since by the obedience of one man, Jesus Christ, the many are made righteous; and since through him, and not through the law, deliverance from the subjective power of sin is effected, therefore it follows that there is no condemnation to those who are in Him.[86]

In other words, Romans 7, Paul's meditation on the imperfection of his sanctification, fundamentally circles around the issue of guilt, of condemnation.[87] While Paul does plead his sincerity throughout, as evidence that he is a true believer (cf. Rom. 7:15, 17, 19, 20, 22), it is not his intention to excuse his own indwelling sin or his culpability for that sin.

A third observation is that Philippians 3:6 ("as to the righteousness which is in the Law, found blameless") ought not refer (as Stendahl and others have argued) to Paul's *current and approving* assessment of his life in Judaism. Rather, Paul is giving us a window into his own prior self-conception as a Jew. Such an understanding of this verse explains why he is bringing out his host of privileges only to reject them (Phil. 3:4–7). Paul, then, is telling us how he perceived his life in Judaism to look once upon a time.

Often, NPP interpreters will suggest that the Reformation tradition of exegesis has understood Paul to claim in Philippians 3:6 a sinless perfection in his life under Judaism. Having raised this view as the only true traditional alternative to their view, they dismiss it and proceed to argue their view. Paul, however, is not making a claim to sinless perfection. He is adopting the Old Testament language of blamelessness and righteousness, which is both commanded (Gen. 17:1) and affirmed (Gen. 6:9; Job 1:1; Luke 1:6). John Calvin rightly observes that by "blameless" Paul means "that righteousness which would satisfy the common opinion of mankind" by which he "was in the judgment of men holy, and free from all censure."[88] In other words, Paul was covenantally faithful and was regarded as such by his fellow Jews. But now, Paul has concluded, that righteousness was insufficient. When seen in view of Christ, his obedience and righteousness lacked the full righteousness that the law requires, *viz.*, "perfect love to God and our neighbours."[89]

Why did Paul fault his former righteousness? He did so because, unlike his "righteousness of [his] own derived from the Law," his "righteousness . . . comes from God on the basis of faith" (Phil. 3:9). His *true* righteousness, in other words, is divine in its origin; has been received by faith; and is not constituted by any status in his possession or by activity that he could perform. Not surprisingly, Paul says of his life in Judaism that "all that is rubbish, and all I value is found in Christ."

The Theological Problems

Confusing Grace, Legalism, and Merit

Recent NPP constructions of Second Temple Judaism muddle the issues regarding grace, legalism, and merit. We are all familiar with the tired battle cries that the Reformers read their own struggles with late medieval Catholicism into Pauline interpretation. Wright is especially egregious in this regard:

> Many people, including many supposedly "Pauline" Christians, would say, off the cuff, that the heart of Paul's teaching is "justification by faith." What many such people understand as the meaning of this phrase is something like this. People are always trying to pull themselves up by their own moral bootstraps. They try to save themselves by their own efforts; to make themselves good enough for God, or for heaven. This doesn't work; one can only be saved by the sheer unmerited grace of God, appropriated not by good works but by faith. This account of justification owes a great deal both to

the controversy between Pelagius and Augustine in the early fifth century and to that between Erasmus and Luther in the early sixteenth century.[90]

Ironically, it is the *ignorance* of historical theology on the part of Wright and other scholars that prompts them to make such affirmations as these. Late medieval Catholicism was not a Pelagian religion—it was *semi*-Pelagian in nature.[91] That is, it most certainly gave a place to God's grace in one's salvation. At the same time, semi-Pelagianism argues that man is weakened but not dead by virtue of man's fall. Man consequently has some remaining ability to cooperate with divine grace, grace that is usually conceived as "moral and suasory," and not "the direct and effectual exertion of the new creative energy of God." What distinguishes "sinner" from "saint," this religion argues, is the individual's "use or abuse of the grace" given to him.[92]

NPP scholars often reason, "Judaism was not a Pelagian religion; Paul, then, must not have been combating Pelagianism; he must have disagreed with Judaism on other grounds." Sanders mistakenly presumes that if Judaism used the language and even occasionally employed the concept of grace, then the religion itself was a religion of grace. He therefore necessarily excluded the possibility of legalism in that religion. As our survey of Sanders's own evidence shows (see chapter 4 above), however, the predominant forms of rabbinic Judaism contemporary to Paul were thoroughly semi-Pelagian in character. They employed the language of the grace of God, but were not themselves wholly gracious in nature.

We can make three observations in this connection: (1) The Reformers were not mistaken in their comparison of late medieval Catholicism with the Judaism contemporary to Paul. For all their differences, late medieval Catholicism and Judaism are both semi-Pelagian in character, and therefore worthy of such comparison. (2) Paul, as we have argued, is no semi-Pelagian, but NPP proponents consistently represent his theology as semi-Pelagian. The predominant semi-Pelagianism among NPP proponents' interpretations of Paul has jaundiced NPP readings of Paul, who is, to speak anachronistically, a thoroughly Augustinian writer. (3) For a number of NPP proponents, to establish that Paul is no Pelagian is sufficient to transcend the historical Augustinian-Pelagian debate and thereby dismiss the relevance of historical theology to Pauline interpretation. These proponents' failure to recognize semi-Pelagianism as a theological category necessary for the study of Paul, his opponents, and his interpreters evidences that this dismissal is shortsighted.

Ignoring Imputation

The NPP systematically rejects or ignores the Pauline doctrine of imputation. Few doctrines of Paul have been more vehemently attacked or systematically overlooked throughout the centuries than the imputation of Adam's sin to his posterity. Even within many of the available criticisms of the NPP, few authors concentrate on this doctrine as a central one in the discussion.[93] The consequences of excising imputation from Paul's thought, however, are dire: (1) Paul's universal condemnation of humanity will not be grounded in man's solidarity in Adam. We are left, rather, to pursue other explanations for Paul's affirmations of universal sinfulness in Romans 1–5. Paul reasons from solution to plight and thereby offers several contradictory accounts of the human condition (Sanders); Paul conceives of no guilt apart from individual transgressions (Dunn); Adam has launched the story of Israel's failure to do what only the Second Adam has done (Wright). What we do not have in each of these explanations are explicit statements of the damage that Adam has wrought by way of the imputation of his sin to his posterity. Such accounts generally trivialize or marginalize Paul's assessment of man's condition, and truncate the radical character of the grace taught by the apostle.

(2) It is not at all surprising, then, to see that in all the NPP proponents that we have observed, the ground of justification is the believer's covenantal obedience (rendered undoubtedly by the assistance of the infused grace of God). This point of soteriology, all sides admit, would make Paul no different from his Jewish contemporaries. Such a conception of Paul's solution, we may observe, follows naturally from the previously considered conceptions of man's plight. Provided that some ability remains in fallen man to please God spiritually, what is to prevent the use of that ability in cooperating with the grace of God in order to produce the ground according to which we are justified?

Pastorally, the implications of these views for the gospel are tremendous. Man is kept ignorant of the full depths of his own sinful condition, while the good news of the gospel (an alien righteousness) is equally withheld from him. Man is told that, in an ultimate sense, his salvation rests on his works. We have, at root, a religion that amounts to a modified covenant of works: do this and live (with a little divine help).

Upsetting the Balance between Forensic and Transforming Grace

The NPP nullifies the Reformation's accomplishment in achieving a balanced understanding of Paul's teaching concerning forensic and transformative grace.

Biblical scholars operating in the critical tradition had lost this balance by the nineteenth century, and showed negligible interest in recovering it in the twentieth century. This tendency is nowhere more evident than in NPP proponents' confounding the offices of faith in justification and sanctification. Dunn functionally defines "faith" in Paul with respect to justification as covenantal faithfulness. Wright, with some qualification, agrees. "Righteousness" and "justification" are forensic terms, but the ground of the believer's final acceptance, Wright says, is his covenantal faithfulness. Since the believer's present justification is made in advance of and as an earnest of his final justification, we may fairly conclude that, for Wright, present justification rests on one's covenantal faithfulness. While Wright may claim that Pauline justification is forensic in character, it is in fact, to Wright, transformative in nature. To argue this way, however, rolls back those necessary distinctions that Protestants of the magisterial Reformation have drawn in order to preserve the biblical distinctions.

Reformed Christians have always argued that faith is ever accompanied by good works. These good works evidence saving faith, distinguishing it from historical faith or temporary faith. The act of believing, however, does not constitute our righteousness in justification, nor ought we to confound our faith in justification with faithfulness. Paul consistently argues that we are justified solely on the ground of Christ's merits. Faith is merely the instrument by which the righteousness of Christ is appropriated. Faith, then, in its office of justification, is entirely receptive. In disentangling these issues, Turretin states the question well:

> The question is not whether solitary faith (i.e. separated from the other virtues) justifies (which we grant could not easily be the case, since it is not even true and living faith); but whether it "alone" concurs to the act of justification (which we assert); as the eye alone sees, but not when torn out of the body. Thus the particle "alone" does not determine the subject, but the predicate (i.e. "faith only does not justify," but "faith justifies alone"). The coexistence of love in him who is justified is not denied; but its coefficiency or cooperation in justification is denied. [Further] the question is not whether the faith "which justifies" works by love (for otherwise it would not be living but dead); rather the question is whether faith "by which it justifies" or in the act of justification, is to be considered under such a relation (which we deny).[94]

Turretin rightly concludes that works are a necessary "concomitant" of faith, but are not thereby to be considered "causes of justification with faith or to do the very thing which faith does in this matter."[95] While many academic proponents of the NPP are not historical theologians, we nevertheless may fairly expect them to demonstrate some awareness of and reasons for the nuances and distinctions involved in the position that they are disputing. The Reformers and their heirs adopted this theological vocabulary for a very specific reason: to preserve vital biblical distinctions. To forfeit this language is not progress but regress in our study of Pauline thought.

Redefining Justification

The NPP mistakenly reinterprets justification as an ecclesiological doctrine, not a soteriological one. The doctrine that Pauline justification is ecclesiological and not soteriological is one of the most remarkable inversions of Paul. No orthodox interpreter of Paul has ever disputed that the doctrine of justification has ecclesiological implications. Paul himself makes these implications explicit in Romans 9–11 and Romans 15. To grasp the sensitivity of both Reformed and

Lutheran commentators to these implications, we may compare the comments of both Hodge and Martin Luther:

> Christ had exhibited the greatest condescension and kindness in coming, not as a Lord or ruler, but as an humble minister to the Jews, to accomplish the gracious promises of God. As this kindness was not confined to them, but as the Gentiles also were received into his kingdom, *and united with the Jews on equal terms*, this example of Christ furnishes the strongest motives for the cultivation of mutual affection and unanimity.[96]

> By all this (summarizing his comment on 15:8–12), the Apostle removes the dissension between the Jewish and the heathen (Christians), so that they should not be at variance with each other, but receive each other, as Christ received them. For out of pure mercy He has received not only the Jews (who therefore should not exalt themselves), but also the Gentiles. Therefore both have reason enough to glorify God and not to contend with each other.[97]

To affirm, however, that Paul's doctrine of justification was *exclusively* ecclesiological and not at all soteriological is to force a dichotomy where Paul (and his orthodox interpreters) has seen none. Given that the doctrine of justification by faith alone is the *raison d'être* of the Protestant movement, one wonders whether ecclesiastical proponents of the NPP have forced this dichotomy in order to permit rapprochement with Rome.[98]

NINE

What's at Stake for Reformed Christianity?

n drawing our study to an end, we want to define the salient issues and press home the importance of our study for what is presently transpiring within Reformed Christianity, specifically in certain quarters of the Presbyterian Church in America (PCA) and of her sister Reformed churches. To do so, we will ask and answer three questions: (1) What doctrines are at stake in this dispute? (2) Why has NPP scholarship been received with such enthusiasm within Reformed Christianity? (3) What theological and practical consequences is the adoption of the NPP having within Reformed Christianity?

The Doctrines in Dispute

We have isolated several doctrines that have come into question or revision in the course of the last quarter century. We will briefly summarize them in part to be reminded that what is at stake strikes at not only the well-being (*bene esse*) of the church, but in some cases the very life and health (*esse*) of the church itself. Nine doctrines merit our attention.

Theological Method

At stake in the discussion is the very nature of revelation and its interpretation. E. P. Sanders and Heikki Räisänen both understand Paul to be inconsistent at points. The latter understands Paul to be radically inconsistent. It is impossible, of course, to reconcile either view with a classical Christian understanding of Scripture as infallible and inerrant. Both views problematize how we may understand Scripture (or some portion thereof) as revelation. J. D. G. Dunn, we have seen, employs the category of metaphor in such a way as to deprive Paul of any propositional foundation. We have seen, rather, that experience yields (imperfect) propositional expression, not vice versa.

N. T. Wright, adopting the epistemological principle of critical realism, argues that worldview lies back of all theological discourse and expression:

> [We must] not simply . . . study Romans as a rag-bag of loci or topoi within Paul's hypothetical *Compendia* or *Summa*, but to show how the letter belongs within, and indeed acts as a window upon, Paul's symbolic world, his nonreflective praxis, his assumed narrative framework, and his fundamental answers to the key questions.[1]

To read Scripture, then, is not to rest content with its poetic sequence (= "the actual argument of the letter") but to dig beneath the letter's language to its narrative sequence (= "the wider worldview and belief system on which Paul draws").[2] Traditional readings of Romans, then, can be modified or discarded by recourse to the purported worldview that is said to underlie the letter. Propositions in Paul are at best mere instantiations of narrative or worldview. They are at worst Western perversions of this Jewish thinker. We have in Wright an aversion to conducting theology in the way that the church has classically conceived theology. We have, in Wright, not only a nonclassical, self-consciously formulated approach to theology, but also an approach to revelation that is antithetical to that of classical Christianity.

Also at stake in this discussion is a related cluster of questions. Will we interpret Scripture as a book that points us to certain eternal verities and to those verities as they have been disclosed by God in time and history? Or will we truncate God's speech to be "horizontal"—concerned predominantly with the here and now, the unfolding of the basic worldview questions, without appreciable concern for the hereafter? Will we divorce history and the heart and say that Paul must be concerned *either* with worldview concerns *or* with experiential categories?

The Doctrine of Scripture

The NPP generally argues that we are to see an intellectual construct of Second Temple Judaism bequeathing to Paul a theological pattern of reading and interpreting Scripture, from which Paul diverged in one or two central points. For Sanders, this construct is termed "covenantal nomism," and is said to be found throughout the rabbinic writings, the Qumran scrolls, and the Apocrypha and Pseudepigrapha. For Wright, this construct is a narrative common to all Jews, *viz.*, that post-exilic Israel remains under exile and awaits divine deliverance from that condition. Either construct makes it functionally impossible for us to distinguish in Paul the normative authority of the Old Testament Scriptures from subsequent Jewish literature, and to acknowledge Paul's full recognition of the divine authority of the former alone.

We have also observed that NPP readings generally require a secondary construct of ancient Judaism to determine questions of Pauline interpretation. Sanders, for instance, precludes certain questions we might ask of Paul (regarding, for example, original sin and soteriological disagreement) because of conclusions that have been previously drawn at this level. Wright argues that the whole of Romans 5–8 is constructed around a retelling of the narrative of Adam and Israel.[3] The traditional soteriological doctrines drawn from these chapters are consequently muted or refuted. We have argued that such approaches bind Protestants, who have thrown off the yoke of a Roman *magisterium* in order to read Scripture aright, to an academic *magisterium* in order to read Scripture aright. It compromises or in some cases denies the sound principle of interpretation that statements of the apostle Paul ought to be interpreted by recourse to other statements of his and by other passages of Scripture that may speak more plainly.

What Is the Gospel?

Wright argues that the gospel is an "announcement about Jesus" that embraces the death of Christ, the resurrection of Christ, the messiahship of Christ, and the universal lordship of Christ.[4] Dunn, on the other hand, concedes that salvation is a central concept in Paul's preaching and thought, but refuses either to assign to it normative content *or* to tie it necessarily and uniquely to the person of Jesus Christ. Traditionally, Protestants have understood the gospel to be an announcement that the God-man Jesus, who has died, who is risen, and who reigns, has effected salvation for his people. We have in effect a wedge driven by both Wright and Dunn between the person and the work of Christ, a wedge that orthodox Protestantism has never recognized.

What Is Justification?

What does Paul mean by the term "justification"? Is justification a *process*? Is it essentially, as Sanders has argued, the same reality as the transformation that follows one's participation in Christ? Is the *act* of justification, as Dunn has argued, God's act in counting the covenant partner as still in covenant? Is justification properly a *series of acts* that succeeds over the course of the covenant-keeper's life? Is the Pauline doctrine of justification, as Wright has argued, focused primarily on the justification that God will make concerning his people in the future, i.e., at the Day of Judgment? Is the believer's present justification derivative of that future declaration? Is justification the "doctrine which insists that all those who have this faith [i.e., in Jesus' lordship] belong as full members of this family, on this basis and no other,"[5] i.e., is it a primarily ecclesiological doctrine?

Or is justification, as the Reformed have consistently maintained, primarily concerned with *soteriology*—how the sinner is declared righteous (not just pardoned) before a holy God? We have observed in Sanders a recognition that, concerning justification, Rome was correct and Protestants were mistaken. Justification is a process of the gradual transformation of the believer. We observed in Dunn and Wright a wedge driven between soteriology and ecclesiology. This wedge has effectively permitted both authors to adopt an understanding of Pauline justification that is sympathetic to Roman Catholic formulations and antithetical to traditional Protestant formulations.

In related fashion, NPP proponents have inquired, "What are the 'works of the law'?" Sanders has argued that the focus of the term was the law as that which distinguishes the Jew from the other. Dunn and Wright have argued that the works of the law are preeminently status markers or boundary markers of the people of God and as such are exclusively concerned with *identity* and not at all with *activity*. Traditionally, however, the works of the law in Paul have been understood to be the deeds of the sinner (in keeping with the law of God) on which he will rest at the Day of Judgment for acceptance before God.

What Is the Office of Faith in Justification?

We have seen that NPP proponents often understand faith in justification to be the equivalent of faithfulness. Hence, the declaration of justification contemplates the subject's faithfulness as a covenant-keeper. For Wright in particular, faith in present justification is the boundary marker that declares a person to be already in the people of God. Faith in future justification embraces one's covenantal faithfulness as the ground of one's acceptance at the Day of Judgment. Traditionally, faith has been seen to be entirely receptive in its office of justification. Faith, in other words, *justifies alone* (although, of course, this faith is *not alone*, i.e., unaccompanied by works that are the fruit of it). Wright, furthermore, defines the believer's righteousness (as in Philippians 3:9) as membership (rightly conceived) within the people of God.[6] We have stressed, however, that for Paul faith lays hold of Jesus Christ and his righteousness, resting upon an alien righteousness *alone* for acceptance with a holy God. It is in this sense that the believer is said to have a "righteousness which comes from God on the basis of faith" (Phil. 3:9).

Why Did Jesus Christ Die?

Dunn has argued that we are to resolve the (tensive) biblical teachings on Christ's death into a series of intangible or poetic metaphors that have no particular bearing on what has transpired in reality. Wright has argued that there *is* a relationship between Christ's death and his people, such that he dealt with sin as power, and provided an example of faithful covenant-keeping. Wright is not especially concerned to affirm who the specific beneficiaries of Christ's death are. That is, has sin as power been canceled only for believers or for everyone? There is a general tendency in NPP writings to downplay Paul's language in affirming Christ's death as expiatory and propitiatory (in part by denying the role of imputation in Paul's thought). We find a concomitant tendency to stress the significance of Christ's death as enabling the believer to render obedience to God now that that believer has been freed from sin's former mastery over him. Traditionalists have followed Paul in giving Christ's death as expiatory and propitiatory its due place in the apostle's thought, and of affirming Christ's death to be the sole ground of the believer's justification in a realistic (not a nominalistic) sense.

The Doctrine of Regeneration

We have seen that Dunn and Wright stress that justification is either God's declaration of our covenant faithfulness or God's declaration of who is to be counted among the inclusive people of God. Covenantal faithfulness is largely seen as living a life that assents to Christ's lordship and is obedient to the terms of the covenant (so defined). The gospel, as Wright defines it, consists of community inclusion and Christ's lordship, not salvation. Necessarily downplayed is a doctrine of regeneration—or the new birth—the decisive transition whereby, according to evangelical religion, the sinner experiences the transition from darkness to light, from death to life. Frequently polemicized in Wright's writings is the pietism to which the Reformation is thought to have given birth, *viz.*, the notion that " 'the gospel' is supposed to be a description of how people get saved; of the theological mechanism, whereby, in some people's language, Christ takes our sin and we his righteousness; in other people's language, Jesus becomes my personal saviour; in other languages again, I admit my sin, believe that he died for me, and commit my life to him."[7] This, Wright stresses, is not "what Paul means" by the "gospel."[8] The gospel, rather, is "at its very heart, an announcement about the true God as opposed to the false gods,"[9] a message "aim[ed] directly at the principalities and powers of the Roman world, from Caesar downwards."[10] When this doctrine is appropriated into the evangelical and Reformed churches, we cannot expect that the doctrine of regeneration will fare well: Wright informs us that traditional understandings of Paul, the gospel, and salvation are utterly misplaced. We need accordingly to reconfigure not just such understandings, but our preaching and teaching as well.

How Can the Believer Have Assurance of Salvation?

When we attempt to construct a doctrine of assurance from Wright, we are left with few and unsettling data. The believer's assurance rests fundamentally in the fact that Jesus is Lord and that the believer is living obediently under the terms of the covenant. In other words, the believer's assurance is grounded essentially in his covenantal faithfulness. This understanding of assurance differs radically from traditional Reformed affirmations that, admitting the necessity of the believer's obedience, fundamentally ground the believer's assurance in God's promises of salvation to the believer in Christ. These promises stem not only from *who* Jesus Christ is, but also from *what* it is that he has accomplished. We may conclude that Wright truncates the role of the work of Christ in a believer's assurance by divorcing the work of Christ from the person of Christ.

What Is the Role of Baptism in the Christian Life?

We have seen that the participatory model (at least in Albert Schweitzer, not so Sanders) can place an inordinate role on the sacraments in the believer's life. Schweitzer, we observed, argued that Paul had adopted a doctrine of baptismal regeneration. The history of religions school, we observed, expressed interest in establishing parallels between baptism and cultic initiation among the Hellenistic mystery religions. This state of affairs at least raises a question for Reformed Protestants. When NPP views, stressing as they do participation and downplaying (if not eliminating) forensic language, are appropriated, how will this affect one's doctrine of baptism? In our studies of Wright, we have seen a significant amount of attention placed on the sacrament of baptism. We have also observed Wright rejecting traditional Protestant conceptions of the efficacy of the sacrament. In a context where he endeavors to explain the fact that many who are baptized nevertheless apostasize, Wright calls believers to "allow the dying and rising of Christ in which we have shared to have its force and way in our own lives."[11] In other words, if we would but cooperate with Christ in whom we participate, then and only then will his transforming power effect change in our lives. For Wright, at least, there is a tangible connection between his understanding of participation in Christ in Paul and an understanding of baptism that, he admits, is elevated beyond many traditional formulations.

The NPP Within Reformed Christianity

Within the last several years, there has been increased openness to the formulations and positions of the NPP within Reformed Christianity. We now offer seven reasons to explain the attraction of the NPP within Reformed Christianity in particular. In doing so, we will focus our attention especially on Wright, the single proponent most responsible for mediating these views into Reformed Christianity.

First, Wright has played a prominent and commendable role in defending the general historicity of the gospel records, the historical and theological continuity between Jesus and Paul, and the legitimacy of the project of New Testament theology. He has thereby attracted a number of younger evangelicals who (rightly) find such defenses welcome. His writings, however, have proven a Trojan horse to the church by virtue of many evangelicals' uncritical appropriation of and appreciation for his scholarship.

Second, Wright purports to offer a way out of the dilemma posed by Sanders without (apparently) forfeiting Sanders's model and the scholarly credibility that comes with it. Sanders stresses that Paul reasons, at the level of his convictions, from solution to plight, even though the apostle has been traditionally understood to reason from plight to solution in Romans. Sanders grounded that argument on a reading both of Jewish texts and of Paul that has seemed persuasive to many of his academic peers.

Wright, however, offers a plausible response to Sanders's model. Wright does so, furthermore, as an academic peer and not as one who could be justly accused of being a "Reformation sympathizer." Wright argues that Paul has reasoned from plight to solution, and that this flow of his thought can be established from the Jewish texts that form the context of Pauline thought. Paul has inherited a narrative model (sin–exile–restoration) from surrounding Judaism. His thought, as we have it outlined in his letters, evidences a series of modifications of that model without disrupting its basic movement. Wright's synthesis, then, affords conservative scholars at least three points of attraction. Wright allows one to maintain both coherency *and* consistency in Paul (against Sanders and Räisänen) as well as a formal adherence to a plight-to-solution movement at both the poetic and rhetorical levels of Pauline thought. Wright formulates both of the preceding in such a way that avoids the label "fundamentalist" and carries academic credibility. While disagreeing with Sanders's solution-to-plight hypothesis, Wright nevertheless embraces Sanders's understanding of Judaism and Paul's relationship to it.

Third, there are formal parallels between NPP interest in the covenant and the interest of the Reformed in the doctrine of the covenant. Operating in a post-Holocaust setting, many NPP proponents have sought rapprochement with Judaism. They have stressed points of continuity between Judaism and the New Testament, and have downplayed or eliminated the points of discontinuity that earlier scholarship had recognized or emphasized. Notwithstanding the differences between the proposals of Ernst Käsemann and W. D. Davies, both men's scholarship was profoundly shaped by the horrors and atrocities perpetrated by the Nazis against the Jews during the Second World War. There has been in the postwar era, then, a tremendous stress on the continuity of the Testaments. Within the overall emphasis on continuity, there have, of course, been a number of differences. Sanders, Dunn, and Wright nevertheless all recognize at a formal level the centrality of the covenant to Pauline thought, and specifically the covenant as inherited from his Jewish background. Men in the Reformed community naturally find this emphasis attractive. In response to the dispensationalism that predominates in American evangelicalism, Reformed students might point to these reputable scholars whose reflections on the covenant could be mustered in support of the unity of the Bible.

Fourth, NPP proponents, in unfolding the covenant, stress that for Paul and for Judaism, obedience to the covenant's terms has played a central and defining role in their respective systems. NPP proponents will consistently maintain that the difference between Paul and his contemporaries did not center on differing views of the role of the law in salvation. For all the differences concerning the extent of the law (i.e., "where shall the boundary markers fall?"; "how much of the law is to be obeyed?"), both parties (Jew and Christian) had no disagreement concerning either the necessity of law-obedience or the place of law-obedience in the economy of salvation. In a climate in American evangelicalism in which antinomianism predominates, "lordship" salvation is being earnestly debated within the church, and many will appeal to the letters of Paul (especially Galatians) in support of antinomianism, a Reformed person might find interest in reputable academic scholars who stress the centrality of obedience to Pauline thought. This, polemically, could be a powerful weapon. One can say to his antinomian opponent: "You see that Paul did not differ with his opponents concerning issues of obedience—what warrant do *you* have to claim Paul as the father of your antinomian errors?" Specifically, we can see the attraction of Wright to folk within the Reformed community. Wright proclaims that the gospel *is* the proclamation of the lordship of Christ. One again might say to antinomians, who often charge orthodox men with "legalism" or a denial, truncation, or compromise of the gospel, "If this is what Paul is saying, then you are not even getting the gospel right—the gospel, as N. T. Wright has argued, *is* the lordship of Christ."

Fifth, NPP thought corresponds well to a growing discomfort with experiential religion in Reformed Christianity. Accompanying the rise of neo-evangelicalism (which pricked the social consciousness of evangelicals beginning in the period after the Second World War)[12] has been an interest among the Reformed in the theologies of such men as Abraham Kuyper and Herman Dooyeweerd. These theologies have often been polemically articulated against the so-called pietistic retreat of fundamentalism and of what is perceived to be the excessive pietism of much of Reformed Christianity. These theologies have stressed the creation and Christ's dominion and have lent a profoundly "this-worldly" focus to Christianity. A subset of this movement has been

Christian reconstructionism (including its theonomic expressions), which has become popular within North American Reformed circles in the last forty-five years, accompanying a period of dramatic civil, religious, judicial, and political changes in North American culture.

With these theologies (whether we look at them in terms of their expressions on the *left* [as the Institute for Christian Studies/Calvin Theological Seminary] or on the *right* [theonomy, reconstruction]) has come a stress on worldviews and a certain conception of history that is worth pondering for a moment. Following H. Richard Niebuhr, these theologies have maintained that Christians must influence history not one heart at a time but one institution or structure at a time. Once the Christian's role in history is conceived in this way, pietism (as it is termed) is seen to be the rejection of history (at worst) or a force that compromises the Christian's interaction with the world (at best).

Individuals who espouse such theologies as these find four points in Wright that are especially attractive: (1) Wright stresses the lordship or dominion of Christ, even to the point of defining this doctrine as the gospel. (2) Wright correspondingly purges soteriological categories from Pauline theological reflection. Rather, Paul is said to be concerned with the flow of history. His interest in Christ's death and resurrection is primarily concerned with how these events have affected the flow of history, specifically the institutional changes that have been wrought in the membership of the people of God. (3) Wright defines Pauline Christianity in such a way as to purge contemplative categories and concerns from the apostle's doctrine. "What must I do to be saved?" and "How do I know that I am saved?" are no longer considered appropriate questions to bring to the study of Paul. (4) Wright conceives Pauline Christianity in such a way as to stress predominantly the active life. Wright understands this active life to consist of the pursuit of ecumenism, the application of Christ's lordship to life, and the pursuit of holiness. Wright generally conceives holiness not contemplatively (meditation, prayer, self-examination), but actively (morality). These observations are not an act of fancy or invention. Wright dedicates his *New Testament and the People of God* to Brian Walsh, author of a celebrated introductory book on evangelical Christian worldview thinking.[13] Walsh also serves as an instructor at the (historically Dooyeweerdian) Institute for Christian Studies, at which Wright is presently listed as a Distinguished Associate.

Sixth, Wright supports a growing tendency among Reformed men to pit biblical theology against systematic theology. Since Geerhardus Vos inaugurated biblical theology as a distinct department of theological endeavor for Reformed men at the turn of the twentieth century (with the *imprimatur* of no less a light than B. B. Warfield), biblical theology has become a staple of Reformed preaching and teaching. During the twentieth century there have been a number of attempts to articulate the relationship between biblical theology and systematic theology. Warfield, Vos, and John Murray were agreed that the former was properly a handmaid to the latter. These three men were good students of historical-critical thought and had remembered how biblical theology in the tradition of J. P. Gabler had decimated systematic theology, both as an ordering principle of biblical data and as a force within the church. Accompanying a revolt against logic and system within Reformed circles, a growing dichotomization within the study and specialization of the theological departments, and the increased credibility of biblical studies as a discipline (coupled with the growing acceptance of evangelical scholars by nonevangelical biblical critics) has come a not unexpected backlash against systematic theology.

To the eager student of biblical theology who shares this growing suspicion of systematic theology, Wright offers at least three attractions: (1) He gives a philosophical justification for pitting narrative against proposition and giving primacy (exegetically and theologically) to the former. In other words, he purports to offer a way of doing theology that is not dependent on the supposedly Greek and philosophically captive categories of systematics. Wright proposes a way of doing theology that is fresh, Hebraic, and biblical. (2) Wright's biblicism ("I'm not bound to the Reformation; I'm just reading Paul") appeals to the biblicism of many within the Reformed biblical-theological movement, as though exegesis could transpire outside any interpretative tradition, as though logic were not something innate to human thought but a cultural imposition of the West upon the text. To conservative men who are ever sensitive of the charge that they are reading their dogmatic or philosophical constructs into the text, and who themselves often share the view that theological systems *necessarily* distort or overhaul the biblical text, such arguments are attractive. (3) Wright provides a biblical-theological construct that is sweeping and comprehensive, is apparently compelling, and seems to satisfy all the necessary academic requirements. In other words, once one jettisons not just the *loci* of systematics, but the entire approach or method of systematics, then one needs to find some way to give expression to the Bible's unity—Wright purports to give just such a construct.

The problem with such an approach is twofold. First, Wright's biblicism neglects the fact that the *loci* of systematics are not the accidental product of Western culture, but key topics that the Bible gives us. One can't help *but* relate these topics in logical and systematic categories. Second, Wright's biblicism masks the fact that he himself is as much a product of an interpretative tradition as Martin Luther, John Calvin, and their heirs. His debts, I hope we have seen, to Schweitzer, Davies, Sanders, and others are patent. The question ought not to be, "Shall I stand inside or outside an interpretative tradition to understand the text correctly?" but "Given that I already stand in an interpretative tradition, (1) do I do so self-consciously and with awareness both of my own position and of rival positions," and (2) "does my interpretative tradition best satisfy all the evidence in the text before me?"

Wright stands just as much in danger of imposing a foreign grid on the Pauline text as the Reformational models he charges of doing the same. We have seen that by importing a biblical-theological construct of "righteousness" to the text of Romans 3, Wright flattens the nuances of Paul's language of righteousness. The result is a distorted reading of Romans 3. Wright's promise, then, of pure exegesis proves to be ill-grounded. The virtue of the Reformational models over Wright is that the former have always been aware of the susceptibility of theological systems to error and of the possibility and reality of progress in doctrine. The motto *semper reformanda reformata est* (reformed [and] always reforming) has rightly captured the spirit of the Reformation's attitude toward the church's understanding of the Scripture. Wright's biblicism, however, renders his results impervious to this kind of scrutiny. There is, ironically, a fundamentalism built into his system that the Reformers have wisely sidestepped.

Seventh, Wright has been found attractive to Reformed men because of the latter's ignorance of historical and systematic theology. The NPP has been embraced by many ministers and teachers who have taken vows to uphold confessional standards that teach the contrary. Such men have accepted NPP formulations either as acceptable expressions of these standards or as improved expressions of these standards. This state of affairs must be owing to these men's ignorance of what their standards teach, since charity forbids us from attributing this failure to malicious duplicity. When we read the writings of certain Reformed men enthusiastic for NPP thought, we see *both* a selective and unpenetrating reading of NPP scholarship, *and* a culpable ignorance of what Reformed doctrine has taught regarding Scripture, the atonement, justification, imputation, and other doctrines. Such individuals, for example, will be satisfied with Wright's formulations concerning Christ's death and its application to the believer (as though they were sufficient to prove the Reformed doctrine) and yet miss the deliberate generalities in which those statements have been framed. What is disconcerting is that the debate has evidenced that a number of our ministers, elders, ministerial candidates, and prospective teachers fail to reflect a competent understanding of the doctrines that they have vowed or are preparing to vow to propagate and defend.

Consequences for Reformed Christianity

What theological and practical consequences is the adoption of NPP having within Reformed Christianity? This, sadly, is not a theoretical question. We may point to the writings of Norman Shepherd and the resolutions passed by the session of Auburn Avenue Presbyterian Church (PCA), Monroe, Louisiana (AAPC), on 26 September 2002.[14] In studying these two parties together, we do not intend to imply that there exists full doctrinal agreement between them. Nor do we mean to say that these two parties have arrived at their conclusions or support their conclusions through a concerted study of the NPP. Shepherd, for example, appears to maintain traditional and non-NPP views concerning first-century Judaism. Nor do we wish to say that these parties would be equally or necessarily supportive of all aspects of NPP scholarship.[15]

What *are* we saying? First, certain issues that we have raised in our study of the NPP find parallels in the writings of the above-mentioned individuals. Second, individuals who have interest in NPP, e.g., might and do (rightly) take interest in Shepherd and the AAPC theology because of certain actual affinities between them (and vice versa). There are at least three affinities between the NPP and the AAPC statement and Shepherd's writings. We focus our attention on the AAPC resolutions and Shepherd's writings because the former is an action of a church court, and because the latter have been authored by one who for nearly two decades taught systematic theology at a flagship Reformed seminary.[16]

1. Shepherd and AAPC each share Wright's "allergy" to the vertical issues pertaining to God and the individual soul that have been emphasized in traditional Pauline interpretation, and share a form of dichotomization of heart and history. We have in this allergy a dichotomy between biblical and systematic theology at a foundational level. AAPC explicitly states this: "It appears that the Bible speaks of salvation, more often than not, in relational and covenantal categories, rather than in metaphysical ones." "Relationships are not static, unchanging entities" but "fluid and dynamic."[17] Shepherd himself argues that "Reformed evangelistic methodology must be consciously oriented to the covenant of grace rather than to the doctrine of election,"[18] and that "the prophets and apostles viewed election from the perspective of the covenant of grace, whereas Reformed theologians of a later day have tended to view the covenant of grace from the perspective of election."[19] Such a stance affects the way in which one conceives salvation. To illustrate this dynamic, we turn our attention to the presentation of two major doctrines in the writings of Shepherd and in the AAPC statement: election and regeneration.

a. *Election.* Shepherd again and again argues that the covenant must determine election, and not vice versa—he faults traditional Reformed doctrine for orienting Reformed evangelism to the doctrine of election and not to the doctrine of the covenant.[20] Consequently, the preacher ought not "address people as a mixed multitude of elect and reprobate, with a view toward separating them. Evangelism addresses people as covenant breakers in rebellion against God and opens up to them covenant life in union and communion with God."[21] One example in which Shepherd's distinctive views become apparent is in his exhortation that "the Reformed evangelist can and must say on the basis of John 3:16, Christ died to save you. . . . Christ did not die for inanimate objects or preternatural beings, nor did he die for abstractions. He died for people, for you and for me."[22] Leaving aside whether in fact John 3:16 affirms that Christ died for all men (it does not), we may observe Shepherd conceding that from the "perspective of election," this statement is "only possibly true, and may well be false"; but because John 3:16 is "embedded in the covenant documents of the New Testament," we have "covenant truth" *simpliciter*, not "an elaboration of the doctrine of election as God views election or a commentary on the extent of the atonement in an absolute sense."[23] AAPC, while taking a higher view of election than Shepherd, argues that the knowledge of one's election effectively resolves into receiving the mark of the covenant and persevering in covenantal obedience:

> All covenant members are invited to attain to a full and robust confidence that they are God's eternally elect ones. Starting with their baptisms, they have every reason to believe God loves them and desires their eternal salvation. Baptism marks them out as God's elect people, *a status they maintain so long as they persevere in faithfulness.*[24]

The AAPC statement claims, then, that election is to be understood as a "status" that is "mark[ed]" by baptism and is a function of one's "persever[ance]."

b. *Regeneration.* Shepherd, in interpreting Jesus' words in John 15:1–8, denies the distinction between a branch that is united to Christ "outwardly" and one that is [truly] united to him " 'inwardly' or savingly."[25] This traditional understanding, he tells us, is the result of conceiving the covenant "from the perspective of election, rather than election from the perspective of the covenant."[26] This raises the question of the doctrine of regeneration in Shepherd's thought.

Shepherd pillories what he terms "regeneration-evangelism." He tells us that if, on this model, we seek to discern marks of regeneration, we will be left with skepticism:

> New obedience is often represented from the [regeneration-evangelist] pulpit as being so minimal and sin so prevailing in the lives of those who are converted, that one is compelled to ask whether there is all that much difference between regenerate and unregenerate people. The work of grace has been done and the sinner has received a new heart, but the graciousness of it all will appear only at death, when he will be perfectly sanctified.[27]

How does Shepherd propose that we escape the deficiencies of this purportedly traditionally Reformed model? He tells us that we must reconceive the marks of a Christian: "Since regeneration is one of the secret things that belong to God, the evangelists in Scripture do not presume to have access to knowledge of it in individual cases. They govern the church in terms of what is open and obvious to all. Christians are those who have been baptized. Unbelievers are those who have not been baptized."[28]

If only we would adopt "covenant-evangelism," Shepherd tells us, then we would understand "regeneration" from the "perspective of covenant," and would see "baptism, as the sign of the covenant, . . . [as] mark[ing] the passage from death to life."[29] On this model, "all who have been baptized and are seeking in faith to do the will of God are to be regarded as Christian brothers and sisters."[30] The problem with this model is not an absolute equation between baptism and salvation (he uses the language of "to be regarded"), nor even that it absolutely rejects the traditional language of regeneration ("The covenantal focus on baptism does not mean that regeneration is discounted."[31]).

The problem with Shepherd's model is that it functionally supplants the doctrine of regeneration with the sacrament of baptism ("When regeneration is understood from the perspective of covenant, it becomes both clear and natural that the sign of the covenant, baptism, should mark the passage from death to life."[32]). The problem with Shepherd's formulation is that there is no overriding concern with the heart, with the religious affections. As the Jewish Paul did (Phil. 3:6), Shepherd would have us confuse the "husk" (covenantal faithfulness) with the "kernel" (a heart that has been renewed by the grace of God). Shepherd, in his zeal to have the covenant swallow regeneration, would have us ignore the vital question of the *nature* of the covenantal faithfulness in view. In this respect we are presented with a stunning departure from Reformed orthodoxy. Shepherd's model promotes the very externalism that the apostle Paul labored so hard to oppose in early Christian circles .

AAPC argues that the traditional distinction between a saving and a nonsaving work of grace is, at best, overdrawn; at worst, a fiction:

> The question [in Hebrews 6] raised does not concern the nature of the grace received in the past (i.e., real regeneration vs. merely common operations of the Spirit), but whether or not the one who has received this grace will persevere. Thus, the solution to Heb 6 is not developing two psychologies of conversion, one for the "truly regenerate" and one for the future apostate, and then introspecting to see which kind of grace one has received. This is a task beyond our competence. The solution is to turn from ourselves and to keep our eyes fixed on Jesus, the Author and Finisher of our faith (Hebrews 12:1f.).[33]

How, then, are we to explain the progress of the Christian life or the reality of apostasy? AAPC prefers covenantal to traditional categories:

> God mysteriously has chosen to draw many into the covenant community who are not elect in the ultimate sense and who are not destined to receive final salvation. These non-elect covenant members are truly brought to Christ, united to Him in the church by baptism and receive various gracious operations of the Holy Spirit. . . . In some sense, they were really joined to the elect people, really sanctified by Christ's blood, really recipients of new life given by the Holy Spirit. God, however, withholds from them the gift of perseverance, and all is lost. They break the gracious new covenant they entered into at baptism.[34]

We may simply note that the vague character of this language (What does "truly brought" mean? Which are the "various gracious operations of the Holy Spirit"? How are members "really recipients of new life given by the Holy Spirit" "in some sense"?) may (and perhaps does) mask genuine error. As with Shepherd, AAPC breaks from the traditional delineation of speaking of those professing faith by using outward (or federal) and inward (or saving) categories. Rather, they simply point to baptism as the point of transition.

In summary, we have in Shepherd and AAPC a stated preference for reformulated covenantal (i.e., horizontal) categories coupled with a functional rejection of the traditional (vertical) doctrines of election and regeneration. This tension between the horizontal and the vertical provides a parallel to the observations drawn above in our study of Wright.

2. A second point of contact with the NPP is a functional adherence in both Shepherd and AAPC to a justifying inherent righteousness. That is, faith in its office of justification is conceived *practically* as covenantal faithfulness. By way of introduction we might note selected theses from those that Shepherd presented to the Presbytery of Philadelphia (OPC) in 1978. Each of the theses cited below departs in some way from traditional Protestant formulations of the doctrine of justification by faith alone.

> 20. The Pauline affirmation in Romans 2:13, "the doers of the Law will be justified," is not to be understood hypothetically in the sense that there are no persons who fall into that class, but in the sense that faithful disciples of the Lord Jesus Christ will be justified (Compare Luke 8:21; James 1:22–25).
>
> 21. The exclusive ground of justification of the believer in the state of justification is the righteousness of Jesus Christ, but his obedience, which is simply the perseverance of the saints in the way of truth and righteousness, is necessary to his continuing in a state of justification (Heb 3:6, 14).
>
> 22. The righteousness of Jesus Christ ever remains the exclusive ground of the believer's justification, but the personal godliness of the believer is also necessary for his justification in the judgment of the last day (Matthew 7:21–23; 25:31–46; Hebrews 12:14).
>
> 23. [G]ood works, works done from true faith . . . though not

the ground of [the believer's] justification, are nevertheless necessary for salvation from eternal condemnation and therefore for justification (Romans 6:16, 22; Galatians 6:7–9).

We may draw five observations from these theses: (1) Shepherd's doctrine of justification is essentially two-staged. Romans 2:13 is not a hypothetical statement (Thesis 20). Consequently, there is a present *and* a future justification particular to believers. (2) Believers have a duty to continue in a state of justification (Thesis 21). Justification is not a single act (the future declaration simply restating and making public the former declaration), but is properly a process. (3) Shepherd categorically refuses to exclude good works (as the fruit of true faith) from consideration in God's declaration of justification. On several occasions, he will call such good works necessary for justification (Theses 21, 22, 23). To be sure, he will affirm that it is Christ and his righteousness alone that are the exclusive ground of the believer's justification, and that these works are not meritorious, *but* if we are to take Shepherd's comments at face value, then he can only mean that it is Christ's righteousness *as it has been infused into the believer* that provides the ground of the believer's justification *because faith in justification is not contemplated apart from its fruit.* (4) Shepherd appears to conflate justification and salvation—committing an error that antinomians commit, but not in an antinomian way. At this point, we might observe this distinction as being carefully drawn by the Westminster Standards. In Westminster Larger Catechism Q&A 32, "holy obedience" is said to be the "way appointed to salvation," but not the "way to justification." Only faith, and that in a manner entirely exclusive of works, is conceived to have such a role in justification.[35] (5) Shepherd confounds two propositions that the Reformed have always affirmed: (a) one's *claim* to justification is contingent on his continuing righteousness; (b) one's justification *itself* is *not* contingent on his continuing righteousness. What's at stake, when we consider works, is not our justification, but the validity of our profession.

In conclusion, Shepherd's affirmations render impossible the traditional view that justification is a decisive and final act at the initial stages of Christian experience whereby Christ's righteousness (and nothing else) is imputed to the believer and received by faith alone, and that final justification (if we may so speak) is rendered certain and unalterable by God's present justification of the believer.

The statement of AAPC does not explicitly dwell on the doctrine of justification. It is impossible, nevertheless, to see how justification, as an irrevocable act of God's grace at the outset of the believer's life, can be reconciled with AAPC's comments on election. How can the decisive and complete act of justification be reconciled with a view of election as a process? We find precisely the same problem in this document as we observed with Shepherd: can I have the reality of grace and then lose it? Do my good works maintain the reality, or the reality my good works?

3. A third point of contact between the NPP and Shepherd and AAPC concerns the doctrine of baptism. Briefly, we may note the parallels between Schweitzer's view of baptismal regeneration, a view that has emerged directly out of his view of mystical participation in Christ, and the high premium placed on baptism in Shepherd's and AAPC's thought. AAPC will stress, in terms very similar to Schweitzer, the view that "by baptism one is joined to Christ's body, united to him covenantally, and given all the blessings and benefits of his work (Galatians 3:27; Romans 6:1ff; WSC 94). This does not, however, grant to the baptized final salvation; rather, it obligates him to fulfill the terms of the covenant. . . ."[36] Both Schweitzer and AAPC, then, affirm a form of baptismal regeneration. Shepherd does not express so exalted a view of the sacrament, but nevertheless points to baptism as that which can replace regeneration and its evidences not *simpliciter*, but as the primary means by which the believer discerns the truth and reality of his relationship with God. Such an argument constitutes an elevation of the role of baptism beyond that expressed in the Westminster Standards.

Conclusion

We may close with the caution with which many older Reformed writers have charged the church. All expressions of Christianity are on the path to one of two destinations, Rome or Geneva. What the NPP offers us is decidedly not "Genevan." The parallel interest, in some Reformed circles, in the redefined categories of covenant and justification, coupled with a new stress (and definition, for some) on baptism and with a consequent diminution of regeneration, does not bode well. It seems that there are elements active in the Reformed churches that wish to lead the church into a sacramental religion, all in the name of being "more Reformed." If we examine their arguments carefully, we see that what they are *really and increasingly* saying is that Luther and Calvin were mistaken, and that Trent was right. May God give us grace that we may not squander the rich theological heritage bequeathed to us by the Reformers, historic British Calvinism, and American Presbyterianism. May we model, in spirit and teaching, that "pattern of teaching" preserved so faithfully by our forefathers.

Select and Annotated Chronological Bibliography

Overviews of the Discussion

The following works are specifically or primarily dedicated to giving surveys of recent scholarship. They have been listed in chronological order—not of the date of these books' publication, but of the subjects that they treat.

Reventlow, H. Graf. *The Authority of the Bible and the Rise of the Modern World*. Philadelphia: Fortress, 1985.

> While not addressing NPP scholarship or questions as such, Reventlow addresses the prior (but no less vital) question—how did we get from the Reformation to F. C. Baur? A helpful survey of how many Protestants in the seventeenth and eighteenth centuries altered their view of the Bible and biblical authority.

Kümmel, W. G. *The New Testament: The History of the Investigation of Its Problems*. Nashville: Abingdon, 1972.

> A standard mid-twentieth-century compendium of critical opinion on questions of academic New Testament studies. Kümmel very helpfully digests the work of nineteenth- and early-twentieth-century scholars, many of whose works either are inaccessible or have not before been translated from the German.

Schweitzer, Albert. *Paul and His Interpreters: A Critical History.* Translated by William Montgomery. London: Adam & Charles Black, 1956.

Akin to Schweitzer's *The Quest for the Historical Jesus*, this work, originally published in 1912, surveys (primarily continental) critical Pauline scholarship from Grotius (de Groot) to Schweitzer. Schweitzer's evaluation of this period is, no doubt, colored by his own peculiar views of Pauline theology. May be profitably read with Ellis, Hafemann, and Westerholm.

Ellis, E. E. *Paul and His Recent Interpreters*. Grand Rapids: Eerdmans, 1961.

An update of Schweitzer's *Paul and His Interpreters*. This noted evangelical biblical scholar surveys Pauline scholarship from Schweitzer through the mid-twentieth century. While dated and brief, Ellis's work is nevertheless helpful to the student of the NPP because of its interest in the question of the origins of Paul's thought (Jewish or Hellenistic).

Neill, Stephen, and N. T. Wright. *The Interpretation of the New Testament, 1861–1986*. 2d ed. Oxford: Oxford University Press, 1988.

Another standard survey of critical opinion on questions of academic New Testament studies. Unlike Kümmel, Neill focuses primarily on English-speaking scholarship. N. T. Wright, an important NPP proponent, has authored the sections pertaining to the years 1961–1986. Chapters 8 and 9 ("Salvation is of the Jews" and "History and Theology") are substantially Wright's reflections on the impact that NPP scholarship has had on various areas of New Testament critical study.

Moo, Douglas. "Paul and the Law in the Last Ten Years." *Scottish Journal of Theology* 40 (1987): 287–307.

A good (but now dated) overview of the issues pertaining to the law in Paul that NPP scholarship raised, and of the scholars who have raised them. By a reputable evangelical scholar, and a critic of the NPP. A good bibliographical companion to Westerholm.

Westerholm, Stephen. *Israel's Law and the Church's Faith: Paul and His Recent Interpreters*. Grand Rapids: Eerdmans, 1988.

A very helpful survey of specifically NPP scholarship in the half century preceding publication. Westerholm particularly focuses on the way in which "law" in Paul has been interpreted by these scholars. Westerholm devotes the first part of the work to exposition of critical opinion and the remainder to a defense of a traditional Lutheran reading of the law. Reformed persons might be interested to know that Westerholm does share and expound Lutheran views of the "third use" of the law. This work has been substantially revised and expanded. See *Perspectives Old and New on Paul*, below.

O'Brien, P. T. "Justification in Paul and Some Crucial Issues of the Last Two Decades." In *Right with God: Justification in the Bible and the World*, edited by D. A. Carson, 69–95. London: World Evangelical Fellowship, 1992.

O'Brien gives a concise overview of discussions (Protestant and Roman Catholic) of justification between ca. 1970 and ca. 1990. He explores the influence of and responses to Ernst Käsemann's formulation of the doctrine. He also gives a brief overview and critique of E. P. Sanders. Unfortunately, O'Brien neglects to address the work of J. D. G. Dunn.

Hafemann, Scott J. "Paul and His Interpreters." In *Dictionary of Paul and His Letters*, edited by Gerald Hawthorne and Ralph Martin, 666–79. Downers Grove, Ill.: InterVarsity Press, 1993.

An outstanding essay that surveys Pauline scholarship since F. C. Baur, centered on the questions that Baur's scholarship has bequeathed to later critical endeavor. Well worth consulting to get an overview of the major figures in academic NPP discussion, and to get a clear and distilled treatment of the issues.

Kruse, Colin G. *Paul, the Law, and Justification*. Peabody, Mass.: Hendrickson, 1997.

This work contains a select survey of the works of pre-NPP and NPP scholars. It also highlights the work of certain critics of the NPP. Although it is now dated, this overview's brevity (about 25 pages) may commend it as an introduction for the beginning student.

Witherington, Ben. *The Paul Quest: The Renewed Search for the Jew of Tarsus*. Downers Grove, Ill.: InterVarsity, 1998.

A fairly recent survey of Pauline scholarship by a prolific evangelical biblical scholar. The work as a whole is more comprehensive than simply NPP issues. Chapters 2 ("The Trinity of Paul's Identity") and 8 ("Paul the Ethicist and Theologian") focus especially on issues pertaining to NPP scholarship, of which Witherington is modestly critical. For Witherington's more detailed engagement of Sanders and Dunn, see his *Grace in Galatia* (Edinburgh: T & T Clark, 1998), 341–55.

Westerholm, Stephen. "The 'New Perspective' at Twenty-Five." In *Jus-*

tification and Variegated Nomism. Vol. 1, *The Paradoxes of Paul*, edited by D. A. Carson, Peter T. O'Brien, and Mark A. Seifrid, 1–38. Grand Rapids: Baker, 2004.

> This essay competently surveys recent Pauline scholarship in the wake of Sanders's scholarship on ancient Judaism and Paul. It both abbreviates and supplements his overview of scholarship in Westerholm's *Perspectives Old and New on Paul*. Westerholm in this essay and in *Perspectives* is especially helpful in grouping the works of contemporary Pauline scholars into "families" of shared sympathies or similar approaches.

Westerholm, Stephen. *Perspectives Old and New on Paul: The "Lutheran" Paul and His Critics*. Grand Rapids: Eerdmans, 2004.

> Westerholm's revision of his 1988 *Israel's Law and the Church's Faith* (above) is perhaps the most recent, comprehensive, and penetrating volume addressing the NPP. Part 1 helpfully offers the reader summaries of Paul as Augustine, Luther, Calvin, and Wesley have read him. Part 2 updates Westerholm's 1988 survey of recent scholarship on Paul. Part 3 expands and revises Westerholm's 1988 exegetical discussion of Paul's understanding of "righteousness," "law," and "justification by faith."

The Historical-Critical Discussion

Judaism

The NPP drew no small measure of its impetus from a revolution in the conception of ancient Judaism among New Testament scholars. While Sanders's writings largely ushered in this revolution in the critical study of Paul, his posture toward and observations of first-century Judaism were by no means unprecedented in the century of scholarship preceding him.

Bousset, Wilhelm. *Die Religion des Judentums in Neutestamentlichen Zeitalter*. Berlin, 1903. [=The Religion of Judaism in the Time of the New Testament]

> An influential (but untranslated) work on the religion of Judaism during the New Testament era. Bousset, drawing from F. Weber's earlier important work on Judaism, bequeathed the model of Judaism that predominated among New Testament scholars through much of the twentieth century through his star pupil, Rudolf Bultmann.

Montefiore, Claude G. *Judaism and St. Paul*. London: Max Goshen, 1914.

An early and important (although neglected) work by a Jewish scholar that attempted to consider Paul's relationship to the Judaism contemporary to him. Montefiore accepts the (then) scholarly consensus that Paul's conception of Judaism is both works-centered and accurate. He does, however, argue that Paul was familiar with and engaged Hellenistic Judaism, not Palestinian (i.e., rabbinic) Judaism. Montefiore then argues that rabbinic Judaism did not reflect the Jewish soteriology reflected in the Pauline correspondence.

Schürer, Emil. *The History of the Jewish People in the Time of Jesus Christ*. 3 vols. Revised and edited by Geza Vermes, Fergus Millar, and Martin Goodman. Edinburgh: T & T Clark, 1973–1987.

A standard and exhaustive adaptation and updating of Emil Schürer's early-twentieth-century survey of Judaism. It reflects traditional (i.e., non-NPP) views about Judaism and remains a benchmark introductory textbook of the history and theology of ancient Judaism.

Jeremias, Joachim. *Jerusalem in the Time of Jesus*. Translated from the 3d German ed. Philadelphia: Fortress, 1969.

Jeremias offers a survey of Judaism that has remained influential among scholars and ministers down to this day. He relies heavily on later rabbinic literature (i.e., fourth century A.D. and following)—before scholars of Judaism, following Jacob Neusner, began to question the value of this evidence for reconstructing pre–A.D. 70 Judaism.

Moore, George Foote. *Judaism in the First Centuries of the Christian Era*. 2 vols. Cambridge, Mass.: Harvard, 1927.

A treatment of Judaism that Sanders found to be an early sympathetic engagement of ancient Judaism and, consequently, a dissenting voice from the Weber model. Moore is less concerned to offer a comparative study of Judaism and the New Testament than to present Tannaitic Judaism positively and on its own merits.

Sanders, E. P. *Judaism: Practice and Belief 63 B.C.E.–66 C.E.* London: S.C.M. Press/Philadelphia: Trinity Press International, 1992.

Sanders's positive construction of ancient Judaism contemporary to the New Testament. An introductory reference work, it reflects the development in the scholarship of ancient Judaism since Jeremias. Sanders is

less concerned here to address Judaism from the standpoint of its implications for the understanding of the New Testament. Traces of his
long-standing debate with Jacob Neusner are evident throughout the
volume.

Neusner, Jacob. Review of E. P. Sanders, *Judaism: Practice and Belief.*
Journal of Studies in Judaism 24 (1993): 317–23.

> A thoroughgoing critique of Sanders's work by a recognized scholar of
> Judaism. Neusner charges the work with "harmonizing" Judaism arti-
> ficially into "one single, equally uniform Judaism." Neusner, who ar-
> gues that scholarship has offered no fewer than four ways to construct
> ancient Judaism, at the very least briefly provides the reader with a sense
> of the complexities that attend the study of ancient Judaism.

Neusner, Jacob. *Judaism in the Beginning of Christianity.* Philadelphia:
Fortress, 2003. *Judaism When Christianity Began: A Survey of
Belief and Practice.* Louisville: Westminster John Knox Press,
2002.

> The former is a reprint of one of Neusner's dozens or hundreds of au-
> thored or edited volumes. The other is a recent survey. They provide a
> succinct overview of Neusner's construction of ancient Judaism. Should
> be read with Sanders (1992) in order to gain a picture of how the two
> most well-regarded scholars of Judaism writing for New Testament
> scholars today differ and agree.

Paul

The following authors rest comfortably in the historical-critical
tradition of reading Paul. The first proponent of the NPP is (arguably)
Krister Stendahl, although each author preceding him is an important
antecedent to the movement. The work of E. P. Sanders reflects a watershed in critical study of Paul. Scholars now frequently speak of "pre-
Sanders" and "post-Sanders" readings of Paul. While the authors listed
below subsequent to 1977 by no means agree with one another on all
points, all reflect to some degree the influence of the NPP.

Baur, F. C. "The Christ-party in the Corinthian Church, the Conflict
Between Petrine and Pauline Christianity in the Early Church, the

Apostle Peter in Rome," *Tübinger Zeitschrift für Theologie* 4 (1831): 61–206.

In many respects, contemporary critical discussion of Paul begins with this essay. Baur, according to Hafemann, defines the three questions that will dominate the next two centuries of Pauline scholarship: (1) the doctrine and identity of Paul's opponents, (2) Paul's understanding of the Mosaic Law, and (3) the center of Paul's thought.

Baur, F. C. *Paul, the Apostle of Jesus Christ, His Life and Work, His Epistles and His Doctrine.* (1845) 2 vols. Translated by E. Zeller and A. Menzies. London & Edinburgh: Williams and Norgate, 1875.

Baur's fullest and most mature expression of his views of Paul.

Lightfoot, J. B. "St. Paul and the Three." In *St. Paul's Epistle to the Galatians: A Revised Text with Introduction, Notes, and Dissertations*, 292–374. 9th ed. London: Macmillan, 1887.

A critique of the "Tübingen School" (i.e., Baur) and its reconstruction of early Christianity by a member of the famed Cambridge Triumvirate (Lightfoot, Westcott, and Hort). This influential essay, which still profits the contemporary reader, helped to stay the influence of Tübingen in Britain well into the twentieth century.

Bousset, Wilhelm. *Kyrios Christos: A History of the Belief in Christ from the Beginnings of Christianity to Irenaeus.* Translated by John E. Steely. Nashville: Abingdon, 1970.

Originally published in 1913, *Kyrios Christos* is a representative work of the "history of religions" school of the early twentieth century. Bousset, breaking from the older "liberals" of the nineteenth century, argues that Paul's thought is grounded in the cultic mystery religions of the Hellenistic world in which Paul lived. Bousset in this work traces his view of the "development" of the church's view of Jesus from Palestine through Paul into the second century A.D.

Reitzenstein, Richard. *Hellenistic Mystery-Religions: Their Basic Ideas and Significance.* Translated from the 3d German ed. by John E. Steely. Pittsburgh: Pickwick Press, 1978.

A classic work, initially published in 1910 (3d ed., 1927), from the history of religions school that endeavored to offer a comparative survey of ancient Hellenistic religions, and to see Paul in that context as a "Hellenistic mystic and Gnostic."

Schweitzer, Albert. *The Mysticism of Paul the Apostle.* Translated by William Montgomery. New York: Holt, 1931.

> As in his book on Jesus, Schweitzer writes this 1931 work in response to the history of religions school. While agreeing with the history of religions school that "justification" was *not* the center of Paul's thought, and that "participation in Christ" *was* the center of Paul's thought, Schweitzer argues that Paul's thought is grounded in Jewish, not Hellenistic, roots. Because E. P. Sanders's construction of Paul is essentially Schweitzer's, proponents of the NPP will have interest in this work.

Bultmann, Rudolf. *Theology of the New Testament.* 2 vols. Translated by Kendrick Grobel. New York: Scribner, 1951, 1955.

> Bultmann, New Testament professor at Marburg, synthesized the language of confessional Lutheranism with the thought of existentialist philosopher Martin Heidegger. Bultmann's magnum opus (originally published in 1948 and 1953) is this work, although he has authored several articles in which he speaks to issues of Pauline theology. Part of Bultmann's influence in critical discussion of Paul stems from the fact that when academic critics of the Reformation speak of the "traditional" (i.e., Lutheran) view of Paul, it is often Bultmann that they have in mind! Unlike Schweitzer, Bultmann argues (with his teacher, Bousset) that the origins of Paul's thought were Hellenistic in nature.

Davies, W. D. *Paul and Rabbinic Judaism: Some Rabbinic Elements in Pauline Theology.* 4th ed. Philadelphia: Fortress, 1980.

> Davies, a Welshman who studied under both Protestants and Jews, offers the first significant attempt to examine the relationship between Paul and contemporary Judaism sympathetically. He endeavors to show that Paul was indebted to Pharisaical Judaism, and Davies's approach is fundamentally comparative in nature. For Sanders's own comparison of his and Davies's views, see Sanders's preface to the fifth edition (a reprinting of the fourth edition), below.

Käsemann, Ernst. "The Righteousness of God in Paul." In *New Testament Questions of Today,* 169–93. Philadelphia: Fortress, 1969.

> *L'enfant terrible* of Bultmann's students, Käsemann dissented from Bultmann's thoroughgoing anthropocentrism and (at least formally) forensic articulation of justification by arguing that the "righteousness of

God" was a "gift of power" with "the lordship of Christ recognized as its peculiar content." He anticipates, in this essay originally published in 1961, the tendency among NPP scholars to reject Paul's language of justification as forensic in character and to conceive of that language as corporate or communal in character.

Käsemann, Ernst. "Justification and Salvation History in the Epistle to the Romans." In *Perspectives on Paul*, 60–78. Philadelphia: Fortress, 1971.

Käsemann's response to Stendahl's proposal that justification was not the center of Paul's thought. Käsemann argues that it *is*, and shows himself to stand between his teacher, Bultmann, and Stendahl, who would inaugurate the NPP in many respects.

Stendahl, Krister. "The Apostle Paul and the Introspective Conscience of the West." In *Paul Among Jews and Gentiles and Other Essays*, 78–96. Philadelphia: Fortress, 1976.

Stendahl's revision of his famous 1961 address before the American Psychological Association in which he argued that the Reformation (following Augustine) had misread Paul. He proceeds to fault Western interpretations of Paul because of their preoccupation with "sin" and "guilt," and because of their overly "sensitive conscience." Stendahl argues that Paul *really* is concerned with the questions of the implications of the Messiah's coming upon the law and upon the boundaries of the people of God. The NPP may rightly be said to have begun with this address.

Stendahl, Krister. "Paul Among Jews and Gentiles." In *Paul Among Jews and Gentiles and Other Essays*, 1–77. Philadelphia: Fortress, 1976.

A slightly later (1963) article in which Stendahl articulates his famous polarities—Paul did not experience a "conversion," but a "call"; he taught not "forgiveness," but "justification"; not "sin," but "weakness"; not "integrity," but "love"; that Christianity was not "unique," but "universal." Here, Stendahl works out in more detail his thesis that Paul was chiefly concerned about the implications of the Messiah's arrival for the law and for the people of God, and *not* about matters of personal salvation.

Sanders, Ed Parrish. *Paul and Palestinian Judaism: A Comparison of Patterns of Religion*. Philadelphia: Fortress, 1977.

The book that officially launched NPP scholarship into the mainstream of Pauline studies. In this massive volume, Sanders convinced most New Testament scholars that Judaism was a "religion of grace" and not a "religion of works." He furthermore launched a project of Pauline interpretation that sought to understand Paul on terms other than soteriological disagreement with Judaism. See our comments above on Schweitzer's *The Mysticism of Paul the Apostle*.

Neusner, Jacob. Review of E. P. Sanders, *Paul and Palestinian Judaism*. *History of Religions* 18 (1978): 177–91.

While appreciative of Sanders's efforts to present ancient Judaism in a more positive light than critical scholarship had hitherto attempted, Neusner argues that Sanders has failed to present Judaism as "an entire religion, parts and all . . . on [its] own merits and . . . own terms" (179). Neusner argues that Sanders has imposed the "issues of Pauline scholarship and Paul" on rabbinic Judaism and, consequently, has distorted the latter (ibid.). Neusner further charges Sanders with "prooftexting" the rabbinic sources, *viz.*, reading them without care to the differences and particularities of the respective documents quoted. For a more sustained critique, see his *Judaic Law from Jesus to the Mishnah: A Systematic Reply to Professor E. P. Sanders* (South Florida Studies in the History of Judaism 84 [Atlanta, Scholars, 1993]).

Sanders, E. P. *Paul, the Law, and the Jewish People*. Philadelphia: Fortress, 1983.

Sanders intended this work to address the "law" in Paul—an issue not thoroughly treated in his *Paul and Palestinian Judaism*. Here, Sanders exegetically defends his thesis that Paul reasons from "solution" to "plight," and that, in view of the apostle's central and coherent convictions concerning Christ and the apostle's call, Paul has left us with nonsystematized reflections on the law and man's plight with respect to the law. A final section treats the question of Paul's identity and relationship with the Jewish people.

Sanders, E. P. *Paul*. Oxford: Oxford University Press, 1991.

This small volume offers a superb introduction to Sanders's understanding of Paul's thought. For the pastor or student intimidated by the length or complexity of *Paul and Palestinian Judaism*, this book is ideal.

Sanders, E. P. Preface to *Paul and Rabbinic Judaism*, by W. D. Davies. 5th ed. Mifflintown, Pa.: Sigler Press, 1998.

One of the briefest and most incisive introductions to Sanders's thought. Written in order to introduce the most recent edition of the ground-breaking work of his mentor and colleague, W. D. Davies, Sanders's preface compares and contrasts Sanders and Davies with respect to Paul and Judaism. It also provides a brief digest of the most salient points of Sanders's proposals concerning Paul.

Beker, Johann Christiaan. *Paul the Apostle: The Triumph of God in Life and Thought.* Philadelphia: Fortress, 1980.

While not adopting the distinctive views of the NPP, Beker stands at the forefront of a number of Pauline scholars who, in the wake of Sanders's formulations, will speak of Paul's "coherence" but not his "consistency." For Beker, "the coherent center of Paul's gospel is an apocalyptic center, as modified by the Christ-event." This "center" is a "reordered field of apocalyptic images," a "symbolic expression of two basic interdependent constituents: the experiential reality of his call on the Damascus Road . . . and the traditional 'in house' apocalyptic language of the world in which he lived and thought as a Pharisaic Jew" (xvii, xviii).

Boyarin, Daniel. *A Radical Jew: Paul and the Politics of Identity.* Berkeley: University of California, 1994.

A post-NPP reading of Paul by a noted contemporary Jewish scholar. Boyarin argues that, for Paul, the "gospel" is "the constitution of all the Peoples of the world as the new Israel" (112). What defines Paul's thought is ecclesiological, not soteriological, concern. Boyarin's work evidences the ways in which the NPP has rendered Paul more palatable to modern Jewish scholarship.

Dunn, J. D. G. "The New Perspective on Paul," *Bulletin of the John Rylands University Library of Manchester* 65 (1983): 95–122. Repr. pages 299–308 in *The Romans Debate.* Edited by Karl P. Donfried. Rev. and enl. ed. Peabody, Mass.: Hendrickson, 1991. Also repr. pages 183–214 in *Jesus, Paul, and the Law: Studies in Mark and Galatians.* Louisville, Ky.: Westminster John Knox Press, 1990.

The groundbreaking essay (a published form of his 1982 Manson Memorial Lecture) in which Dunn coined the name that the movement has come to adopt. Dunn expresses appreciation for Sanders's break from Reformational categories and conclusions regarding Paul. He argues, however, that Sanders's Paul remains too anthropocentric. In this essay, Dunn lays out his sociologically informed approach to Paul by offering a new definition of the "works of the law" (i.e., as social "boundary markers") and its implications for the relationship between Paul and the Judaism of his day.

Dunn, J. D. G. "Works of the Law and the Curse of the Law (Galatians 3.10–14)," *New Testament Studies* 31 (1985): 523–42. Repr. pages 215–41 in *Jesus, Paul, and the Law: Studies in Mark and Galatians*. Louisville, Ky.: Westminster John Knox Press, 1990.

An article in which Dunn restates, expands, and defends his "works of the law" position first advanced in his 1983 article. He then applies his findings to Galatians 3:10–14 in particular (see also his commentary on Galatians below). Well worth consulting in conjunction with the previous entry. Dunn's subsequent responses to critics of this article may be found in "Yet Once More—'The Works of the Law': A Response," *Journal for the Study of the New Testament* 46 (1992): 99–117 and in his *Theology of Paul the Apostle*, 354–71.

Dunn, J. D. G. *Romans 1–8, 9–16*. Word Biblical Commentary 38A–38B. Waco, Tex.: Word, 1988.

A magisterial and comprehensive reading of Romans from the "New Perspective." This massive (lxxii + 976 pp.) work affords the reader a chance to explore an NPP reading of passages touching the "law," "works of the law," "faith," "justification," and the death of Christ. Although its format is cumbersome (separate sections devoted to "comment" and "explanation" afford temptations to repetition), a careful reading of this work would well repay the interested student of the NPP. Be forewarned—although WBC advertises itself as a repository of evangelical biblical scholarship, Dunn arrives at many conclusions that are anything but evangelical.

Dunn, J. D. G. *Jesus, Paul, and the Law: Studies in Mark and Galatians*. Louisville, Ky.: Westminster John Knox Press, 1990.

In this collection of previously published essays that have been updated and revised, Dunn addresses questions concerning Jesus and the law (chapters 1–3) and Paul and the law (chapters 4–9). Of particular interest is chapter 4 (" 'A Light to the Gentiles,' or 'The End of the Law?': The Significance of the Damascus Road Christophany for Paul"), which provides the reader appropriate background to Kim's work (below). Chapter 6 gives Dunn's analysis of the controversy at Antioch (Gal. 2), while chapters 7 and 8 provide the reader a reprint of Dunn's "New Perspective" and "Works of the Law" essays (above).

Dunn, J. D. G. *A Commentary on the Epistle to the Galatians*. Black's New Testament Commentary. London: A. C. Black/Peabody, Mass.: Hendrickson, 1993.

One of the most comprehensive readings of Galatians from the NPP by one of its mature proponents. Readers can explore how the NPP addresses the "works of the law" as well as questions of human (in)ability to keep the law (cf. Gal. 3:10–13; 5:3; 6:13). While not as thorough as his earlier work on *Romans*, it certainly merits study.

Dunn, J. D. G. *The Theology of Paul the Apostle*. Grand Rapids: Eerdmans, 1998.

Another sizable (xxxvi + 808 pp.) contribution by Dunn. Here, Dunn synthesizes Paul's thought under several topical *loci*. One of Dunn's strengths in this work is his ability to digest prior scholarship competently and clearly, and to write in an engaging style. Readers may consult here overviews of Dunn's thoughts on the "law," "salvation," and the "death of Christ" in Paul. For weaknesses and critique, be sure to consult the important and penetrating review of Dunn by Gaffin (below). Note as well the reviews of Schreiner (below) and Thielman (below).

Hays, Richard B. *Echoes of Scripture in the Letters of Paul*. New Haven: Yale, 1989.

Readings of both citations and "echoes" of Scripture in the writings of Paul, as well as an attempt to explore the hermeneutics of Paul's readings of the Old Testament. The second chapter offers an important reading of the language of "righteousness" in Romans from a standpoint sympathetic to the NPP.

Räisänen, Heikki. *Paul and the Law*. Wissenschaftliche Untersuchungen zum Neuen Testament 29. Tübingen, Germany: Mohr—Siebeck, 1983.

A devoted critic of Reformational readings of Paul, Räisänen claims to have followed Sanders's thesis with more consistency than Sanders has (albeit in a different direction than Dunn has pursued). He argues that Paul is not at all "consistent," and that Paul deliberately misrepresented Jewish soteriology as legalistic. Few have followed Räisänen's flat and uncharitable readings of Paul, but he remains an important NPP proponent. For representative criticisms, consult the titles by Westerholm (above), Schreiner (below), Thielman (below), and Moo (below).

Wright, N. T. *The Climax of the Covenant: Christ and the Law in Pauline Theology.* Philadelphia: Fortress, 1991.

> A collection of unrelated essays by Wright on a number of passages in Paul, centering on the topics of "Christ" and the "law." Those who are interested in Wright's earlier work will have interest in this work. A more extended version of his argument (in his "Romans" commentary) that *peri hamartias* (Rom. 8:3) should be translated "for a sin offering" may be found in chapter 11 of this work. Readers may also find treatments of Galatians 3:10–14 (chapter 7) and Romans 7 (chapter 10), an early overview of Romans 9–11 (chapter 13), and Wright's views on "The Nature of Pauline Theology" (chapter 14).

Wright, N. T. "Romans and the Theology of Paul." In *Pauline Theology,* vol. 3, edited by David M. Hay and E. Elizabeth Johnson, 30–67. Minneapolis: Augsburg Fortress, 1991.

> An early attempt of Wright to offer a comprehensive outline of the epistle to the Romans. It helpfully and concisely provides the reader with Wright's understanding of the main themes and concerns of this letter. Wright's recourse to the narrative of "sin–exile–restoration" as underlying this epistle anticipates later and more detailed efforts to discern the "narrative sequence" informing Pauline thought. Includes a valuable and not uncritical response by Richard Hays.

Wright, N. T. "On Becoming the Righteousness of God: 2 Corinthians 5:21." In *Pauline Theology,* vol. 2, edited by David M. Hay, 200–208. Minneapolis: Augsburg Fortress, 1993.

> An article on a verse that has historically been understood as a *locus classicus* for double imputation in justification. Examining the second half of the phrase, Wright concludes that the verse means that the apostle "has become, by the Spirit, the incarnation of the covenant faithfulness of God" (206), a view argued again in *What Saint Paul Really Said* (below).

Wright, N. T. "The Law in Romans 2." In *Paul and the Mosaic Law: The Third Durham–Tübingen Research Symposium on Earliest Christianity and Judaism,* edited by J. D. G. Dunn, 130–50. Tübingen, Germany: Mohr-Siebeck, 1996/Grand Rapids: Eerdmans, 2001.

An important NPP study of Romans 2 wherein Wright argues (1) that the individuals of 2:25–29 *and* 2:13–14 are Gentile Christians, (2) that the "keeping of the law" of 2:25–29 refers not to "achievement" or "ethics," but to "status," (3) that in 2:17–24, Paul is indicting Israel as a nation, not individual Israelites, and (4) that we are to understand a narrative of sin–exile–restoration to lie beneath Romans 2.

Wright, N. T. *The New Testament and the People of God: Christian Origins and the Question of God*. Vol. 1. Philadelphia: Fortress, 1996.

The first installment of N. T. Wright's projected multivolume New Testament theology. He argues for "critical realism," *viz.*, an epistemology wherein narrative (and not proposition) is fundamental to human thought. Wright argues at length here that early Christians inherited from Second Temple Judaism a narrative and a worldview that were reconfigured around the person and work of Jesus.

Wright, N. T. *What Saint Paul Really Said: Was Paul of Tarsus the Real Founder of Christianity?* Grand Rapids: Eerdmans, 1997.

At present, the fullest topical treatment of Paul that Wright has offered the reading public. Although it is a popular-level treatment, this book addresses such issues as "righteousness," "the righteousness of God," and "justification." It is here that the reader is most likely to discern the contrasts between Wright's project and the accomplishments of the Reformation, as well as to learn what Wright perceives to be the practical outworking of his reading of Paul.

Wright, N. T. "New Exodus, New Inheritance: The Narrative Structure of Romans 3–8." In *Romans and the People of God: Essays in Honor of Gordon D. Fee on the Occasion of His 65th Birthday*, edited by Sven K. Soderlund and N. T. Wright, 26–35. Grand Rapids: Eerdmans, 1999.

Another (and later) effort to articulate Wright's conception of the narrative organization and cohesion of a significant portion of Romans. Here, Wright argues that the Exodus narrative, as adopted and transformed by Paul, is evident at such places as Romans 5:12–21 (where Paul resolves the problem of Adam and Israel by telling the story of the "New Israel," of Christ), Romans 6 (where "baptism" is said to be a reading of the Red Sea crossing), and Romans 7:1–8:11 (a passage centered on the reception of the law at Sinai). Thus, it provides a good example of the program announced in *The New Testament and the People of God*.

Wright, N. T. "Romans." In *New Interpreter's Bible: Acts–First Corinthians*, vol. 10, edited by Leander E. Keck. Nashville: Abingdon, 2002.

> By far, Wright's lengthiest exegetical contribution to date. Although briefer than Dunn's *Romans* commentary, it ranks with Dunn's *Romans* as an important NPP reading of this letter. Readers will observe many similarities between Dunn's and Wright's exegetical conclusions. Wright affords the student the opportunity to explore his views on the "law," "works of the law," "faith," "justification," and the death of Christ as these terms surface in Romans. Wright is also concerned explicitly to address the practical and pastoral implications of his revisionary readings of Romans for the church.

Critiques of the New Perspective(s) on Paul

The following are published critiques of the NPP. (While I have intentionally restricted myself to works that have gone to press, I by no means wish to intimate that there are not fine criticisms available on the Internet.) I have listed them (for the most part) chronologically, with same-year entries ordered alphabetically. Not all the works listed below are identical in their criticisms of the NPP: some are more appreciative of the NPP than others. Nor are all of these works supportive of all the soteriological doctrines of the magisterial Reformation. I have attempted to note where appropriate the extent to which these works are critical of the NPP and are supportive of confessional Protestantism.

Moo, D. J. " 'Law,' 'Works of the Law,' and Legalism in Paul," *Westminster Theological Journal* 45 (1983): 90–100.

> While conceding (with Westerholm) that "*nomos*" in Paul ordinarily means the Jewish Torah, Moo in this article upholds (also with Westerholm) the idea that "works of the law" clearly embrace human activity, *viz.*, the activity required by the Mosaic Law. For a more thorough and recent statement of Moo on this point, be sure to consult his *Romans* commentary (below).

Moo, D. J. Reviews of Heikki Räisänen, *Paul and the Law* and E. P. Sanders, *Paul, the Law and the Jewish People. Trinity Journal* 5 (1984): 92–99.

This review (read with Westerholm) will give the reader both awareness of the place of Räisänen in the NPP discussions as well as helpful and concise criticisms of his project.

Schreiner, Thomas. "Is Perfect Obedience to the Law Possible? A Re-Examination of Gal 3:10," *Journal of the Evangelical Theological Society* 27 (1984): 151–60.

Unlike his 1985 article (which concentrates on Sanders and on a variety of passages), Schreiner here directs his attention to Galatians 3:10 and the efforts of recent scholars (most notably Daniel Fuller) to argue that one ought not supply an implied premise ("no man is able perfectly to observe the Law") between the two halves of Galatians 3:10. Schreiner defends here the "implied premise" view. Compare also chapter 2 ("Why the Works of the Law Cannot Save") of *The Law and Its Fulfillment* (below).

Gundry, Robert H. "Grace, Works, and Staying Saved in Paul," *Biblica* 66 (1985): 1–38.

An important and early critique of Sanders's *Paul and Palestinian Judaism* and *Paul, the Law, and the Jewish People*. Gundry succeeds in refuting Sanders's thesis that Paul and Judaism were in agreement on the doctrines of grace and works, and in ably defending the traditional view that "Palestinian Judaism [was] centered on works-righteousness and . . . Paul's theology [was] centered on grace" (6). This article well repays the student's careful study.

Schreiner, Thomas. "Paul and Perfect Obedience to the Law: An Evaluation of the View of E. P. Sanders," *Westminster Theological Journal* (1985): 245–78.

Schreiner both expounds Sanders's view that "Paul did *not* teach that it was impossible to keep the law perfectly" (246), and engages Sanders in an extensive exegetical critique. Schreiner's review may be read profitably alongside chapter 2 ("Why the Works of the Law Cannot Save") of *The Law and Its Fulfillment* (below).

Thielman, Frank. *From Plight to Solution: A Jewish Framework to Understanding Paul's View of the Law in Galatians and Romans.* Supplements to *Novum Testamentum* 61. Leiden: Brill, 1989.

A revised form of the author's dissertation, this work attempts to counter Sanders's argument that Paul reasoned from "solution to plight." Thielman contends that Paul reasoned from "plight to solution," and that this movement parallels a broader Jewish pattern of expecting deliverance from foreign rulers and transgressions of the law. See also his more comprehensive *Paul and the Law* (below).

Schreiner, Thomas. "Works of the Law in Paul," *Novum Testamentum* 33 (1991): 217–44.

A post-NPP evaluation of a Pauline phrase ("works of the law") much debated within NPP scholarship. This article is useful in its collocation of the relevant passages and their discussion within recent scholarship. Readers will find a comparable discussion in *The Law and Its Fulfillment* (below).

Schreiner, Thomas. "Israel's Failure to Attain Righteousness in Romans 9:30–10:3," *Trinity Journal* 12 (1991): 209–20.

Critics of the NPP have long observed that this passage presents problems for the view that Paul was not faulting Israel for striving for a righteousness of law observance. Readers may also find Schreiner's treatment of this passage (and his interaction with T. David Gordon, "Why Israel Did Not Obtain Torah-Righteousness: A Translation Note on Rom 9:32," *WTJ* 54 [1992]: 163–66) at *The Law and Its Fulfillment*, 104ff.

Silva, Moisés. "The Law and Christianity: Dunn's New Synthesis," *Westminster Theological Journal* 53 (1991): 339–53.

A critical overview of Dunn's published opinion (through 1990) concerning the relationship of Paul and the law (above). In the second part of this review article (347–53), Silva gives a brief but useful analysis and critique of the theses of both Sanders and Dunn. A very clear and distilled introduction to the key issues at stake in the debate.

Schreiner, Thomas. "Did Paul Believe in Justification by Works? Another Look at Romans 2," *Bulletin of Biblical Research* 3 (1993): 131–55.

Romans 2 has played an important role in NPP exegesis of Paul's view of the law—whether to "prove" that Paul had contradictory views of the law (Sanders, Räisänen) or that Paul believed in some form of justification grounded on human obedience (Dunn, Wright). Here Schreiner gives a survey of the exegetical options and concludes that Paul's statements regarding the law and justification in Romans 2 do not contradict the Reformational doctrine of justification. See also his parallel discussion in chapter 7 ("Did Paul Teach Justification by Works?") of *The Law and Its Fulfillment*.

Schreiner, Thomas R. "Paul's View of the Law in Romans 10:4–5," *Westminster Theological Journal* 55 (1993): 113–35.

Romans 10:4–5 has played an important role in the discussions concerning Paul and the law: in what sense is Christ the "end" (Greek *"telos"*) of the law? What is the "righteousness which is based on the Law" of which "Moses" speaks? Notice also Schreiner's treatment of this passage at *The Law and Its Fulfillment*, 104ff.

Schreiner, Thomas. *The Law and Its Fulfillment: A Pauline Theology of Law*. Grand Rapids: Baker, 1993.

A work that synthesizes (but by no means simply reproduces) a decade of Schreiner's scholarship on the law. A helpful overview of the issues raised by NPP scholarship with a strong exegetical defense of many of the traditional positions and critical interaction with representative NPP works. This work provides a good complement to Thielman, *Paul and the Law*. Reformed Protestants will observe that Schreiner does not believe that Paul taught what has come to be known as the "third use" of the law.

Seifrid, Mark A. "Blind Alleys in the Controversy over the Paul of History," *Tyndale Bulletin* 45 (1994): 73–95.

One of Seifrid's earlier contributions to the criticism of the NPP. Seifrid critiques in this piece (1) Dunn's distinctive view of the "works of the law" in Paul and (2) Wright's argument that Paul (and other early Christians) inherited a Jewish narrative of "sin–exile–restoration." Because of the paucity of criticisms focusing on the latter issue, this article is an especially valuable one.

Thielman, Frank. *Paul and the Law: A Contextual Approach*. Downers Grove, Ill.: InterVarsity, 1994.

An overview of recent Pauline scholarship (concentrating on the contributions of NPP proponents) on the subject of the law in Paul. The first chapter is a concise overview of Pauline scholarship from Aquinas through Westerholm. The second chapter addresses the Jewish context in which Paul wrote (here the reader will see certain sympathies with Wright's portrait of Judaism). The remaining chapters address the Pauline letters *seriatim* on the question of the law. Thielman is a competent scholar who raises many (but by no means all) important objections against the findings of NPP scholarship. This book is a helpful introduction to the issues at hand.

Moo, Douglas. *The Epistle to the Romans*. New International Commentary on the New Testament. Grand Rapids: Eerdmans, 1996.

While not a "critique" of the NPP per se, Moo's recent commentary on Romans not only provides the reader with extended exegetical interaction with NPP readings of this letter, but also generally defends traditional readings of Romans. Its length (xvii + 1,012 pages) and its bibliographical thoroughness will commend this important work to the interested student.

Schreiner, Thomas. *Romans*. Exegetical Commentary on the New Testament. Grand Rapids: Baker, 1998.

This massive (xxi + 919 pages) commentary complements Moo's commentary on Romans as a (generally) traditional exegetical response to NPP readings of Paul (although Moo's work is more comprehensive bibliographically). Readers should be aware of Schreiner's note in his *Paul, Apostle of God's Glory in Christ* (p. 192 n.2) that he has subsequently departed from his view expressed in this commentary (pp. 63–71) that "righteousness" in Paul is transformative. When read with Moo, the student will have as thorough an exegetical response (from the epistle to the Romans) to the NPP as one could desire.

Thielman, Frank. "Paul as Jewish Christian Theologian: The Theology of Paul in the Magnum Opus of James D. G. Dunn," *Perspectives in Religious Studies* 25 (1998): 381–87.

A review of Dunn's sizable Pauline theology by the author of *From Plight to Solution* and *Paul and the Law*. Thielman is a critic of the NPP on a number of points, but would be more appreciative of NPP scholarship than other evangelical critics.

Schreiner, Thomas. Review of James D. G. Dunn, *The Theology of Paul the Apostle*. *Trinity Journal* 20 (1999): 95–100.

An appreciative yet not uncritical survey of Dunn's most thorough treatment of Paul to date. Points of Schreiner's criticism include Dunn's conception of Paul's Christology, the "works of the law," justification in Paul, the death of Christ in Paul, and Paul's ecclesiology and conception of the sacraments.

Smith, Robert. "Justification in 'the New Perspective on Paul,' " *Reformed Theological Review* 58 (1999): 16–30.

A brief overview of what NPP proponents (Sanders, Dunn, and Wright) have taught concerning justification in Paul. Smith, sympathetic to the Reformational doctrine, also outlines the main points of difference between the "Reformation paradigm" and the NPP.

Smith, Robert. "A Critique of the 'New Perspective' on Justification," *Reformed Theological Review* 58 (1999): 98–113.

The companion piece to the above article. Smith, after outlining points of appreciation, offers one of the most penetrating and thoroughgoing critiques of the NPP that I have encountered in such a small space. I would urge interested readers to make the study of these articles a priority.

Carson, D. A., Peter T. O'Brien, and Mark A. Seifrid, eds. *Justification and Variegated Nomism*. Vol. 1, *The Complexities of Second Temple Judaism*. Grand Rapids: Baker, 2001.

A post-Sanders survey of Second Temple literature that considers the viability of Sanders's "covenantal nomism" thesis in the face of more specialized study of the evidence than Sanders offered in *Paul and Palestinian Judaism*. The authors, who represent a variety of academic and theological traditions, arrive at different conclusions—conclusions that Carson helpfully synthesizes in a concluding chapter. In fairness, it should be mentioned that some critics have argued that Carson's conclusions are not supported by the findings of the individual contributors in the volume. Carson nevertheless argues compellingly in this chapter that the findings of the scholars in this volume as a whole do not sustain Sanders's thesis.

Gaffin, Richard B. "Paul the Theologian," *Westminster Theological Journal* 62 (2000): 121–41.

Authored by the long-standing professor of biblical and systematic theology at Westminster Theological Seminary (Philadelphia), this review essay of Wright's *What Saint Paul Really Said* (above) and Dunn's *Theology of Paul the Apostle* (above) gives brief and well-digested overviews of both books. Another strength of this review is the precision and depth of its critique of these two writers. Gaffin addresses necessary theological issues (revelation, Adamic imputation, and Christology, for example) that few other critics of the NPP have broached in print.

Seifrid, Mark A. *Christ Our Righteousness: Paul's Theology of Justi-fication.* Leicester: Apollos/Downers Grove, Ill.: InterVarsity, 2000.

> A substantial work mounting critical exegetical interaction with the NPP on such diverse topics as "conversion," the "righteousness of God," the "law," and "justification by faith." Seifrid will disappoint the con-fessional Protestant in at least two of his positions: (1) that faith is not exclusively receptive in the act of justification, and (2) his doubts con-cerning the adequacy of the language of imputation in regards to justi-fication. Important also in this regard is Seifrid's " 'The Gift of Salvation': Its Failure to Address the Crux of Justification," *Journal of the Evan-gelical Theological Society* 42 (1999): 679–88.

Seifrid, Mark A. "The New Perspective on Paul and Its Problems," *Themelios* 25 (2000): 4–18.

> In a brief but illuminating article, Seifrid offers the reader several points of criticism with respect to the NPP. He problematizes Sanders's "covenantal nomism" as a descriptive term of first-century Judaism; nicely contrasts and defends the traditional soteriological readings of Paul against the communitarian readings of the NPP; and raises doubts concerning Wright's thesis of the "continuing exile" in first-century Jew-ish thought. Readers will also be introduced to Seifrid's own view of justification, discussed at length in his book *Christ Our Righteousness* (above).

Stuhlmacher, Peter. *Revisiting Paul's Doctrine of Justification—With an Essay by Donald A. Hagner.* Downers Grove, Ill.: InterVar-sity: 2001.

> A brief book containing Stuhlmacher's 2000 Biblical Studies Lectures at Beeson Divinity School, Birmingham, Alabama, with Hagner's essay ("Paul and Judaism: Testing the New Perspective") appended. Stuhlmacher argues that the NPP has mistakenly read Paul's doctrine of justification and the "works of the law," mounting a brief, incom-plete critique. Stuhlmacher's positive exposition of "justification," how-ever, evidences the influence of Käsemann, and lacks the precision that Reformed Protestants might wish to find. Hagner's appended essay, while one may disagree with his conclusions, is outstanding in its pres-entation of the relevant issues and its updated bibliography.

Talbert, Charles H. "Paul, Judaism, and the Revisionists," *Catholic Biblical Quarterly* 63 (2001): 1–22.

Delivered as the 2000 Presidential Address of the Catholic Biblical Association, this article represents an academic and critical post-NPP assessment of Paul and his relationship to Judaism. While Talbert concludes that neither the Reformers nor the NPP has adequately captured this relationship, he nevertheless concedes that "Paul's theological struggle is between divine grace and human self-sufficiency" and that "some ancient Jews were legalists" (15). Talbert's Pauline soteriology, unfortunately, is decidedly sympathetic to Roman Catholic readings of Paul, a fact that, for confessional Protestants, compromises his conception of the differences between Paul and ancient Judaism.

Gathercole, Simon. *Where Is Boasting? Early Jewish Soteriology and Paul's Response in Romans 1–5*. Grand Rapids: Eerdmans, 2002.

A critique of Sanders's assessment of the Second Temple literature by a young scholar. Gathercole focuses on the language of "boasting" in the rabbinic literature and in the Pauline letters. He concludes that this body of evidence demonstrates (*pace* Sanders) that Paul and rabbinic Judaism materially differed on the question of whether man has the ability to render obedience to the law.

Kim, Seyoon. *Paul and the New Perspective: Second Thoughts on the Origins of Paul's Gospel*. Grand Rapids: Eerdmans, 2002.

A recent critique of the NPP by the author of *The Origin of Paul's Gospel*. Valuable to the reader is its concentration on Dunn's readings of Paul. Kim argues, against Dunn, that Paul's encounter with Christ on the Damascus Road is not only the origin of Paul's *call*, but also the origin of his doctrine of *justification*. Kim also argues that NPP formulations of the "works of the law" are mistaken and that, *contra* NPP constructions of Judaism, by this term Paul affirms first-century Judaism to be a "covenantal nomism with an element of works-righteousness" (83–84).

Piper, John. *Counted Righteous in Christ: Should We Abandon the Imputation of Christ's Righteousness?* Wheaton, Ill.: Crossway, 2002.

A valuable exegetical and theological defense (against Robert Gundry) of the doctrines both of Adamic imputation and of the imputation of Christ's righteousness to the believer in justification. In the wake of some critiques of the NPP that are defective on this latter point (e.g., Stuhlmacher, Seifrid, and the early Schreiner), Piper's contribution is most welcome to friends and defenders of these vital doctrines.

Schreiner, Thomas. *Paul, Apostle of God's Glory in Christ: A Pauline Theology*. Downers Grove, Ill.: InterVarsity/Leicester: Apollos, 2002.

One of the few recent Pauline theologies authored by an evangelical scholar. Schreiner's sizable (504 pp.) work gives the reader sustained interaction with the NPP in the context of a positive presentation of Paul's thought. While Schreiner in this work now maintains that "righteousness" in Paul is forensic in nature (see the comments on his *Romans* commentary above), he still holds that Paul did not teach what has become known as the "third use" of the law. Readers might also observe that Schreiner does not appear to understand faith to be entirely receptive in justification (see pp. 209–11) nor to embrace traditional Reformed views of Adamic imputation (see p. 146ff.). These comments notwithstanding, this work is well worth the study of an interested student of the NPP.

Carson, D. A. "Atonement in Romans 3:21–26." In *The Glory of the Atonement: Biblical, Historical, and Practical Perspectives. Essays in Honor of Roger Nicole*, edited by Charles E. Hill and Frank A. James III, 119–39. Downers Grove, Ill.: InterVarsity, 2004.

Carson gives the reader an accessible and well-digested discussion of a passage critical to NPP discussions. Interacting with NPP readings of Romans 3:21–26, Carson offers a concise defense of traditional readings of "righteousness," "faith," and "propitiation." He also persuasively positions his reading of Romans 3:21-26 within the larger argument of Romans 1-3.

Carson, D. A. "The Vindication of Imputation: On Fields of Discourse and Semantic Fields." In *Justification: What's at Stake in the Current Debates*, edited by Mark Husbands and Daniel J. Treier, 46–78. Downers Grove, Ill.: InterVarsity, 2004.

This essay is a careful and measured survey of the biblical and theological issues touching on the imputation of Christ's righteousness to the believer. Although Carson does not primarily engage NPP readings in this essay, the passages he considers have played a crucial role in NPP discussions. Carson offers readings of Romans 3:27–31; 4:4–5, 6–8; 1 Corinthians 1:30; and 2 Corinthians 5:19–21 in which he defends the traditional doctrine of imputation as Pauline.

Carson, D. A., Peter T. O'Brien, and Mark A. Seifrid, eds. *Justifica-tion and Variegated Nomism*. Vol. 2, *The Paradoxes of Paul*. Grand Rapids: Baker, 2004.

Following the 2001 companion volume that addressed Second Temple Judaism, this volume concentrates on the biblical and theological issues touching the issues that the NPP have raised concerning the interpreta-tion of Paul. Among the many fine essays in this volume are thorough exegetical studies of Romans 1:18–3:20 (Seifrid); 3:21–4:25 (Gather-cole); 5–11 (Moo); and a treatment of Paul's language of faith and works in Galatians (M. Silva). O'Brien argues in two separate essays that Paul was not a covenantal nomist, and that Paul was called *and* converted at the Damascus Road. Yarbrough and Carson attempt positively to define Paul's relationship to the Old Covenant. T. George offers a con-temporary defense of the Reformation's (and particularly Luther's) read-ing of the apostle Paul. Each student of the NPP should make a careful reading of this volume a priority.

Notes

Chapter 1: "How the Mighty Have Fallen": From Luther to Schweitzer

1. The following discussion is indebted to Richard Muller, "Biblical Interpretation in the 16th & 17th Centuries," in *Historical Handbook of Major Biblical Interpreters*, ed. Donald McKim (Downers Grove, Ill.: InterVarsity, 1998), 123–51.

2. Muller, "Biblical Interpretation," 124.

3. Quoted in W. G. Kümmel, *The New Testament: The History of the Investigation of Its Problems* (Nashville: Abingdon, 1972), 111.

4. Muller, "Biblical Interpretation," 124.

5. Ibid.

6. The following discussion is indebted to Scott J. Hafemann, "Paul and His Interpreters," in *Dictionary of Paul and His Letters*, ed. Gerald Hawthorne and Ralph Martin (Downers Grove, Ill.: InterVarsity, 1993), 666–79, and to the unpublished lectures of Richard B. Gaffin addressing the history of Pauline interpretation.

7. Hafemann, "Paul and His Interpreters," 666.

8. F. C. Baur, "The Christ-party in the Corinthian Church, the Conflict Between Petrine and Pauline Christianity in the Early Church, the Apostle Peter in Rome," *Tübinger Zeitschrift für Theologie* 4 (1831): 61–206.

9. Hafemann, "Paul and His Interpreters," 667.

10. Ibid.

11. Ibid.

12. Ibid.

13. Ibid.

14. Ibid., 668.

15. I owe these questions to Hafemann, ibid.

16. Herman Ridderbos, *Paul: An Outline of His Theology*, trans. J. R. DeWitt (Grand Rapids: Eerdmans, 1975), 16.

17. Hafemann, "Paul and His Interpreters," 668. Lightfoot's essay may be found in *St. Paul's Epistle to the Galatians: A Revised Text with Introduction, Notes, and Dissertations*, 9th ed. (London: Macmillan, 1887), 292–374.

18. Hafemann, "Paul and His Interpreters," 668–69.

19. The following discussion is indebted to the analysis both of Gaffin's unpublished lectures on the history of Pauline interpretation and of Ridderbos, *Paul*.

20. Ridderbos, *Paul*, 17–18.

21. Ibid., 19. Ridderbos in these words is summarizing Otto Pfleiderer's conception of Paul.

22. Richard B. Gaffin, Unpublished Lectures on Acts and the Pauline Epistles (Spring 1997).

23. Ridderbos, *Paul*, 18.

24. Gaffin, Lectures on Acts and the Pauline Epistles.

25. Quoted in Kümmel, *The New Testament*, 193.

26. Ridderbos, *Paul*, 20.

27. Wilhelm Bousset, *Kyrios Christos: A History of the Belief in Christ from the Beginnings of Christianity to Irenaeus*, trans. John E. Steely (Nashville: Abingdon, 1970); Richard Reitzenstein, *Hellenistic Mystery-Religions: Their Basic Ideas and Significance*, trans. John E. Steely (Pittsburgh: Pickwick Press, 1978).

28. Ridderbos, *Paul*, 23.

29. Quoted in Kümmel, *The New Testament*, 274–75.

30. Kümmel, *The New Testament*, 188.

31. Albert Schweitzer, *Paul and His Interpreters: A Critical History*, trans. William Montgomery (London: Adam & Charles Black, 1956); *The Mysticism of Paul the Apostle*, trans. William Montgomery (New York: Holt, 1931).

32. From *Paul and His Interpreters*, quoted in Kümmel, *The New Testament*, 243.

33. Both sacraments derived strictly from Jewish eschatological roots. For Schweitzer's argument of this point, see chapter 11 of *The Mysticism of Paul the Apostle*.

34. Ibid., 261.

35. Ibid., 262.

36. Ibid.

37. Ibid., 275.

38. Ibid., 286–87.

39. Ibid., 272.

40. Ibid., 225.

41. Ibid.

Chapter 2: Into the Twentieth Century: Bultmann, Davies, and Käsemann

1. Rudolf Bultmann, *Theology of the New Testament*, trans. Kendrick Grobel, 2 vols. (New York: Scribner, 1951, 1955).

2. W. G. Kümmel, *The New Testament: The History of the Investigation of Its Problems* (Nashville: Abingdon, 1972), 350.

3. Bultmann, *Theology of the New Testament*, 1:187.

4. Ibid., 1:189.

5. Ibid., 1:124.

6. Ed Parrish Sanders, *Paul and Palestinian Judaism: A Comparison of Patterns of Religion* (Philadelphia: Fortress, 1977), 39, 47.

7. For which, see ibid., 44–46.

8. Bultmann, *Primitive Christianity*, 68, quoted in Sanders, *Paul and Palestinian Judaism*, 45.

9. Bultmann, *Primitive Christianity*, 69, quoted in Sanders, *Paul and Palestinian Judaism*, 45.

10. Scott J. Hafemann, "Paul and His Interpreters," in *Dictionary of Paul and His Letters*, ed. Gerald Hawthorne and Ralph Martin (Downers Grove, Ill.: InterVarsity, 1993), 676.

11. Bultmann, *Theology of the New Testament*, 1:279–80.

12. Stephen Westerholm, *Israel's Law and the Church's Faith: Paul and His Recent Interpreters* (Grand Rapids: Eerdmans, 1988), 74–75.

13. E. P. Sanders, Preface to W. D. Davies, *Paul and Rabbinic Judaism*, 5th ed. (Mifflintown, Pa.: Sigler Press, 1998).

14. W. D. Davies, *Paul and Rabbinic Judaism: Some Rabbinic Elements in Pauline Theology*, 2d ed. (New York and Evanston: Harper and Row, 1957), xvii.

15. Bultmann, *Theology of the New Testament*, 1:264.

16. Ibid., 15.

17. Ibid., 223. These and the following quotations have been drawn from Sanders's preface.

18. Ibid., 222.

19. Ibid., 223.

20. Ibid.

21. Ibid., 69ff.

22. Ibid., 74.

23. Ibid., 73.

24. Ibid.

25. Sanders, *Paul and Palestinian Judaism*, 435. In what follows, I am indebted to Sanders's analysis.

26. Ernst Käsemann, "Justification and Salvation History in the Epistle to the Romans," in *Perspectives on Paul* (Philadelphia: Fortress, 1971), 60–78.

27. Ibid., 76.

28. Ibid., 64.

29. Ernst Käsemann, "The Righteousness of God in Paul," in *New Testament Questions of Today* (Philadelphia: Fortress, 1969).

30. Ibid., 180.

31. Ibid., 170 *et passim*.

32. Ibid., 172ff.

33. Ibid., 174.

34. Ibid., 176.

35. Ibid.

36. Ibid., 180. We may observe parenthetically that, for Käsemann, Paul does not adopt the covenant of the Old Testament. Paul, rather, conceives of a covenant with the whole creation, to which God pledges his faithfulness in Christ. Many proponents of the NPP will differ with Käsemann on this point.

37. Ernst Käsemann, "The Faith of Abraham in Romans 4," in *Perspectives on Paul*, 74.

Chapter 3: Enter the New Perspective: Krister Stendahl

1. "The Apostle Paul and the Introspective Conscience of the West," in *Paul Among Jews and Gentiles and Other Essays* (Philadelphia: Fortress, 1976), 78–96; "Paul Among Jews and Gentiles," in *Paul Among Jews and Gentiles and Other Essays* (Philadelphia: Fortress, 1976), 1–77.

2. Stendahl, "The Apostle Paul and the Introspective Conscience of the West," 82ff.

3. Ibid., 86.

4. Ibid., 95.

5. Ibid., 85.

6. Ibid., 87.

7. Ibid., 87–88.

8. Ibid., 85.

9. Ibid., 83.

10. Ibid., 84.

11. Ibid.

12. Ibid., 86.

13. Stendahl, "Paul Among Jews and Gentiles," 23.

14. Ibid., 28.

15. Ibid., 3.

16. Ibid., 4.

17. Ibid., 7–22.

18. Ibid., 9.

19. Ibid., 8.

20. Ibid., 7.

21. Ibid., 8.

22. Ibid., 8–9.

23. Ibid., 12–13.

24. Ibid., 13.

25. Ibid.

26. "For we must all appear before the judgment seat of Christ, so that each one may be recompensed for his deeds in the body, according to what he has done, whether good or bad. Therefore, knowing the fear of the Lord, we persuade men, but we are made manifest to God; and I hope that we are made manifest also in your consciences."

27. Stendahl, "Paul Among Jews and Gentiles," 14.

28. "Let a man regard us in this manner, as servants of Christ and stewards of the mysteries of God. In this case, moreover, it is required of stewards that one be found trustworthy. But to me it is a very small thing that I may be examined by you, or by any human court; in fact, I do not even examine myself. For I am conscious of nothing against myself, yet I am not by this acquitted; but the one who examines me is the Lord. Therefore do not go on passing judgment before the time, but wait until the Lord comes who will both bring to light the things hidden in the darkness and disclose the motives of men's hearts; and then each man's praise will come to him from God."

29. Stendahl, "Paul Among Jews and Gentiles," 15.

30. Ibid., 14.

31. Ibid.
32. Ibid., 23–40.
33. Ibid., 24–25.
34. Ibid., 25.
35. Ibid., 23–24.
36. Ibid., 24–25. The fact that at Romans 4:9 Paul quotes Genesis 15:6 (another Old Testament passage) in order to introduce a topic ("righteousness") that Stendahl correctly understands to be central to Paul's argument in Romans 4 belies Stendahl's inconsistency in stressing that the quotation of Psalm 32 at Romans 4:7 is incidental to the argument and therefore may be dismissed.
37. Stendahl, "Paul Among Jews and Gentiles," 24.
38. Ibid., 27.
39. Ibid.
40. "The real center of gravity in Romans is found in chapters 9–11, in the section about the relation between Jews and Gentiles, the mystery of which had been revealed to Paul, Romans 11:25 and Galatians 1:12; cf. Romans 16:25" (ibid., 28).
41. Ibid., 29.
42. Ibid., 30.
43. Ibid., 34.
44. Ibid., 31.
45. Ibid.
46. Ibid., 33.
47. Ibid., 40–52.
48. Ibid., 52.
49. Ibid., 44.
50. Ibid., 50–51.
51. Ibid., 47ff.
52. Ibid., 52–67.
53. Ibid., 66.
54. Ibid., 67.
55. Ibid., 66.
56. Ibid., 29.
57. Ibid., 34.

Chapter 4: *Ad Fontes*?: E. P. Sanders on Judaism

1. E. P. Sanders, *Paul and Palestinian Judaism: A Comparison of Patterns of Religion* (Philadelphia: Fortress, 1977).
2. E. P. Sanders, *Paul, the Law, and the Jewish People* (Philadelphia: Fortress, 1983).
3. E. P. Sanders, *Judaism: Practice and Belief 63 B.C.E.–66 C.E.* (London: S.C.M. Press/Philadelphia: Trinity Press International, 1992).
4. Wilhelm Bousset, *Die Religion des Judentums im Neutestamentlichen Zeitalter* (Berlin: 1903); H. Strack and P. Billerbeck, *Kommentar zum Neuen Testament aus Talmud und Midrasch*, 4 vols. (Munich: C. H. Beck, 1922–28); Joachim Jeremias,

Jerusalem in the Time of Jesus, translated from the 3d German ed. (Philadelphia: Fortress, 1969); Emil Schürer, *The History of the Jewish People in the Time of Jesus Christ* (1885–1891); Emil Schürer, *The History of the Jewish People in the Time of Jesus Christ,* rev. and ed. Geza Vermes, Fergus Millar, and Martin Goodman, 3 vols. (Edinburgh: T & T Clark, 1973–1987).

    5. Sanders, *Paul and Palestinian Judaism,* 12.

    6. Ibid., 69.

    7. Ibid., 69–70.

    8. *The Rabbinic Traditions about the Pharisees Before 70,* 3 vols. (Leiden, The Netherlands: Brill, 1971).

    9. Sanders, *Paul and Palestinian Judaism,* 63.

    10. Ibid., 422.

    11. Ibid., 87.

    12. Ibid., 88ff.

    13. Ibid., 87.

    14. Ibid., 88–89, citing *Mekilta Bachodesh.*

    15. Ibid., 87.

    16. Ibid., 88, citing *Sifre Deuteronomy* 343.

    17. Ibid., 87.

    18. Ibid., 89, citing *Mek. Pischa 5* (on Ex. 12:6).

    19. Ibid., 92, citing *Sifre Deuteronomy* 311.

    20. Ibid., 88.

    21. Ibid., 99, citing *Mek.* of R. Simeon b. Yohai (on Ex. 6:2).

    22. Ibid., 91.

    23. Ibid., 235.

    24. Ibid., 99.

    25. Ibid., 101.

    26. Ibid., 98.

    27. Ibid., 107.

    28. Ibid., 107–16.

    29. Ibid., 114–15.

    30. Ibid., 133, citing *Makkoth* 3.15.

    31. Ibid., 133, referencing *Sifra Chobah* 12.10 (Lev. 5:10).

    32. Ibid., 124.

    33. Ibid.

    34. Ibid., 129, citing *Kiddushin* 1.10a.

    35. Ibid., citing *T. Kiddushin* 1.13.

    36. Ibid., 130, citing *T. Kiddushin* 1.14.

    37. Ibid.

    38. Ibid.

    39. Ibid., 131.

    40. Ibid., citing *P. Kiddushin* 61d (1.10).

    41. Ibid., 132.

    42. Ibid.

    43. Ibid., 143.

44. Ibid., 134.
45. Ibid., 137.
46. Ibid., 138.
47. Ibid., 139, cited from Finkelstein, *Akiba*, 186.
48. Ibid.
49. Ibid., 139, 141.
50. Ibid., 143.
51. Ibid., 142, citing *T. Sanhedrin* 13.3.
52. Ibid., 147.
53. Ibid., 157.
54. Ibid., 142, citing *Sifre Deueronomy*. 307.
55. Ibid., 160.
56. Ibid., 158–59, citing *Mek. Bachodesh* 7.
57. Ibid., 159, citing *T. Yom Ha-Kippurim* 4.5.
58. Ibid., 174.
59. Ibid., 176.
60. Ibid., 178.
61. Ibid., 158, citing *Mek. Bachodesh* 7.
62. Ibid.
63. Ibid., 167.
64. Ibid., 158–59, citing *Mek. Bachodesh* 7.
65. Ibid.
66. Ibid., 168, citing *Mek. Mishpatim* 9.
67. Ibid., 170.
68. Ibid., 172.
69. Ibid., 158, citing *Mek. Bachodesh* 7.
70. Ibid.
71. Ibid., 174.
72. For Sanders's evidence, see ibid., 220–23.
73. *Berakoth* 28b, cited in Sanders, *Paul and Palestinian Judaism*, 225.
74. Sanders, *Paul and Palestinian Judaism*, 229.
75. Ibid.
76. Ibid., 230, 229.
77. Consult, for example, the work of George Foote Moore, *Judaism in the First Centuries of the Christian Era*, 2 vols. (Cambridge, Mass.: Harvard, 1927).
78. Sanders, *Paul and Palestinian Judaism*, 225.
79. Readers of John Bunyan's *Pilgrim's Progress* will be familiar, for example, with the trials that Christian encounters and, by divine grace, overcomes at the hour of his death.

Chapter 5: Schweitzer *Revivus*: E. P. Sanders on Paul

1. For the extent of Sanders's appreciation of Schweitzer, see *Paul and Palestinian Judaism: A Comparison of Patterns of Religion* (Philadelphia: Fortress, 1977), 434–42.

2. For Davies's understanding of his differences with Sanders, see his "Preface to the Fourth Edition," in *Paul and Rabbinic Judaism* (Philadelphia: Fortress, 1980). For Sanders's response to Davies's articulation of those differences, see Sanders's "Preface to the Fifth Edition," in *Paul and Rabbinic Judaism* (Mifflintown, Pa.: Sigler Press, 1998).

3. Sanders, *Paul and Palestinian Judaism*, 427.

4. Ibid., 441–42.

5. Ibid., 513.

6. Ibid., 514.

7. E. P. Sanders, *Paul, the Law, and the Jewish People* (Philadelphia: Fortress, 1983), 208.

8. Sanders, *Paul and Palestinian Judaism*, 514.

9. Ibid.

10. Ibid.

11. Sanders, *Paul, the Law, and the Jewish People*, 207.

12. Ibid.

13. Ibid.

14. Ibid.

15. Ibid., 208.

16. Ibid.

17. Ibid., 154–55.

18. Sanders, *Paul and Palestinian Judaism*, 552.

19. Ibid., 475, citing Rudolf Bultmann, *Theology of the New Testament*, trans. Kendrick Grobel, 2 vols. (New York: Scribner, 1951, 1955), 1:249.

20. Ibid.

21. Sanders, *Paul, the Law, and the Jewish People*, 73.

22. Ibid., 70ff.

23. Ibid., 73.

24. Ibid.

25. Ibid.

26. Ibid.

27. Ibid., 74–75.

28. Ibid., 74.

29. Ibid., 75.

30. Ibid., 76.

31. Sanders, *Paul and Palestinian Judaism*, 474, citing Bultmann, *Theology of the New Testament*, 1:227.

32. Ibid.

33. Sanders, *Paul, the Law, and the Jewish People*, 123.

34. Ibid., 124.

35. Ibid.

36. Ibid., 125.

37. Ibid.

38. Sanders, *Paul and Palestinian Judaism*, 488.

39. Ibid., 488–89.

40. Ibid., 489–90.

41. Ibid., 490.

42. Ibid., 490–91.

43. Ibid., 491.

44. Ibid.

45. Ibid., 492.

46. Ibid., 443.

47. "He reasoned to sin's dominion as the reverse of his soteriology and Christology, and he was then easily able to work 'sinning' in—either as the *cause* of the dominion for argumentative purposes (as in Romans) *or* as the *result* of being in the flesh (Galatians 5.19–21). This very variation in considering transgression as cause or result of bondage to sin indicates that it was not his starting point." Ibid., 501.

48. We may observe parenthetically that Sanders is himself unclear on the meaning of "righteousness" in this passage ("whatever the precise meaning of 'righteousness' is here"). Ibid., 502.

49. Ibid., 544.

50. Ibid., 471.

51. Ibid.

52. In support of this claim, Sanders cites Romans 6:7, "for he who has died is freed [*dedikaiōtai*] from sin," which he sees as an equivalent to Romans 6:18, "having been freed [*eleutherōthentes*] from sin." Ibid., 471–72.

53. Ibid., 472.

54. Ibid., 503.

55. Ibid.

56. Ibid.

57. Ibid.

58. Ibid.

59. Ibid.

60. Ibid.

61. Ibid.

62. Ibid.

63. Ibid., 504.

64. Ibid.

65. Ibid.

66. Ibid., 505.

67. Ibid., 504–5

68. Ibid., 505.

69. Ibid., 506.

70. Ibid.

71. Ibid.

72. Ibid., 508.

73. Sanders, *Paul, the Law, and the Jewish People*, 45–48.

74. Ibid., 46.

75. Ibid., 21.

76. Ibid., 25.

77. Ibid., 26.
78. Ibid., 22.
79. Ibid., 22–23.
80. Ibid., 26.
81. Ibid., 27.
82. Ibid.
83. Ibid., 28–29.
84. Ibid., 29.
85. Ibid., 23.
86. Ibid., 31–32.
87. Ibid., 32.
88. Ibid., 33.
89. Ibid.
90. Ibid., 34–35.
91. Ibid., 35
92. Ibid.
93. Ibid.
94. Ibid., 35–36.
95. Ibid.
96. Ibid., 37.
97. Ibid., 37–38.
98. Ibid., 38.
99. Ibid., 42.
100. Ibid.
101. Ibid.
102. Ibid.
103. Ibid., 43.
104. Ibid., 44.
105. Ibid.
106. Ibid., 45.
107. Sanders, *Paul and Palestinian Judaism*, 497.
108. Sanders, *Paul, the Law, and the Jewish People*, 76.
109. Ibid., 145.
110. Ibid., 147.
111. Sanders, *Paul and Palestinian Judaism*, 463.
112. Ibid.
113. Ibid., 498–99.
114. Ibid., 465.
115. Ibid., 466.
116. Ibid., 499.
117. Ibid., 449–500.
118. Ibid., 500.
119. Ibid., 506.

Chapter 6: After Sanders: Räisänen and Dunn

1. One of the most vigorous and vocal opponents of Sanders's scholarship on Judaism has been Jacob Neusner. For a brief specimen of Neusner's interaction with Sanders, see his review of *Judaism: Practice and Belief*, by E. P. Sanders, *Journal of Studies in Judaism* 24 (1993): 317–23.

2. Heikki Räisänen, *Paul and the Law*, Wissenschaftliche Untersuchungen zum Neven Testament 29 (Tübingen, Germany: Mohr-Siebeck, 1983), 4. By "patent harmonization" and "the dialectical approach," Räisänen has in mind the projects of C. E. B. Cranfield and Peter Stuhlmacher, respectively.

3. Ibid., 6.

4. Ibid., 11–12.

5. Ibid., 16.

6. Ibid., 18–21.

7. Ibid., 25.

8. Ibid., 26ff., 199.

9. Ibid., 28.

10. Ibid., 69.

11. Ibid., 71.

12. Ibid., 82.

13. Ibid., 77.

14. Ibid., 109.

15. Räisänen sees this text as a piece of "propagandist denigration" and true evidence of Paul's lack of love "for those who disagree with him." Ibid., 101.

16. Ibid., 103.

17. Ibid., 107.

18. Ibid., 118.

19. Ibid., 133.

20. Ibid., 152.

21. Ibid., 154.

22. Ibid., 176.

23. Ibid., 176–77.

24. Ibid., 177.

25. Ibid., 178.

26. Ibid.

27. Ibid., 187.

28. Ibid.

29. E. P. Sanders, *Paul and Palestinian Judaism: A Comparison of Patterns of Religion* (Philadelphia: Fortress, 1977), 551.

30. Ibid.

31. Räisänen, *Paul and the Law*, 256ff.

32. Ibid., 265.

33. Ibid., 266.

34. Ibid., 200.

35. Ibid., 262.

36. J. D. G. Dunn, "Works of the Law and the Curse of the Law (Galatians

3.10–14)," *New Testament Studies* 31 (1985): 524. Repr. in *Jesus, Paul, and the Law: Studies in Mark and Galatians* (Louisville, Ky.: Westminster John Knox Press, 1990), 215–41.

37. J. D. G. Dunn, "The New Perspective on Paul," *Bulletin of the John Rylands University Library of Manchester* 65 (1983): 95–122; repr. in *The Romans Debate*, ed. Karl P. Donfried, rev. and enl. ed. (Peabody, Mass.: Hendrickson, 1991), 299–308; also repr. in *Jesus, Paul, and the Law: Studies in Mark and Galatians* (Louisville, Ky.: Westminster John Knox Press, 1990), 183–214. Except where noted below, we will be using the Donfried pagination.

38. J. D. G. Dunn, *The Theology of Paul the Apostle* (Grand Rapids: Eerdmans, 1998); *Romans 1–8, 9–16*, Word Biblical Commentary 38A-B (Waco, Tex.: Word, 1988); *A Commentary on the Epistle to the Galatians*, Black's New Testament Commentary (London: A. C. Black/Peabody, Mass.: Hendrickson, 1993).

39. Dunn, "The New Perspective on Paul," 299.

40. Ibid.

41. Ibid., 300.

42. Ibid.

43. Ibid.

44. Ibid., 301.

45. Ibid., 300.

46. Ibid., 303, 304.

47. Ibid., 305.

48. Ibid., 306.

49. Ibid.

50. Ibid., 307.

51. Ibid.

52. Dunn, *The Theology of Paul the Apostle*, 341.

53. Ibid., 342.

54. Ibid.

55. Ibid., 344.

56. Dunn, *Romans*, 1:40.

57. Ibid., 1:41.

58. Ibid.

59. Ibid., 1:42.

60. Ibid.

61. Ibid.

62. Ibid., 1:43.

63. Ibid., 1:48.

64. Ibid., 1:177.

65. Ibid.

66. Dunn will cite the high incidence of *hapaxlegomena* in these verses, on which see ibid., 1:163ff.

67. Ibid., 1:164.

68. "God's action on behalf of those whom he has pledged himself," citing Romans 1:17; 3:5. Ibid., 1:173.

69. Ibid.

70. Ibid., 1:174–75.

71. Ibid., 1:182.

72. Ibid., 2:587.

73. Ibid., 2:595–96.

74. Ibid., 2:595.

75. Ibid.

76. Ibid., 2:596.

77. Ibid.

78. Dunn, *The Theology of Paul the Apostle*, 344.

79. Dunn, *A Commentary on the Epistle to the Galatians*, 134.

80. Ibid., 134–35.

81. Dunn, *Jesus, Paul, and the Law*, 190.

82. Dunn, *The Theology of Paul the Apostle*, 345.

83. Ibid., 347.

84. Ibid., 348.

85. Ibid.

86. Ibid., 349.

87. Ibid., 350.

88. Ibid., 351.

89. Ibid., 353, 352.

90. Ibid., 354.

91. Ibid., 371.

92. Ibid., 355.

93. Ibid.

94. Ibid., 357–58.

95. Ibid., 358.

96. Ibid., 372.

97. Ibid., 379.

98. Dunn, *Romans*, 1:97–98.

99. Ibid., 1:97.

100. Dunn, *The Theology of Paul the Apostle*, 386.

101. Ibid., 386.

102. Dunn, *Romans*, 1:172.

103. Ibid., 1:181.

104. Ibid., 1:172–73.

105. Ibid., 1:241.

106. Ibid.

107. Dunn, *The Theology of Paul the Apostle*, 361.

108. Dunn, *A Commentary on the Epistle to the Galatians*, 171.

109. Ibid., 172.

110. Dunn, *The Theology of Paul the Apostle*, 362.

111. Dunn, *A Commentary on the Epistle to the Galatians*, 266.

112. Ibid., 266–67. Interestingly, Dunn polemically cites an understanding of the "typical Jewish mind-set" regarding "doing the law," of "the striving of an individual

for (in effect) an attainable sinless perfection," as "the very denigration of Judaism which has caused so much pain in Jewish and Christian attempts to understand each other." Ibid., 266.

113. Ibid., 339.
114. Dunn, *The Theology of Paul the Apostle*, 365.
115. Dunn, *Romans*, 2:582.
116. Ibid.
117. Ibid., 2:582–83.
118. Ibid., 2:639.
119. Ibid.
120. Ibid.
121. Dunn, *The Theology of Paul the Apostle*, 367.
122. Dunn, *Romans*, 1:204.
123. Ibid.
124. Ibid., 1:228.
125. Ibid.
126. Ibid., 1:205.
127. Ibid.
128. Ibid.
129. Dunn, *The Theology of Paul the Apostle*, 349.
130. Ibid., 350.
131. Ibid.
132. Ibid., 369.
133. Ibid., 370.
134. Ibid., 371.
135. Ibid., 472–73.
136. Ibid., 474.
137. Dunn claims that Romans 7:25b "can hardly be read otherwise more naturally than as indicating a continuing state—a state of continuing dividedness of the 'I' who says, 'Thanks be to God through Jesus Christ our Lord!'," and will continue until the "resurrection of the body." Ibid., 474, 476.
138. Ibid., 99.
139. Ibid.
140. Ibid., 98–99.
141. Ibid., 98.
142. Dunn also appears to use the term "metaphor" interchangeably with "image." ("We should note that Paul also drew his images from religion" [ibid., 330]; "Finally in this brief categorization we can refer to metaphors drawn from the major events of life" [ibid., 331].) We should register, then, that there is imprecision in his terminology.
143. Ibid., 328–29.
144. Ibid., 331.
145. Ibid., 332.
146. Ibid.
147. Ibid., 333.

148. Ibid., 332.
149. Ibid.
150. Ibid.
151. Ibid.
152. Ibid.
153. Ibid., 333.
154. Ibid., 212–18.
155. Dunn cites Romans 8:3 to establish this particular connection in Paul. Ibid., 216.
156. Ibid., 212.
157. Ibid., 214–15.
158. Ibid., 225.
159. Ibid., 231.
160. Ibid.
161. Ibid.
162. Ibid., 231, 232.
163. Ibid., 233.
164. Dunn argues that "there is little evidence that Paul preached for conviction of sin or to stir up feelings of guilt." Ibid., 332.

Chapter 7: Enter the Church: N. T. Wright

1. See Heikki Räisänen, *Beyond New Testament Theology* (Harrisburg, Pa.: Trinity Press International, 1990).
2. N. T. Wright, *The New Testament and the People of God: Christian Origins and the Question of God*, vol. 1 (Philadelphia: Fortress, 1996).
3. Ibid., 5.
4. Ibid., 6.
5. Ibid., 45.
6. Ibid., 36.
7. Ibid., 38.
8. Ibid., 77–78.
9. Ibid., 79.
10. Ibid.
11. Ibid., 221.
12. Ibid., 222.
13. Ibid., 224.
14. Ibid., 237.
15. Ibid., 243.
16. Ibid., 369–70.
17. Ibid., 458.
18. N. T. Wright, *What Saint Paul Really Said: Was Paul of Tarsus the Real Founder of Christianity?* (Grand Rapids: Eerdmans, 1997); "Romans," in *New Interpreter's Bible: Acts–First Corinthians*, vol. 10, ed. Leander E. Keck (Nashville: Abingdon, 2002).

19. Wright, *What Saint Paul Really Said*, 96.
20. Wright, "Romans," 398.
21. Wright, *What Saint Paul Really Said*, 96.
22. Wright, "Romans," 399.
23. Ibid.
24. Ibid., 400.
25. Wright, *What Saint Paul Really Said*, 97.
26. Ibid., 98.
27. Ibid.
28. Ibid., 99.
29. Wright, "Romans," 401.
30. Wright, *What Saint Paul Really Said*, 99.
31. Ibid.
32. Wright, "Romans," 401.
33. Ibid.
34. Ibid., 402, 403.
35. Ibid., 403.
36. Ibid., 403–4.
37. Ibid., 426.
38. Ibid., 405.
39. Ibid., 467.
40. Ibid.
41. Ibid.
42. Contrast the translation of the NASB ("even the righteousness of God through faith in Jesus Christ . . .").
43. Wright, "Romans," 467.
44. Ibid., 468.
45. Ibid., 646, 654, 646.
46. Ibid., 655.
47. Ibid.
48. Wright, *What Saint Paul Really Said*, 114.
49. See here Wright's comments on Romans 3:28 in "Romans," 481–82.
50. Wright, *What Saint Paul Really Said*, 113.
51. Ibid., 117.
52. Ibid., 115.
53. Wright, "Romans," 468.
54. Wright, *What Saint Paul Really Said*, 117.
55. Wright, "Romans," 468.
56. Wright, *What Saint Paul Really Said*, 120.
57. Ibid., 122.
58. Ibid., 125.
59. Wright, "Romans," 468 n.106.
60. Ibid., 481.
61. Ibid.
62. Ibid.

63. Ibid., 482.

64. Ibid., 649. Wright acknowledges his sympathy with Dunn on this point at ibid., 461.

65. Ibid., 461.

66. Ibid.

67. Ibid., 482.

68. Ibid., 440.

69. Ibid., emphasis mine.

70. Ibid., 519.

71. Ibid., 580.

72. Ibid., 477.

73. Ibid., 519.

74. Ibid., 529.

75. Ibid.

76. Ibid.

77. Ibid.

78. Ibid., 503.

79. Ibid., 504.

80. Wright, *What Saint Paul Really Said*, 124.

81. Wright, "Romans," 649.

82. Ibid.

83. Ibid.

84. Ibid., 654.

85. Wright, *What Saint Paul Really Said*, 124–25, citing Philippians 3:9.

86. Wright uses the terms "wickedness" and "catalog of vices" to describe Paul's discussion of unrighteousness in Romans 1:18–32. "Romans," 434.

87. Wright, *What Saint Paul Really Said*, 125.

88. Ibid.

89. Ibid., 160.

90. Wright, "Romans," 420.

91. Ibid.

92. Ibid.

93. Wright, *What Saint Paul Really Said*, 129.

94. Ibid.

95. Ibid., 123.

96. Ibid., 104–5. See also N. T. Wright, "On Becoming the Righteousness of God: 2 Corinthians 5:21," in *Pauline Theology*, vol. 2, ed. David M. Hay (Minneapolis: Augsburg Fortress, 1993), 200–208.

97. Wright, "Romans," 578.

98. Ibid.

99. Ibid., 579.

100. Ibid.

101. Wright, *What Saint Paul Really Said*, 106 *et passim*.

102. Wright, "Romans," 474.

103. Ibid., 476.

104. Ibid. I owe these quotations to Daniel Kirk.
105. Wright, *What Saint Paul Really Said*, 48.
106. Ibid., 47.
107. We might at this juncture briefly comment on an unpublished lecture of Wright, "The New Perspectives on Paul." Appeal is sometimes made to this lecture to show that Wright embraces something resembling a traditional doctrine of imputation. It is true that rhetorically Wright's comments in this lecture on the traditional doctrine of imputation are far more irenic than those previously published in *What Saint Paul Really Said*. Neither Wright's exegetical arguments nor his conclusions, however, have substantially modified his previously published statements. It is unclear that this essay establishes a theological shift in Wright's doctrine of imputation.
108. Ibid., 60.
109. Ibid., 35.
110. Ibid., 36.
111. Ibid., 37.
112. Ibid., 36.
113. Wright, "Romans," 461.
114. Ibid.
115. Ibid., 551.
116. Ibid., 552.
117. Ibid.
118. Ibid.
119. Ibid., 552.
120. Ibid., 552.
121. Ibid., 553.
122. Ibid., 554.
123. Ibid., 555.
124. Ibid.
125. Wright, *What Saint Paul Really Said*, 116–17.
126. Ibid., 159.
127. Ibid.
128. Wright, "Romans," 533.
129. Ibid., 534–35.
130. Ibid., 535.
131. Ibid.
132. Ibid.
133. Ibid., 548.
134. Wright, *What Saint Paul Really Said*, 158.
135. Ibid., 159.
136. Wright, "Romans," 491.
137. Ibid., 491–92.
138. Ibid., 492.
139. Ibid.
140. Ibid.
141. Ibid., 579.

Chapter 8: A Critique of the New Perspective

1. *Aboth* 3.15, cited at E. P. Sanders, *Paul and Palestinian Judaism: A Comparison of Patterns of Religion* (Philadelphia: Fortress, 1977), 132.

2. Two recent examples include D. A. Carson, ed., *Justification and Variegated Nomism*, vol. 1, *The Complexities of Second Temple Judaism* (Grand Rapids: Eerdmans, 2000); and Simon Gathercole, *Where Is Boasting? Early Jewish Soteriology and Paul's Response in Romans 1–5* (Grand Rapids: Eerdmans, 2002).

3. Carson, *Justification and Variegated Nomism*, 543–48.

4. Ibid., 543.

5. Ibid., 544, 545.

6. For details, see chapter 2 of Guy Prentiss Waters, " 'Rejoice, O Nations, With His People': Deuteronomy 27–30, 32 in the Epistles of the Apostle Paul" (Ph.D. diss., Duke University, 2002).

7. Mark A. Seifrid, "Blind Alleys in the Controversy over the Paul of History," *Tyndale Bulletin* 45 (1994): 91, cf. 89.

8. Robert H. Gundry, "Reconstructing Jesus," *Christianity Today*, April 27, 1998, 78.

9. Richard B. Gaffin, "Paul the Theologian," *Westminster Theological Journal* 62 (2000): 134.

10. E. P. Sanders, *Paul, the Law, and the Jewish People* (Philadelphia: Fortress, 1983), 46.

11. N. T. Wright, *What Saint Paul Really Said: Was Paul of Tarsus the Real Founder of Christianity?* (Grand Rapids: Eerdmans, 1997), 99.

12. N. T. Wright, "Romans," in *New Interpreter's Bible: Acts–First Corinthians*, vol. 10, ed. Leander E. Keck (Nashville: Abingdon, 2002), 482.

13. Seifrid, "Blind Alleys," 77–85. See also Mark A. Seifrid, "Righteousness Language in the Hebrew Scriptures and Early Judaism," in *Justification and Variegated Nomism*, 415–42.

14. Seifrid, "Blind Alleys," 80–81.

15. "Can it be that . . . there are some ethnic Jews who have succeeded in obeying Torah, 'attaining their own righteousness' (10:3), and establishing a status of covenant membership based on their belonging to Abraham's physical family and maintaining its distinctive outward markers? No. These two verses [i.e., 11:5–6] make it clear that this 'remnant' is not a small minority for whom the way of national status actually worked. . . . No: the present 'remnant' is 'chosen by grace.' " Wright, "Romans," 676.

16. Douglas Moo, *The Epistle to the Romans*, New International Commentary of the New Testament (Grand Rapids: Eerdmans, 1996), 678.

17. Ibid.

18. Sanders, *Paul, the Law, and the Jewish People*, 46.

19. J. D. G. Dunn, *Romans 1–8, 9–16*, Word Biblical Commentary 38A-B (Waco, Tex.: Word, 1988), 1:158.

20. Ibid.

21. Ibid., 1:159.

22. Ibid.

23. Wright, "Romans," 649, commenting on 3:28.

24. Ibid., 461.

25. Ibid.

26. Robert Smith, "A Critique of the 'New Perspective' on Justification," *Reformed Theological Review* 58 (1999): 106.

27. Dunn, *Romans*, 1:204.

28. Stephen Westerholm, *Israel's Law and the Church's Faith: Paul and His Recent Interpreters* (Grand Rapids: Eerdmans, 1988), 113.

29. Ibid., 119.

30. Sanders, *Paul, the Law, and the Jewish People*, 42.

31. Dunn, *Romans*, 2:582.

32. On these options and their relative merits, see Thomas Schreiner, *Romans, Exegetical Commentary on the New Testament* (Grand Rapids: Baker, 1998), 537; and Moo, *Romans*, 622.

33. See Schreiner, *Romans*, 536, and the literature cited at 536 n.8.

34. Ibid., 544.

35. Sanders, *Paul, the Law, and the Jewish People*, 41.

36. Dunn, *Romans*, 2:601.

37. Ibid., 2:612.

38. Ibid., 2:612.

39. Wright, "Romans," 660.

40. Ibid., 662.

41. The following argument is indebted to Schreiner, *Romans*, 551–55.

42. Ibid., 552.

43. Ibid., 553.

44. Ibid., 554.

45. Moo, *Romans*, 648.

46. Charles Hodge, *Commentary on the Epistle to the Romans* (New York: A. C. Armstrong and Son, 1896), 531.

47. Westerholm, *Israel's Law and the Church's Faith*, 203–4, citing Romans 10:5; Galatians 3:10, 12; 5:3.

48. J. D. G. Dunn, *The Theology of Paul the Apostle* (Grand Rapids: Eerdmans, 1998), 362, 261.

49. Francis Turretin, *Institutes of Elenctic Theology*, trans. G. M. Giger, ed. James T. Dennison Jr., 3 vols. (Phillipsburg, N.J.: P&R Publishing, 1992–1997), 2:641 (=L.16.2.11).

50. Sanders, *Paul and Palestinian Judaism*, 506.

51. Dunn, *Romans*, 1:241.

52. Wright, "Romans," 440.

53. N. T. Wright, "The Law in Romans 2," in *Paul and the Mosaic Law: The Third Durham–Tübingen Research Symposium on Earliest Christianity and Judaism*, ed. J. D. G. Dunn (Tübingen, Germany: Mohr-Siebeck, 1996/Grand Rapids: Eerdmans, 2001), 144.

54. Robert L. Dabney, *Syllabus and Notes of the Course of Systematic and*

Polemic Theology Taught in Union Theological Seminary, Virginia, 5th ed. (Richmond: Presbyterian Committee of Publication, 1927), 639.

55. Ibid.

56. Such parallel expressions evidence the error of Wright's *ad absurdum* argument that "imputed righteousness" in 1 Corinthians 1:30 requires "imputed wisdom" and "imputed sanctification." Paul on more than one occasion speaks of imputed righteousness, but never once conclusively speaks of "imputed wisdom" and "imputed sanctification." See here John Piper, *Counted Righteous in Christ: Should We Abandon the Imputation of Christ's Righteousness?* (Wheaton, Ill.: Crossway, 2002), 86 and n.32.

57. As also, rightly, ibid., 105–6.

58. This argument has been raised by Wesleyan Arminians; see Dabney, *Syllabus and Notes,* 637–38.

59. Ibid., 637.

60. Ibid., 638.

61. Wright, "Romans," 492.

62. Sanders, *Paul, the Law, and the Jewish People,* 124.

63. Hodge, *Commentary on the Epistle to the Romans,* 82.

64. E.g., Moo, *Romans,* 142.

65. Ibid.

66. Ibid., 147–48.

67. Ibid., 168.

68. *Pace* Schreiner. Schreiner, commenting on Romans 2:13, observes that "we must await, however, the discussion in 2:25–29 to grasp how Paul can conceive of obedience that justifies." *Romans,* 119.

69. *Paul and Palestinian Judaism,* 466, citing D. E. H. Whiteley, *Theology of St. Paul* (Oxford: Oxford University Press, 1964), 134–37.

70. N. T. Wright, "On Becoming the Righteousness of God: 2 Corinthians 5.21," in *Pauline Theology,* vol. 2, ed. David M. Hay (Minneapolis: Augsburg Fortress, 1993), 200–208.

71. Dunn, *The Theology of Paul the Apostle,* 221–22.

72. knew no sin/sinful; became sin/became the righteousness of God; on our behalf/in Him.

73. Cited in John Piper, *Counted Righteous in Christ,* 82–83.

74. Hodge, *Commentary on the Epistle to the Romans,* 142.

75. Ibid., 144.

76. John Murray, *The Epistle to the Romans,* 2 vols. (Grand Rapids: Eerdmans, 1968), 1:118–20.

77. E.g., ibid., 1:119–20; Piper, *Counted Righteous in Christ,* 74.

78. E.g., Piper, *Counted Righteous in Christ,* 74. Note the (unsuccessful, in my judgment) compromise measure proposed by Moo, *Romans,* 74.

79. Hodge, *Commentary on the Epistle to the Romans,* 44.

80. Dunn, *The Theology of Paul the Apostle,* 97.

81. N. T. Wright, "Romans and the Theology of Paul," in *Pauline Theology,*

vol. 3, ed. David M. Hay and E. Elizabeth Johnson (Minneapolis: Augsburg Fortress, 1991), 46.

82. For a more detailed survey of these verses, see the recent treatments of Piper, *Counted Righteous in Christ*, 90–114; and John Murray, *The Imputation of Adam's Sin* (Grand Rapids: Eerdmans, 1959), 64–95.

83. Piper, *Counted Righteous in Christ*, 94–100.

84. See ibid., 100.

85. The following list has been drawn from ibid., 102.

86. Hodge, *Commentary on the Epistle to the Romans*, 391.

87. Ibid.

88. John Calvin, *Commentaries on the Epistles of Paul the Apostle to the Philippians, Colossians, and Thessalonians*, trans. and ed. John Pringle (Edinburgh: Calvin Theological Society, 1851), 92.

89. Ibid.,

90. Wright, *What Saint Paul Really Said*, 113.

91. The following comments are indebted to the analysis of Archibald Alexander Hodge, *Outlines of Theology* (New York: Robert Carter, 1879), 108.

92. Ibid.

93. A notable exception is Gaffin, "Paul the Theologian," 121–41.

94. Turretin, *Institutes*, 2:677 (L.16.8.6, 7).

95. Ibid., 2:680 (L.16.8.13).

96. Hodge, *Commentary on the Epistle to the Romans*, 685, emphasis mine.

97. Martin Luther, *Commentary on Romans*, trans. J. Theodore Mueller (Grand Rapids: Zondervan, 1954), 214.

98. As does Wright, *What Saint Paul Really Said*, 158–59.

Chapter 9: What's at Stake for Reformed Christianity?

1. N. T. Wright, "Romans and the Theology of Paul," in *Pauline Theology*, vol. 3, ed. David M. Hay and E. Elizabeth Johnson (Minneapolis: Augsburg Fortress, 1991), 32.

2. Ibid.

3. Dunn, as we have observed, argues the same for portions of Romans.

4. N. T. Wright, *What Saint Paul Really Said: Was Paul of Tarsus the Real Founder of Christianity?* (Grand Rapids: Eerdmans, 1997), 60.

5. Ibid., 133.

6. Ibid., 124.

7. Ibid., 41.

8. Ibid.

9. Ibid., 59.

10. Ibid., 57.

11. Wright, "Romans," in *New Interpreter's Bible: Acts–First Corinthians*, vol. 10, ed. Leander E. Keck (Nashville: Abingdon, 2002), 548.

12. Cf. Carl Henry, *The Uneasy Conscience of Modern Fundamentalism* (Grand Rapids: Eerdmans, 1947).

13. Brian Walsh and Richard Middleton, *The Transforming Vision: Shaping a Christian World View* (Downers Grove, Ill.: InterVarsity, 1984).

14. "Summary Statement of AAPC's Position on Covenant, Baptism, and Salvation."

15. These comments are all the more important in view of a not infrequent tendency within the church to apply the label "New Perspective" to the teachings of Norman Shepherd and the theology of the Federal Vision. While Shepherd and the Federal Vision share some of the concerns expressed by the NPP, it is inaccurate to categorize the three as a single movement.

16. A substantial literature promoting and criticizing the theology of the Federal Vision has arisen in the last two or three years. It is beyond the scope of this project to engage thoroughly the concerns and views of the Federal Vision. Having read much of this literature, I can affirm that the discussion that follows is a fair, if incomplete, representation of the views expressed by the session of the Auburn Avenue Presbyterian Church.

17. "Summary Statement," § 12.

18. Norman Shepherd, "The Covenant Context for Evangelism," in *The New Testament Student and Theology*, ed. John H. Skilton (Nutley, N.J.: Presbyterian and Reformed, 1976), 57.

19. Ibid., 60.

20. Norman Shepherd, *The Call of Grace* (Phillipsburg, N.J.: P&R Publishing, 2000), 91.

21. Ibid., 84; cf. Shepherd, "Covenant Context," 61.

22. Shepherd, "Covenant Context," 61.

23. Ibid., 61, 62.

24. "Summary Statement," Summary, emphasis mine.

25. Shepherd, "Covenant Context," 65.

26. Ibid.

27. Shepherd, *Call of Grace*, 99.

28. Ibid., 101.

29. Ibid., 102. Shepherd had earlier said that "baptism *rather than regeneration* is the point of transition from lostness in death to salvation in life" ("Covenant Context," 66, emphasis mine). He altered that statement in the light of subsequent criticism from Sinclair Ferguson (see "More on Covenant Evangelism: A Reply from Norman Shepherd," in *The Banner of Truth* 170 [November 1977]: 25).

30. Shepherd, *Call of Grace*, 104.

31. Shepherd. "Covenant Context," 72.

32. Ibid.

33. "Summary Statement," n.1.

34. Ibid., Summary.

35. Westminster Larger Catechism Q&A 70, 71, 72, 73.

36. "Summary Statement," § 7.

Index of Scripture

Index of Subjects and Names

Guy Prentiss Waters is assistant professor of biblical studies at Belhaven College. He is a graduate of the University of Pennsylvania (B.A., Greek and Latin), Westminster Theological Seminary (M.Div.), and Duke University (Ph.D. in religion, with concentrations in New Testament, Old Testament, and ancient Judaism). At Duke he studied under Richard B. Hays and E. P. Sanders, two leading expositors of the New Perspectives on Paul.

Dr. Waters is a member of the Society of Biblical Literature and the Institute for Biblical Research. He is an ordained minister of the Presbyterian Church in America.